# From
# DARK DUNGEONS
# To
# DAZZLING DAWN

# From DARK DUNGEONS To DAZZLING DAWN

## A Life-Long Struggle with the Christian Hierarchy (An Autobiography)

Rev. Abraham Vellamthadathil
M.A.; M.Ph.; M.Th.

SHIPRA

Price: Rs. 995 US$ 49.75

ISBN: 978-81-7541-813-4

First Published in India 2016

*From Dark Dungeons to Dazzling Dawn*



*Published by:*
**SHIPRA PUBLICATIONS**
LG 18-19, Pankaj Central Market, I.P. Ext.
Patparganj, Delhi-110092, India
Tel: 91-11-2223 5152, 2223 6152
E-mail: info@shiprapublication.com
www.shiprapublication.com

*Dedicated*

*To*

*All my students, witnesses of my struggles,*

*especially the Third Year B.A. Literature*

*Students of 2010-2011*

*Girideepam Institute of Advanced Learning, Kottayam*

*Who honoured and rewarded me with the*

*following precious Award.*

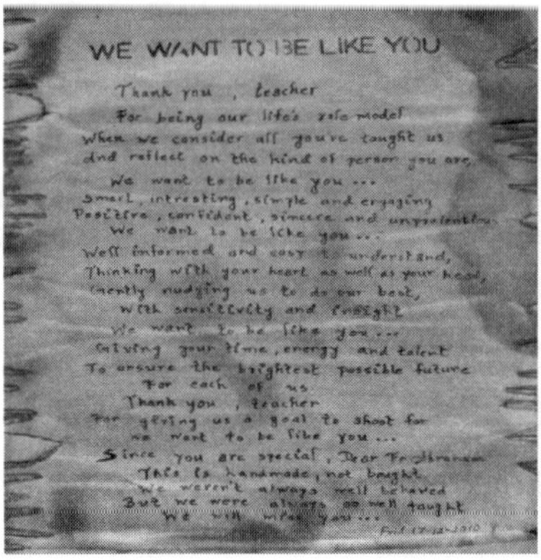

*'We Want To Be Like You*
*Thank you, teacher*
*For being our life's role model.*
*When we consider all you've taught us*
*And reflect on the kind of person you are,*
*We want to be like you...*
*Smart, interesting, simple and engaging*
*Positive, confident, sincere and unpretentious*
*We want to be like you...*
*Well informed and easy to understand*
*Thinking with your heart as well as your head,*
*Gently nudging us to do our best,*
*With sensitivity and insight*
*We want to be like you...*
*Giving your time, energy and talent*
*To ensure the brightest possible future*
*For each of us*
*Thank you, teacher*
*For giving us a goal to shoot for*
*We want to be like you...*
*Since you are special, Dear Fr Abraham*
*This is handmade, not bought*
*We weren't always well behaved*
*But we were always so well taught*
*We will miss you...' Friday 17-12-2010.*

Anumol George
John Mathew George
Josin J. Kudakassery
Kurian John
Nelson Varghese
Shamila T. S.
Shimon K. Chacko
Sonia P. Jacob
Subin Thomas
Varsha Selvaraj

# Foreword

*From Dark Dungeons to Dazzling Dawn* is the poignant yet fascinating story of a former Roman Catholic priest, Fr Abraham Chacko [Fr Abraham Vellamthadathil] who fought a relentless battle for nearly half a century against injustice, oppression and persecution in personal and professional life. Fr Abraham was a brilliant scholar who was selected to study in the famous Papal Seminary at Poona where after eight years of study he secured the degrees of Master of Philosophy and Master of Theology. Later he joined the Karnataka University at Dharwar and secured a Master's degree in English Literature.

Fr Abraham's alleged offence which provoked the power-drunk dictatorial church authorities was his 'audacity' to think independently, when they asked the question: 'Who are you to think when we are here?'Fr Abraham asserted that he was opposed to the commercialization of the 'Faith in God, ritualistic structure, placing Christ at its head and the distortion of Christian values and the claim of infallible dogmatic divine right'.

Little wonder then, that Fr Abraham became an 'enemy' of the Church. And there followed innumerable ways of harassing and persecuting him and subjecting him to uncivilized, inhuman and unchristian treatment.

Corruption of the best is the worst,' Fr Abraham asserts. He is right. Corruption in the Church, in all denominations of the Church has taken many forms and at every level tarnishing the pristine glory and unsullied reputation of the true Church. And it appears that there is no way to get out of this pernicious and all embracing malady.

Fr Abraham was practically driven out of the Catholic Church. Seeking peace of mind and minimum comfort, he embraced the Church of South India (C.S.I.). Although at first he was received well, soon he found that it was like getting out of the frying pan and falling into the fire. Although he was made a Professor and later Principal of the College, he found that unless he was prepared to become a party to the corrupt caucus that controlled the Administration of the College he had no place there. Morality, truth, justice and love had no place in the hands of a set of corrupt men who were after illegal and immoral monetary gain. And Fr Abraham did not bend before anybody and bluntly refused to do any wrong.

Finally thanks to a few justice-loving and kind top officials of the University and the forthright stand of the High Court, he came out victorious.

Today he is a happy family man.

The sordid and melodramatic vindictive torture Fr Abraham Chacko had to face in his career is an unusual story like a page from the Arabian Nights. It is a challenge to the present day Christianity and its almighty dogmatic authority.

This is a work which must be read by every Christian priest and of course, by every layman.

I take pleasure in recommending it to all.

Padmabhushan Emeritus
**Prof Dr. M.V. Pylee**
Former Vice Chancellor of
Cochin University of Science & Technology
Cochin-683 503.

# An Appreciation

Any unbiased truth-seeker who closely studies the origin and early phase of Christianity will undoubtedly arrive at the clear conclusion that law, cult and power do not belong to its core. Unfortunately these three seem to constitute the very essence of present-day Churches, which claim to be founded by Jesus Christ himself.

What is most attractive, addictive and seductive to the Church Authorities is power. Here, one is reminded of the well-known words of John Acton: 'Power tends to corrupt, and absolute power corrupts absolutely'. The assessment of Bernard Shaw too is pertinent: 'Power does not corrupt man; but fools, if they get into a position of power, corrupt power.'

Fr Abraham Chacko's 'From Dark Dungeons to Dazzling Dawn' is his memoirs depicting in brilliant colours the story of his barbarous victimization by oppressive and power-addict hierarchs, and of his triumph as glorious victor from the state of pathetic victim.

Birds of the same feather flock together, and hierarchs of authoritarian mind-set cling together. These are unceasingly busy validating their defensive and apologetic stance by selectively quoting and cunningly distorting biblical verses in their own favour.

They are blind to the numerous verses calling explicitly

for their duty to serve in humility and humaneness; on the other hand they see every where in the Bible capital-written words of God granting them unqualified license for despotic and tyrannical rule over their subjects. Too small are for their eyes the letters of Jesus' words: 'You know that the rulers of the Gentile lord it over them, and their great men exercise authority over them. It shall not be so among you; but whoever would be great among you must be your servant and whoever would be first among you must be your slave; even the Son of man came not to be served but to serve and to give his life as a ransom for many' (Mathew 20: 25-26). Truly, they resemble the cranes sitting at sluices, devouring the small fishes and conniving at the big ones.

The crystalline records of Fr Abraham's bitter experiences indicate that 'crook,' which is a synonym of bishop's crosier, is perhaps a reminder that some bishops can even be crooks. They immolate their helpless and defenseless subjects on the altar of their egotism, under the pretext of offering pleasing sacrifices to the sadistic and Shylockian firmamental Deity.

Who pays the piper calls the tune! The Bishops, who claim to feed the poojari-priests demand from them blind obedience and slavish service, and decide upon and dictate to them all the details of the mode of their life and behaviour. Those who do not comply with their orders and injunctions, and do not mind their interests and idiosyncracies, will be deprived of their livelihood as pujaris. Nobody has the right to question them, because practically they are the legislature, judiciary and executive at the same time.

Against the background of his painful experiences under authoritarian hierarchs, Fr Abraham repeatedly highlights the significant difference modern theologians make between Religion and religions, and Christianity and Churchianity. He is of the firm conviction that 'God is to be sought in the thick of human civic and family life', and not in the rigid Church-structure with its dogmatic labyrinths or in the suffocating systems of the institutionalized religions; consequently, he fights vehemently against the squalid commercial ritualization of faith and religion, and the horrible Gnostic, Manichean and puritanical tendencies in Christianity.

'From Dark Dungeons to Dazzling Dawn' is an excellent crime-thriller exposing the filthy interiors of the pyramidal ecclesiastical structures, and an exciting narrative capable of captivating the readers and keeping them spell-bound till the end. Since it is written by a priest who is Master of English, Philosophy and Theology, it is also a precious piece of beautiful literature to be enjoyed and used by people of all walks.

As the autobiographic narrative of a cleric who calls a spade a spade, and had to endure excruciating torments and tortures under despotic Church leaders before his final and glazing victory, this book will bring to the boil the blood of freedom fighters in all the Episcopal Churches. They should never miss this valuable Handbook for Non-violent Fight against the enslaving systems within the Churches.

I am sure, the truth-missiles launched by the author will hit at the intended targets, namely the bunkers of spiritual terrorists and religious tyrants.

Warmly I do commend this book to all lovers of freedom and justice in the institutionalized and structuralized Churches all over the world.

**Dr. James Gurudas, CMI**
Director
'Snehavani', Centre for Interreligious Fellowship,
Thellakom,
Former Dean of Studies
Bhopal Theological Seminary,
Ashta, Kottayam-686630

# Message

Most Rev. Philipose Mar Chrysostom, Metropolitan. Before passing your judgment on his view try to understand it. I think God is using him to challenge the church to look at the Bible in the light and context of the development of research and science.

May God blessyou all.

Philipose Mar Chrysostom

# Preface

From 'Dark Dungeons to Dazzling Dawn' is my autobiography, spoken out through live records. It unfolds an almost nightmarish struggle with Church hierarchy for nearly 50 years as a priest including 40 years as a college Professor and Principal. The sordid drama of this octopus grip of vindictiveness was enacted during my interim legal helplessness when the University Appellate Tribunal was struck down and consequently the college 'domestic enquiry procedure' emerged absolute. My 'offense' which provoked the vindictiveness is implied in their question: 'Who are you to think when we are here?' This melodrama with traumatic episodes was ended in a happy denouement with the help of honest and justice-loving officials of the rank of Vice Chancellor and court interventions which washed away the slanders and mud slung at me, ordered compensation for damages and rescued me and family by enabling me to retire honourably.

My motive to publish this is not so much the traumatic episodes of this unequal battle as the awareness this experience led me to the awareness that there is only ONE Religion—the Universal Natural Human Morality, based on Faith in God, the Moral Imperative, who is Truth, Justice and Love, the source of all moral values. I think this awareness is deeply significant in the context of our civic society, drained of all moral values and turned into a veritable rumbling volcano, a veritable 'hell' on this Earth, with its human morality completely drained and replaced by the sonorous hullabaloo of the dogma-generated weird ritual practices. It led me to the awareness, shared with Holger Kersten, that Jesus' message has been distorted beyond recognition. Jesus, morally indignant at the ritualistic commercialization of Faith in God, demolished the 'religious' commercial ritualism which was the means of livelihood for the high-priestly class. And they plotted against and did away with Jesus and threw the blame upon the anonymous criminal, the 'sins of the world'. And, ironically enough, they re-instated those very ritualistic structures – and did it with a vengeance – and placed Jesus as its foundation and claimed monopoly over these very rituals and arrogated the insulation of 'divine-right' infallible dogmatic authority.

'Corruption of the best is the worst'. Corruption of the best ritualistic religions is the worst pest on the gullible faithful. These religions black out the God-given light of reason, and lead the devotees by the blind man's rod of blind faith and ruthlessly exploit them and deprive them of their God-given chances of 'abundant life here on earth' guaranteed under the rule of the Religion of Natural Human Morality. The devotees are conditioned by the ritualistic pujaris and purohitas by din of the repeated dogmatic faith-formulae and make them look skyward for a heaven after death far above there somewhere.

Each religion holds its own set of dogmas and rituals as *above* reason and those of others as *against* reason; but in either case they are *alien* and therefore *irrelevant* to reason. To black out the light of reason and to condition the rational humans in dogmatic darkness and thereby to exploit them is perhaps the greatest crime against humanity. God created man in His own image and likeness – rational and moral. But the ritualistic religions created God in the image and likeness of perverted and covetous humans to be at the beck and call of and ordered about by the intermediary priests and pujaris.

# Contents

# Introduction

## Not Known, but Worth Knowing

Let me begin this chronicle with a humble acknowledgement of the absolute sovereignty of Almighty God, the Moral Imperative, the Almighty Source of everything visible and invisible.

Here in my son Jeslie's residence, Apt. A4, 5053, Madison Avenue, Okemos, Ml 48864, Michigan, it is now 13:30 hours, Friday 31 December 2010. Quite unexpectedly the sun appears, and appears indeed quite bright. At this very moment, my home parish Vadavathoor C.S.I. Church in Kottayam, Kerala, is gathered in prayerful silence with lighted candles, waiting for the last stroke of the midnight clock to bid farewell to 2010 and to usher in 2011. I join them in spirit in silent prayer to thank God for the graceful divine Providence hitherto guiding us and to surrender me and mine to the same graceful divine Providence during the moments of life ahead as designed from above.

Autobiographies have their justification on the merit of the fame and outstanding achievements of the authors concerned. Speaking of the lives of the great personalities mentioned in *The Worldly Philosophers* (Revised 7th Edition,1999) its author Robert L. Heilbroner says: 'By all the rules of school-boy history books, they were non-entities: they commanded no armies, sent no men to their deaths, ruled no empires, took little part in the history making decisions. A few of them achieved renown, but none was ever a national hero; a few were roundly abused, but none was quite a national villain. Yet what they did was more decisive for history than many acts of statesmen who basked in brighter glory, often more profoundly disturbing than the shuttling of armies back and forth, across frontiers, more powerful for good and bad than the edicts of kings and legislators. It was this: they shaped and swayed men's minds.

'And because he who enlists a man's mind wields a power even greater than the sword or the scepter, these men shaped and swayed the world...they worked, in the main, as scholars – quietly, inconspicuously, and without much regard for what the world had to say about them. But they left in their train shattered empires, and exploded continents; they buttressed and undermined political regimes; they set class against class, and even nation against nation – not because they plotted mischief, but because of the extraordinary power of their ideas'. [Introduction, page 13].

I have no claim of any such justification. Pearls lying hidden undetected and trodden underfoot can be more valuable than those polished and exhibited on lovely necks. There are highly illustrious and media-projected personality magnets who play the jury and choose worthies for great awards and who in turn are chosen as worthies for the same awards next year. Ideas and visions born of life-experiences may be profound, exciting and highly transformative, if recognized and accepted. But centers of power, political as well as religious in the mutually back-scratching and clandestine alliance, would rather maintain the existing order of politico-religious affairs in its 'pristine purity' and share the spoils thereof, looking upon these ideas with suspicion, disdain and trepidation, and therefore would black them out using every possible influence including the powerful and crowd-pulling media.

I am persuaded to believe that during the last 74 years of my life I have experienced an immensely great and relevant evolution in my beliefs and ideas. It has been an experience of passing through long, dark dungeons of dogmatic faiths and ideas generated through them and emerging out into a dazzling dawn. I am strongly persuaded to believe that this evolution of beliefs and ideas as I have experienced in my life has immense relevance to life social, political and religious. That is the justification, if any at all, I claim for this venture.

Dogmatic beliefs and ideas which they generate are indeed numerous. More often than not they are mutually opposed and contradictory and aggressively repulsive to each other. If they ever come to any agreement for peaceful co-existence, it is only for the sheer need for self existence and is nothing more sustainable than 'Hindi Chini Bhai Bhai'. [The ceremonious and much publicized diplomatic peace-talk between Prime Minister Jawaharlal Nehru and his Chinese counterpart, the then Premier Chou En Lai, over Peaceful Co-existence generated a much media-celebrated catchphrase 'Indians – Chinese Brothers, Brothers'. But hardly had the ink dried when China invaded India without any warning.] Dogmas of one's own are held as dogmas above reason and those of others as against reason. But in either case they are alien to reason. And what is alien to reason can have very little effective beneficial role in the lives of rational beings. Nay, they can and even do play havoc in normal human life because involving oneself in areas where, light of reason having been blacked out, darkness and disputes prevail, can and often turn out our human society into one that 'seems to lie before us like a land of dreams, so various, so beautiful, so new, Hath really neither joy, nor love, nor light, nor certitude, nor peace, nor help for pain. And we are here as on a darkling plain swept with confused alarms of struggle and flight, where ignorant armies clash by night' (Mathew Arnold, *Dover Beach)*. Ideas generated from dogmas are themselves dogmatic because plus cannot come from minus, nor can light issue forth from darkness. Dogmas and dogma-generated ideas are ruled by dint of dogmatic teaching authority. The authority, particularly when it arrogates divino jure infallibility, orders to take in what it gives without questions. What then is the norm for distinguishing 'true' faiths from 'false' ones I am yet to be told. If no such distinction needs to be made, blind faith can slip into blind fanaticism. The mushroom growth of diverse, mutually repellent faiths that cut out crisscross paths of weird ritualistic diversity, can and do result in utter confusion and chaos, creating social turbulence and communal clashes in the socio-rational human family.

## Events Witnessed by Live Documents

The evolution of ideas, indicated above, has been caused by certain events. These events are recorded through authentic live documents kept safely and are expected to testify these events as related in this chronicle. I am indebted to an elderly and very gentleman priest, the late Fr Philip Visakhanthara, for the file of these valuable documents. Fr Visakhanthara, a member of the Kottayam Diocesan Congregation of Oblates of Sacred Heart, OSH, was a tall, dark-skinned, but very white-souled man. He was capable of cracking boisterous jokes with a hidden meaning that pierced you like a rapier. To quote but one such joke: during my early petit seminary student life at Sacred Heart Mount, [S.H. Mount], Fr Visakhanthara very affectionately called me to him. Pressing me close to him with his left hand he remarked: 'Before you enter the seminary, you feel natural. In the seminary you feel supernatural. Out of the seminary as a priest when you begin your priestly ministry under your Bishop, you begin to feel unnatural'.

And prophetic indeed those words were as far as I was concerned. Then came a valuable piece of advice from him: 'Son,' he said pressing me closer to him, 'You may not grasp fully now the depth and significance of the tip I am going to give you. But later on you will surely realize its full relevance. It is this: keep all the letters or written instructions you receive from the Bishop or any of your higher ecclesiastical superiors safe for future reference. And keep a copy of all your communications to them'. I took his advice with a smile of gratitude and kept it very faithfully. And now I realize how deeply significant this piece of advice was!

One of the chief sources of inspiration for me to venture out on this chronicle came from the office of Menon and Bhanu, Advocates, Kottayam. The late Mr Kumarakom Sankunni Menon was a renowned criminal lawyer of Kottayam Bar. He and his then junior, now a senior advocate of Kottayam Bar, Mr P.K. Chithra Bhanu, were handling my cases related to the Catholic Management of St Stephen's College, Uzhavoor, defending me against the onslaughts of the Management. As such both of them knew me and my struggle against the blind traditional concept of dogmatic religion and how the 'colossal institutional and socio-political power' was out there to teach me the dire consequences of daring to think independently and to question dogmas and dogma-supported church authorities. Adv. Sree Sankunni Menon, who knew my habit of preserving the file of correspondence carefully, suggested that I should venture out the chronicle of my life experiences authenticating it with documents. I express my heavy debt of gratitude to both these eminent advocates.

I also express my deep indebtedness to the late Dr A.V. Varghese, the then Vice-Chancellor of Kerala University. St Stephen's College was at that time affiliated to Kerala University. He advised me and decisively helped me to extricate myself from the octopus-clutches of the college management, during the brief period of the non-existence of University Appellate Tribunal, which had been struck down under the legal complications involving Minority Rights. 'You, with a family that is dependent on you, are grossly unequal to fight back a center of colossal institutional and socio-political power' he advised me and helped me to relinquish service under this management and take up service in the soon-to-be sanctioned Henry Baker College, Melukavu. But for this advice and decisive help, I would have ended my life, after having been pushed out of college service, as a casual head-load labourer priest, of course in my priestly robe, working as a head-load labourer at Kottayam market, as I had been visualizing my future. My indebtedness to that great man remains un-exonerated.

I wish I were able to adequately pay back the debt of gratitude I owe to Padmabhushan Emeritus Prof Dr. M.V. Pylee for the Foreword he has written to this Chronicle. The fact that he wrote such a sharply worded Foreword is a confirmation and guarantee that 'From Dark Dungeons to Dazzling Dawn' is the record of a traumatic experience worth reading through and reflecting on.

I am also extremely grateful to Rev. Dr James Gurudas, C.M.I. for his profoundly significant 'Appreciation'. A man of such erudition and depth as he is in the Catholic Christian theology and in matters biblical, in addition to his versatility in resource languages such as Greek, Latin, Syriac German etc., Dr. Gurudas makes sure that he attaches his finger print only on matters that deserve it.

Last and certainly not least, I humbly thank the Most Rev. Metropolitan Mar Chrysostom for the short but poignant MESSAGE couched in his characteristically double-edged words.

In this venture of my unfolding the saga of my life-struggle I have absolutely no intention of casting aspersions on any person or of paying back any old score. What I had to undergo might have been triggered off by those concerned because they might have thought it their duty to do so in order to protect, preserve and perpetuate what they might have honestly thought to be sacred and unquestionable: the dogmas and the dogma-generated ideas over which, they thought, they had the divine mandate of exclusive and inalienable custodianship. Nor do I have any intention whatsoever of projecting out my life and experiences. They are nothing more than just ordinary and inconspicuous. My only modest ambition is to share my conviction that rational human beings as we are, we have a duty to strive for and bring under the rule and guidance of the light of reason the human affairs small or large in the prevailing darkness and confusion brought about by diverse and more often than not mutually repellent dogmatic beliefs and blind traditions of weird ritualism: darkness of religious and communal fanaticism in which gullible but innocent people of God clash and perish.

# 1

# My Early Memories

When I turn back, searching into my childhood memories, the one image that I badly miss is that of my mother. Her name was Annamma, as I have been told by my immediate relatives. As I write this, my eyes and nose are flowing, of course, due to the cold and snow-bound surrounding of my dwelling in Okemos, Michigan. I take my wet eyes and flowing nose as symbolic of my soul's sorrow at the absence of any trace of memory or image of my mother's face. I have seen her womanly shape in several dreams I had of her, but not the faintest image of her face. Probably photography came to be known only after her interment. Even if photography facilities were available, they must have been unaffordable to my family which was of lower middle class level. She died when I was about two years old. I remember having heard my father often relate how I approached the bier wherein my mother's body was laid in our parish church, Holy Kings' Catholic church, Piravom, for the last rites, and poked her to get up and give me food – a scene that reportedly provoked suppressed sobs and tear drops in the bystanders.

My father, late Mr Chacko, or Chackopilla as I remember my grand parents and my elderly neighbours used to call him, was about thirty years old when my mother died. He was advised and urged by many, including even by my grand parents, to marry again. But he refused to do so reportedly because he would not leave us, his three motherless children, to the care of a step-mother. He took it upon himself to bring us up. My grand father, late Mr Mathai, or kaikkaran Mathaichettan as he used to be called by our neighbours because for many years he had served as the trustee of our parish church, joined us and came to my father's help in bringing us up.

I said we were three brothers. I have been told that the eldest child born of my parents was a girl. But she died as an infant of six months. I grew up with my two brothers, Joseph or Kochu and Mathai or Mathachan under the joint care of my father and grand father, exclusively in masculine company until my eldest brother at the age of eighteen got married to Mariakutty aged sixteen. Ever since then she was to me a mother and sister-in-law.

My father had an education only up to primary level. A small-scale farmer of low middle class level, working on a landed property of about two acres, his ambition was to produce enough paddy and tapioca as well as yam and vegetables to meet the family's annual food requirements and enough fodder for a pair of oxen maintained for ploughing. But often enough unexpected rainfalls or the lack of it used to leave his annual budget in the red, and cause strains in the family. I was interested in and I used to go fishing with a line and hook at free times. I would take pride if I could catch half a pound of fish from the nearby ponds. A pound of beef or pork once a month would be a great luxury. The main condiment resource was jackfruit seeds and mangoes. Seasoning this menu item would have considerably added to its taste; but then two ounces of coconut oil a week would be an inaccessible luxury. When I look back at this period of my childhood from the perspective of the present God-given condition and amenities of life I feel that period was one of very strenuous privations and wants. But the most significant aspect of it is that in the midst of such 'strains and privations of life', we never ever had any feeling of poverty or privation. It never gave us a sense of bitterness, grudge or depression-complexes. It never affected or tainted the village simplicity or innocence, the mood of cheer and playfulness that was characteristic of my childhood life. In fact I look upon the experience of such strains and privations and later experiences of struggles and strains as a great blessing of God in disguise as they enabled me to understand life in general, to sympathize with those in untold and silent grip of privations, pains and sorrows. In short, the greatest wealth and health that we inherited from my father was this rustic simplicity, innocence and cheer, and contented attitude to life around us. We worked, played, laughed, dived into deep ponds around us, swam across the river nearby and enjoyed the intimate fellowship of all the neighbours who also were moulded more or less in the same attitude and atmosphere of life in Karakode village of Piravom Panchayat. Like the snow-flakes that are falling around me now in Okemos village are the innumerable other sweet memories of and experiences with the neighbours that crop up into my mind. With a word of apology to all of them for my inability to mention all of them in this short account, I here draw the curtains on all those nostalgic memories.

The sight of the white satin-covered virgin scenery outside my bedroom window is fascinating. The heavens seem to bless the scenery by sprinkling the jasmine petals of snow flakes over it. I would love to sit in my rotating chair enjoying it. But I have to turn to my home childhood memories once again. As I hinted earlier, I was brought up in an exclusively male-dominated family atmosphere. Naturally I too had to get involved in the routines of such a family. I slowly imbibed the art of household duties such as cleaning, cooking, boiling etc., including even boiling paddy, drying it in the sun and de-husking it by beating it in a large mortar with a long pestle. 'Ural and Ulakka' we used to call them. Grinding and de-husking mills were unheard of at that time. Our art of cooking consisted of boiling rice or tapioca or yam and making condiment of jack-fruit seeds and mangoes fresh or salted. The modern sophisticated cuisine art of varied branded and highly specialized cooking process and variety food items too were equally unheard of.

## The Spirituality of Village Innocence

Quarrelsome and mischievous as boys are, we three brothers too used to get involved in small skirmishes and little fights.

Being the youngest, I rarely got involved. But my elder brothers used to have tough fights in the absence of my father. At times their wrangles used to frighten me and make me cry aloud. And often enough I would report the matter to my father. He would then hold a case trial. The judgment and the award of punishment would be based entirely on my deposition as the sole witness. The happiest thing for me was that neither the judge nor the accused had any doubt about the honesty and truthfulness of my deposition and consequently my brothers never had any grudge against me on account of my deposition. That natural honesty and truthfulness, I believe, was the product of the village simplicity and innocence that surrounded our home and was one of the greatest gifts of God. It equipped me with the necessary defense and enabled me to stand intrepid against the onslaughts of the 'colossal religious and socio-political power centers' in my life.

# 2

# The Sunday-School Instilled Religious Spirituality

However, the most important factor of my childhood memories which, I think, needs to be emphasized is the 'religious spirituality' that ruled and regulated our home life and even our social life. This spirituality had absolutely no role in the shaping of the natural and spontaneous honesty and truthfulness mentioned above. That I got from the nature of the village innocence, simplicity and guileless neighbourly fellowship we were fortunate enough to be surrounded with. But the 'religious spirituality' was entirely ruled, shaped and conditioned by the Catholic parish church. It was an impenetrable super layer that seemed to fall on our life from regions above nature and cover up the entire life. It consisted of minute and careful rituals and came to be firmly established by dint of the by-hearted prayer-formulae and ritualistic practices as prescribed and drilled into us by the parish priest. My father, being a man of no higher education than primary level, as I have already hinted, was unable nor could he afford, in the humdrum routine and hard work to make both ends meet, to indulge in speculative philosophy or in the principles of rational thinking and scrutinize the meaning and relevance of these prayer formulae he was instructed to learn by heart and repeat it at regular times. The words of the prayers rolled out from memory while the mind could be engaged in any other matter. Gullible and simple, he totally accepted and faithfully followed the authority of the church and the periodical instructions of the parish priest. On his turn he faithfully imparted to us this impenetrable and above-natural layer of ritualistic spirituality through his faithful practice and through the Sunday school teaching at church. Sending children to regular Sunday school catechisms was one of the greatest church-imposed parental duties. And my father was scrupulously faithful in discharging this religious duty. Thus we the children, too, learned the church-drilled and the traditionally by-hearted and repeated prayer-formulae from the mouth and practice of my father and by dint of the Sunday school exercises.

The 'Ten Commandments' of God are seen summarized and synthesized into the 'Two greatest of all commandments', that is 'Love God with all your strength and mind and Love your neighbour as yourself'. These two are again distilled into faithfulness to Natural Human Morality of which Nature is the norm. As the Thomistic Catholic philosophy has it: 'Natura est Norma Moralitatis': Nature is the norm of morality. And what is Nature and its Laws? I consider Nature as the Universal common Sacred Scripture in which is the Word of God found recorded unpolluted, un-interpolated and un-mutilated. What else shall I say about the white-carpeted Nature's brilliance that I view from my room if not that it is the 'Sacred Scripture of the Unwritten Word of God'? Unfortunately this common, universal 'Holy Scripture' has hardly any regulatory role in the Church-designed and ritual-centered spirituality that we were conditioned in from our infancy, or that wrapped my early childhood life in. In fact, the spirituality of ritual exercises was almost entirely designed and ruled by the 'Five Commandments of the Holy Church' elaborately detailing the all-important rituals to be unquestionably adhered to, and faithfully observed. Significantly enough, the 'church commandments' conclude with the duty of the 'tithes and payment of the share of income as decided and decreed by the 'High Priest', (the Bishop, I presume) from time to time'. The other four commandments prescribe and make mandatory the various ritual practices like attendance at Mass on Sundays and other prescribed days, abstinence from meat on Fridays, annual confession and communion and ban on marrying from outside the ghetto. Any violation of these five commandments is nothing less than a deadly 'mortal' sin inviting the punishment of eternal condemnation to hell after death – a hell of unquenchable flame of fire and undying worms and obnoxious pests! The unearthly emphasis which these rituals are charged with in Sunday school teachings and in sermons develops an acute and depressing sense of sinfulness resulting from failures in adhering to these ritual practices. However, hardly any sense of sin is developed for failures and negligence of duties civic, social and of natural morality. This attitude of unconcern about the social and moral aspect of human life and the inordinate emphasis on the performance of ritualistic duties is what I could learn from the practice of making ritualistic confessions and later from hearing confessions as a priest for hours at a stretch.

## Sex the Greatest Sin-generative Sector

There is a distortion added to this sense of sin. Along with the sin-generative area of the church-prescribed rituals there is another equally generative of more 'degenerate' sin! It is the area of sex. Any indulgence in the area of sex is not only a sin, it is designated as 'impure' sin. It would appear that violation of commandments relating to any other area would be 'pure' sin! The 'deadly' impure act of sex is looked upon as an inevitable evil that is to be tolerated only among married couples and that too as a tool or machine work only to procreate. And the impure sin of sex is given a special treatment in the 'Principles of Moral Theology'. The principles of moral theology say that three ingredients are necessary for the constitution of a mortal sin: full awareness of the evil nature of the act, full willingness or freedom and gravity in the matter of violation. For example, stealing one rupee may constitute a venial or small sin, because it is not a grave matter, whereas stealing a hundred rupees could be a mortal or grave sin. However, according to the same principles of moral theology, in matters relating to the sixth divine commandment (area of sex) gravity of matter does not enter into the fray as an ingredient of the 'impure' mortal sin. 'In rebus de sexto, nulla datur parvitas materiae' is the relevant principle. In short, the religion that I was grounded in from my infancy was given shape to and dominated more by the five commandments of 'Holy Mother the Church' than by the Ten Commandments of God. It covered two areas: the area of rituals and any violation thereof generated sin and the area of sex, where any indulgence, however insignificant it may be, would generate 'impure' mortal sin. Thus, poor ordinary mortal as I am, my life was haunted by a sense of sin, but haunted to a nightmarish level by the sense of the 'impure' sin in a gradually increasing degree as I drew nearer to the stages of puberty and adulthood. And it continued to haunt me for quite a number of years even after I left the Catholic Church in1975 at the age of 38 after twelve and a half years of Catholic priestly ministry, until I arrived at the delightful daylight after the long peregrination of groping through the dark dungeons of dogma-ruled religion. Of course, the Catholic church has prescribed medication for the disease of this haunting sense of sin which it has generated and provided spiritual physicians who only can administer it, the sacramental confession, priests equipped with theological expertise and certified and authorized and installed to practice through ritualistic priesthood. Rev. Dr James Gurudas in his 'Mochana Kahalam' (a powerful satire on this 'otherworldly and anti-sex spirituality') published in 2011 refers to 'sacramental confession' as a device to compensate through 'auricular pleasure' what the Catholic priests lost through the 'Law of Celibacy'

## My Sunday School Experience

The memories of my Sunday school experience highlight how such a load of dogmatic sediments piled in my mind and began to weigh me down and shut out the light of reason. I have in my mind a fantastic world called 'Heaven' situated far above somewhere. There is the god-family where the old father-god is found seated on a throne. His head is covered with long, snow-white, thick and curly hair and his face with a bushy, white long beard reminding me of some of the Metropolitans both of the Orthodox as well as the Catholic churches. Seated on his right is the son-god with long hair and beard and dress, all of a style similar to that of a middle-aged handsome healthy Jew. The Nicene Creed theologises the origin of the son-god as 'begotten' and 'not made' by the father-god ('genitus, non factus' as the creed has it worded). The third member of the god-family is the dove-shaped connecting god with feathery wings spread out between the father-god and the son-god. The Nicene creed again theologises the connection by the phrase 'proceeding from the father and the son' with maximum emphasis on 'and the son' because there is a heated controversy among the theologians: the 'filioque' controversy. According to the theology of the Roman Catholic Latin or western theologians, the connecting god proceeds from the father-god and the son-god, whereas according to the theology of the Oriental Catholic Church and according to the Oriental Syro-Malabar Catholic Church since 3 July 1962 – the date of the restoration of the de-Latinised Syro-Malabar Rite into its pristine purity—the connecting god proceeds only from the father-god. The 'filioque' issue has been a perennial controversy and a still undecided hot dispute among the Latin Catholic and the Oriental Catholic theologians. But how the latter group connect the father-god and the son-god without the 'filioque' and come to the sum total of the 'Triunity god' must be another dogmatic mystery.

This highly interesting spectrum of the god-family is summarily described through the most fundamental and crucial formula in the whole of Christian theology: the mystery concept of the Triune God, – the Three-One God, the 'three-eka-deivam! I have been told that mathematics is the source and basis of all sciences. The concept of the Triune God – the Three-One God – simply topples the world of science. To the science of mathematics the concept of the 'Triune' is as self contradictory as the concept of 'square circle' is to geometry. But what does that matter? Science is the world of the light of reason whereas theology is the world of dogmatic faith and 'philosophy ends where theology begins'! The sum total of the triune god thus reached with or without the 'filioque' seems to be a blindly pragmatic and light-heartedly concocted compromise between the Hindu concept of the 'Trinity God' and the staunch Jewish concept of the 'Monotheistic God' into a 'Triunity God'. The first element, i.e., the Hindu concept of the Trinity God, stands the theologians in good stead to weave the crucial story of the Christian religion. The Trinity God is also helpful to support the attendant spectrum of the various rituals very similar in essence to the Hindu rituals: the story of the father-god sending the son-god to take human incarnation and to be sacrificed as an eternal sacrifice to appease the father-god in adequate atonement for the original and the personal sins of the world and thus to become the sole redeemer of the world. Without this basic story, Christian religion becomes simply non-existent. The second element of the 'triunity', i.e. the Jewish concept of the strict monotheism stands in good stead as the ground for the claim of the honour and uniqueness of the Jewish monotheism.

The colossal spectrum of the dogmatic Christian faith generated from this core faith in the square-circular 'Triune' god is masterfully synthesized and shaped into power-packed capsule form in the Sunday school programme in the form of catechism questions and answers, easy for even the small children to swallow. I had been almost overdosed with such power packed mystery capsules in my childhood Sunday school programme. It comes in the very simple form of elementary questions and answers that the child has to swallow by heart. The very first question I was confronted with was: 'Which are the chief mysteries of our faith?' Take careful note of the words 'mystery' and 'faith'. They indicate the direction the wheels of the Sunday school programme are steered to. And pat comes the answer to be picked up and learnt by rote: 'Unity and trinity of God, the human incarnation, death by crucifixion, the resurrection of our Lord Jesus Christ, and the redemption of the human race'. This capsular formula of the fivefold mystery which defines the hardcore essence of the Christian faith is further clinched and conditioned by dint of sheer repetition of it at the beginning and at the end of every prayer composed and administered by the Church authorities or other pious laymen. But then in the latter case these prayers must be impressed by the Episcopal censure seal and certificate of 'nihil obstat' (nothing objectionable) and 'imprimatur' (it may be printed). The simple believers are to learn them by heart and repeat. The hardcore essence of this fivefold mystery formulae is further corroborated through the innumerable repetition, almost to the extent of sheer boredom, of the triunity formula in the Mass and in all other liturgical ritual prayers: 'for ever father, son and holy ghost, god almighty for ever, amen'. This capsular summary of the faith formula is further insulated against any threat from the regions of rational light within the impenetrable even bullet-proof immunization cover of the dogma of ecclesiastical infallible teaching magisterium. Under such immunizing, protective and precautionary measures, no ordinary mortal believer would ever think of or feel the need of scrutinizing the meaning of those formulae in the light of reason to see how they are relevant in the lives of rational, moral human beings.

The picturesque description of the divine abode of the god-family, namely the Heavens situated far above there somewhere, is further embellished by the images of the infinite number of winged angels flying about like the snow flakes flying about in the Okemos open air outside my room. The throne of the Triune God is surrounded by saints of all hues and in divers religious habits, corresponding to the religious orders they came from and by the prophets and chief priests mentioned in the old and in the new testaments including John the Baptist dressed in the camel's skin and all the saints officially declared by the Pope as saints, all of them repeating the incessant angelic chorus of 'glory, Honour Hallelujah'! I am reminded of those eminent Jesuit professors on the faculty of Philosophy of the Pune Papal Vidyapeeth: Professors like Fr Richard V. De Smet, Fr Gasper Koelman, Fr Antony Sabino etc. They used to teach me about God in concepts like Spirit, Omnipotent, Immutable, absolutely simple, pure Infinite Reality, pure absolute Knowledge, Bliss, Truth etc. They have confirmed that I correctly understood their concepts about God because they have awarded me a first rank with distinction in the post graduation degree examination in Philosophy. I wonder how they could comfortably get on well with this spectroscopic description of the god-family of Christian theology. The revered dean of the faculty of theology in the same Papal Vidyapeeth, Fr Joseph Neuner, used to repeat the norm and guiding principle in the methodology of theology: 'Philosophy ends where theology begins'! Probably those eminent professors of philosophy also know how to black out the light of reason in order to usher in the darkness in which dogmas can grow and multiply. So I started to usher in the thick darkness of the dogma-dominated religious capsules administered to me in catechism classes; nay, I gladly accepted them as salutary to my soul from my infancy. The habit slowly got corroborated and drilled by dint of our daily family practice of by-hearted prayer formulae, by faithful observance of prescribed rituals, and by indoctrination through Sunday school programmes and hardcore dogmatic sermons for years till later when my church authority confronted me with the attitude: 'Who are you to think when we are here?' And then I was tempted to answer back—with a small amount of arrogance, I fear—'God is not in anybody's long pocket'! With that confrontation the cozy comfort and ease in swallowing the power-packed faith formulae pills crashed and crumbled. It added acceleration and momentum to my effort to get out of the peregrination and groping through the dogma - generated dark dungeons to the delightful daylight similar to the brilliance of the mid sunny day here in Okemos, outside my room, snow flakes flying about like the winged angels!

**Pilgrim Stampede Flashed**

Look there! Asianet News channel flash. Here, in Okemos, Michigan, now it is about 10 a.m. Friday, 21 January 2011. Asianet News channel begins the telecast. Let me listen. Wow! The news of prime importance: the Ambalamedu Makara Jyothi Stampede tragedy, took the lives of more than a hundred innocent and gullible Sabarimala pilgrims. Here is another event, the most recent, showing to what extent of social tragedy blind religious beliefs can take us! Moths in thousands are attracted to the brightness of flame and get consumed in the fire!

The season of Sabarimala pilgrimage in Kerala reaches the climax and begins the anti-climax with the vision, or 'darshan', as the pilgrims respectfully call it, of 'the Makara Jyoti' *(Note: South Indians have a tendency to add an 'h' after the 't' but I am sticking to general Indian spelling.)* a light that is believed to appear miraculously by divine intervention above the thick forest of Ambalamedu that is visible from Sabarimala. The 'miracle' takes place in the first half of every January at the exact moment pre-announced. Pilgrims, this year tens of thousands in number, were standing densely crowded with loud pious invocations for the 'darshan'. Suddenly a vehicle, parked somewhere up in the neutral gear started rolling towards the crowd. It triggered off the unfortunate stampede that claimed such an alarming number of human lives. The telecast brought out a heated debate on the issue between a representative of the 'Rationalist Association' on one side and S.N.D.P. chief Vellappally Nadesan and the Hindu Aikia Vedi Spokesperson Sasikala on the other.

A few years ago a group of rational thinkers, contemptuously referred to as atheists by the venerable religious dogmatists, had challenged the miraculous or divine halo attributed to the appearance of the Makara Jyoti. They had contented that the event was a mere product of sheer human manipulation and it had nothing to do with anything miraculous or divine. They held that the victims of such innumerable pilgrimage tragedies are the gullible devotees either in search of relief from various maladies and misfortunes or in pursuit of undue prosperity and satisfaction of insatiable greed for wealth. Their weaknesses are cruelly exploited by the proprietors and custodians of pilgrim centres through stories of miraculous signs and effects supposed to be performed by divine intervention. But in reality they are products of crafty human manipulations. Such stories have been woven by centres of dogmatic religious creeds and practices. The rationalist thinkers look upon such practices as nothing less than criminal public cozenage. So they had challenged the veracity of the story of divine intervention in the case of Makara Jyoti. They also decided to conduct an on-the-spot investigation. Sensing the possible devastating setback to the colossal annual income from the pilgrims, the creators of the miracle story contended that it was well within their 'freedom' of faith and religion and whipped up 'Hindu religious sentiment' to counter the rationalist challenge and to resist the proposed on-the-spot investigation edeavour.

Foreseeing a communal clash and consequent catastrophe and law and order disturbance that could ensue, the then Chief Minister, the late Mr E.K. Nayanar, defused the explosive situation by openly confessing that the appearance of the Jyoti had nothing to do with any divine intervention but was only humanly manipulated by persons appointed and paid for it with the knowledge of the government and under supervision of the electricity department. With this official explanation the storm and rumbling of a near civil war subsided. But the light of reason lit by the Rationalist Group could not outlive the dark story of this 'miraculous' event. The story had already been solidified and the darkness thickened by generations of traditional indoctrination which continued through annual boisterous propaganda and media celebrations of the event each year. Significantly enough, other religious sects including the Christian ones chose to take the path of diplomatic silence lest they should burn their own finger and spoil the benefits of their own practices of pilgrimages and took an attitude of 'we are not of this region'! Soon the oil of the light lit by the rationalists dried up and the light was extinguished, while the solidified darkness continued its triumphant march through the winds and waves of propaganda pageantry and crowd-pulling media celebration. This triumphant march of the deliberately created religious blindness continued to claim every year the toll of several more lives of innocent pilgrims due to various calamities like pollution, accident, diseases, weather inclemency etc until the present stampede that claimed more than a hundred lives. The events that followed the tragedy, as indicated by the Asianet Telecast, are even more foreboding. The 'atheistic' rationalists approached the High Court with a petition to intervene against this criminal cozenage of ignorant and gullible masses. This has provoked heated debates as relayed in the Asianet news telecast. The religious stalwart Vellappally Natesan and Sasikala were heard staunchly and brazenly defending the 'religious freedom' of creating dark faith in the 'miraculous divine halo' around the purely humanly manipulated appearance of Makara Jyoti and harping upon the unconstitutionality of the judiciary intervening against deceiving the public and exploiting their blissful ignorance in the name of 'religious freedom'! If propagation of religious faith means spreading of ignorance of facts, what credibility is there in dogmatic faiths? What is then the meaning and purpose of civic education? If the Makara Jyoti affair is not a massive social cozenage legitimately demanding the intervention of the judiciary, how could it be argued, as was heard in the same telecast, that the judiciary should effectively intervene in the case of the conduct of state lotteries, be it Kerala State or Sikkim State, because it is public gambling and sheer pick-pocketing of the public and therefore criminal mass cheating? Does it all mean that when it comes to the matter of amassing revenue, whether by the State or by the religious power centers, there is nothing like civic rights, legal protection, civic education or spreading of enlightened citizenship? What a mess of civic life has been generated by our 'secular' democratic party politics and religions of dogmatic faiths through their clandestine unholy alliance? Sure enough, the prospects of our democratic civic community are bleak and foreboding! Let me go back to my early memories.

# 3

## My Early Education

Unlike my father and my two brothers, I was fortunate enough to have an education beyond the primary level, thanks to the strenuous efforts of and privations suffered by my grandfather, father and brothers. My brothers could go only up to the primary level of formal education, as schooling for them beyond that level was not affordable. Besides, my father needed my brothers' help to ease his hectic schedule of work, domestic as well as agricultural. My formal education started at the age of four, I think, with learning the Malayalam alphabet. Unlike English, Malayalam is a phonetic language having fifty six linguistic sounds and consequently as many letters or graphic symbols of those sounds. I started the acquisition of literacy under a primary master whom we respectfully called Kuzhyil Aasan. Kuzhyil is his surname and Aasan is a variant of Guru. The class room was the cow dung smeared open verandah of his thatched house about two miles away from my similar house. I used to walk this distance every class day with my second brother who after dropping me at Aasan's house proceeded to his primary government school at Onakoor, about two miles further down. He had to wade through a small stream called Kariyila Thode. Thode means more or less a brook. This thode played an important role in my village of Karakode because the thin and narrow flow of water shared by all the villagers in turn and used for the irrigation of small plots of paddy cultivation came from this thode. On return from Onakoor after class which ended at 4 p.m. my brother picked me up from my study center and we walked back home for Lunch at about 5.00 p.m.

Our method of learning to write was entirely different from that followed in modern kindergarten or pre-primary classes. We had no papers, pencils or even slates. We carried with us an unbroken, coconut shell with its inside scraped clean and which contained sand with sugar-like grains. We spread it on the cow-dung smeared floor. Squatting behind the spread sand, leaning on the mud-wall behind, we reproduced the letter already graphed by Aasan on a long dried palm leaf with a thin sharp pointed iron rod and articulated the sound which the letter represented. The most significant part of this process of literacy was that Aasan made sure of the absolute clarity and purity of each linguistic sound represented by the phonetic symbol which the letter is. Unfortunately, in the modern practices in kindergarten and pre-primary literacy exercises, the care and effort taken by Aasan for the clarity and purity of linguistic sounds is missing, I fear. And this neglect can be seen conspicuously reflected on modern spoken Malayalam. For example, 'Bharatam' is heard as 'Baratham' and 'Bhavi' as 'Bavi'.

## At the Primary School

After the literacy course under Aasan, I joined the first standard in Government L.P. School, Onakoor, about two miles further from Aasan school. I walked all this distance of four miles with my second brother who was two classes ahead of me. My four-year course of primary education was quite uneventful, without the embellishments of modern democratic culture like strikes, bandhs, hartals, party clashes leading to vandalism etc. Our country at that time was Travancore, which is now one third of the present Kerala State. Our sovereign king was His Highness Sree Chithira Thirunal Bala Rama Varma Maha Raja, brother of the living Sree Marthanda Varma. To my memory, the independence struggle under the leadership of Gandhiji, Nehruji and other jis had not gathered any momentum. All that we were taught was that our king had sovereign power and could declare war, literally war, on any neighbouring country such as Kochi or Malabar – these, with Travancore, are now part of the State of Kerala. What I have heard of this our Sovereign Maha Raja was that every morning he took a ritual dip in the Sree Padmanabha Swamy Temple pool and stood with wet clothes before the temple Sree Kovil (the sanctum sanctorum or sanctuary) to invoke God's blessings upon him and his subjects (including me, of course) before he approached his throne of authority. The most unforgettable of my primary school memories was the celebration of our king's birthday. On that day we would reach the school, each with a sugar cane flower bunch – we had no flags to flourish nor could we afford to have one. Flourishing this flower bunch we would go round the school in a procession shouting the rhythmic slogan 'C.h.i-T.r.a-Chithira-Chithira-Chithira–Sree Balarama Varma Maha Raja Ki jai'. At the end of this sonorous procession we were supplied with a 'vatta ila' (a round leaf similar to a lotus leaf) full of aval (fried beaten rice sweetened with scraped coconut and jaggery) and a half coconut shell full of black coffee, and all these at the king's personal expense. We loved him and felt that he too loved us and cared for us. I am inclined to think that he wielded his sovereignty which, he believed, was given to him from the God he worshiped every day, not for himself but for his subjects. He did so with the right and responsibility of a trustee. Far from being power-addicted or blinded, he was ready to relinquish it and hand it over to whomsoever it might suit. Thereby he made it possible to bring about a wider union of one State out of three 'sovereign countries' and block the possibility of any war between these 'sovereignties'. For him there was only one sovereign authority and that was God Almighty. His is an example set in motion, which, if emulated and imitated by all the power-drunk sovereigns all over the world, would have opened up wider unions until this wave, started by this humble God-fearing sovereign king, would have transformed the entire world nations into one world community of human beings, under one world government. It would have eliminated once for all the possibility of any world war or even any war at all. It would have saved 60 to 70 per cent of the national income of all the present 'sovereign' countries set apart in their annual budget for 'national defense and army maintenance' which could have been used to form a world nation, free from war-tensions – a world geared to ever greater prosperity, peace and happiness, as 'atheist rationalist' Bertrand Russel had dreamt, for which he was banished. But he was rationally strong enough to retaliate: 'Not that you banish me, but I banish you'! And he called himself a 'citizen of the world'.

Sorry, I strayed far away from my primary school memories of Onakoor. Let me come back. There are four persons related to my primary school experiences and conspicuous in my memory: first, Markose Sir (as we used to call him), our Headmaster – a rather serious looking, moderately fat and more than average bellied man. Then comes Chemmanat Chacko Sir, a member of my own Piravom Knanaya Catholic Parish. Next is Raman Pilla Sir, a tall, rather lean, medium sized man with a broad forehead fully and thickly smeared with sandalwood paste (kalabham). And finally, Raman Pilla Sir's daughter and my fellow student Saraswathy Amma. She must have been a very beautiful girl, but I was not adult enough to assess her beauty sufficiently and accurately from close quarters. Every day when the bell rang for the beginning of classes, Saraswathy intoned the 'Desa vandana Prayer song 'Vanchi Bhoomi Pathe Cheeram'....I felt all her qualification to be assigned to this prestigious regular duty was that she was Raman Pilla Sir's daughter! I remember to have visited Markose Sir at his residence to offer him my 'dakshina' of gratitude after receiving the T.C. along with the certificate of promotion from the fourth and final year of primary education.

Having been promoted from the fourth and final year of primary education, I had two choices in front of me: one, to join the one year course of 'Preparatory Class' in the M.K.M. (Mar Kurilose Memorial) Upper Primary school, under private management; the other, to join the fifth class in the Government Upper primary school, both in Piravom town. The government school was slightly more distant from my home than the M.K.M. school. But the M.K.M. school levied a monthly fee of two rupees or so from every student while there was no fee in the government U.P. school. In either case the next promotion would be to the first form which was the first of the three year Upper Primary course and it would be free of any fee. Naturally my choice was the fifth class in the government school because the monthly fee of Rs. 2 in the M.K.M. preparatory class was prohibitively unaffordable to my father. I was then ten years old and it was the year 1946, the pre-independence year. We the students were getting information about meetings, processions, demonstrations, slogan-shouting, student-police clashes etc. related to the national struggle for Independence under the leadership of Gandhi ji, Pandit ji, Patel ji and many other ji's. We decided to show our solidarity with the national independence movement. One day during the pre-noon class interval, some of us gathered at the school gate and began shouting laudatory 'Ki jay's to all the movement leader ji's and condemnatory slogans like 'down, down with British rule', 'Koothattukulam Lathi charge, shame shame' etc. We had been informed that the police had lathi-charged a group of nationalist enthusiasts. The headmaster came to our class after the interval and enquired with an air of contempt: 'You, stupids, what did you understand about these slogans you shouted?' Indeed we did feel stupid.

Promoted from the fifth class in the government school, I joined the M.K.M. to complete the first, the second and the third forms comprising the entire course of upper primary education free of any fee. Meanwhile, India gained Independence without much commotion or rumblings of national sentiments in our still boyish minds. The only memory, perhaps, worth mentioning here, about this period of my U.P. Education is that I always looked forward eagerly to and immensely enjoyed the English classes handled by one John Sir. I forget his initials. I had special regard for him because he was our English teacher. I checked up the time table every morning and that morning of the day was exceptionally bright and happy which had an hour of English. Another amusing memory was that of Mathew Sir the tallest and P.U. Chacko Sir, the shortest of the members of the teaching staff. It was amusing to see how both of them managed to see each others face for any short close conversation. Mathew Sir would bend his head forward at an angle of 90 degrees to look down and Chacko Sir would bend his head backward at an angle of 90 degrees supporting the backside of his head with his two palms kept tight with the fingers intertwined to look up and thus their eyes would meet each other and we would enjoy the scene from a little distance with a slight nudge at each other.

## At High School

The three years of the U.P. course having been completed, and that too successfully, by the grace of God, I joined the fourth form (the present eighth Standard) in St. Joseph's High School, Piravom. It was rather close to where my grandmother lived. I was able to have noon meal at my grandmother's. Our headmaster, Fr C.T. Kuriakose, was formerly of the Syrian Orthodox Church and therefore a married priest, but later became a Catholic through the historical event of the 'Reunion' of a section of the Orthodox Church with the Catholic Church under the leadership of Bishops Mar Ivanios, Mar Severios and others. As with the English teacher John Sir of M.K.M., I had a special liking for Mrs. Elizabeth Maret, again, our English teacher. The subjects that I disliked most were history, geography and to some extent, arithmetic. The policy of our Government Education Department of the late twentieth century and early twenty first century is all promotion in schools. Several schools are flashed in medias as achieving nearly ninety per cent pass with distinction, five per cent with a First Class and three percent with a Second Class and the rest with Third Class, at any rate a hundred per cent pass. Most recently this all-pass system has further been reformed into the most modern 'grading system' of all-pass with grades ranging from A to E, the last grade pass mark being zero! I remember what a University expert told me about five years ago: 'Let the students write something. You give them marks'! However in the 1950s, if the best school had half a dozen first classes, (with 60 per cent of the total marks) that would be a record. One day during the final year (1953) of my high school education, Elizabeth teacher came to our class and called up four of us – P.T. John, E.T. Baby, K. George and myself – and said, 'If you work a little harder, you four could get a first class'. Her assessment was almost correct: all of them got first class that year except me. I got only a third class with marks a little below the second class. And I thanked God for such a good result, coming, as I did, from a home background as mentioned earlier and walking about four miles to school and back.

As for the outcome of these two methods of assessment, we, of the older type, were able to analyze into clauses showing their kind and construction an understandable sentence of any length, as I did in the entrance test taken for admission to Petit Seminary in June 1953. As for the level of standard promoted by the all-promotion policy, let me quote a sentence produced by one of my first year degree students of the 2010 batch: 'All student are spoking well English goodly'! He was appreciating the Spoken English Course introduced into the syllabus in the place of the usual 'grammar course' that had been in the degree syllabus. Such a sentence is good enough English, according to the most current principle of the language teaching: the purpose of language is to convey ideas. If the idea is conveyed, the language used for it is good enough. 'All student are spoking well English goodly' conveys the idea, I believe.

Another event that added to my grief and heaviness of heart was the demise of my grandfather, which took place in the last year of my high school life.

# 4

## At the Petit Seminary

The idea of turning to priestly studies after my S.S.L.C. was implanted in my mind by our Parish Priest, Rev. Abraham Kochuparambil. It was further nourished by his successors and cherished by my own family members because having a priest and/or a nun in the family brings extraordinary prestige and honour to it.

By the by, the number of my home members had increased as my brothers got married, and the eldest became a father. I did not have to think much as to my future course that I should turn to: to priestly ministry for the greater glory of God and 'for the service of the Church'. I decided to apply for the course of priestly studies. I have heard my father gloat over his privilege and honour of having given his third son to the greater Glory of God and for the service of the Church. It was only later, in fact after years of my priestly service or rather struggle that my poor father, bothers and I myself came to the belated understanding that God's glory could not be added to and that the Church service I was destined to do was service rendered to quite extraordinarily mortal humans wielding church authority covered under the self arrogated halo of divinity. I had decided to become a priest having been convinced by dint of the thick Catholic atmosphere, tradition and catechism that becoming a priest was a direct call from God. I was already at the gate of adulthood to suspect and fear the pungency of celibacy attached to the catholic priesthood. But what of that? Sex was only a necessary evil, so went the contemporary catholic idea, but tolerated only in marriage for the procreation of children and for the continuation of the human species. Celibacy meant the voluntary renunciation of this necessary evil, part of the mortification of all the desires and participation in the redemptive suffering of the Incarnate Son of God, Jesus! And mortification of all desires and total renunciation of the worldly and the bodily and voluntary and even self-inflicted endurance of suffering were the hallmarks of the holy life of Christian Faith. That was the dogma that ruled me then.

My next step towards the achievement of my chosen career was to apply for admission to the two-year course offered in the diocesan Petit Seminary at S.H. Mout, Kottayam. It was a course offered by every Catholic diocese in those years to prepare the priest aspirants for the seven or more years of priestly studies offered by the major regional seminaries. The preparatory Petit Seminary course consisted of learning three languages: Latin, which was the prescribed exclusive medium of instruction in major seminary studies; Syriac, the language of priestly rituals, and English for general use. Admission to the Petit Seminary course was determined on the basis of an entrance examination conducted to test the level of standard of English acquired in the S.S.L.C. examination. The test covered all the major steps of English grammar culminating in the analysis of sentences of considerable length into clauses stating their kind and construction, an exercise in grammar that is hardly seen or heard in the modern systems of grammar. I took the entrance test successfully and got admitted to the Petit Seminary attached to and within the campus of the Monastery of the Oblates of the Sacred Heart (O.S.H.).

The Oblates of the Sacred Heart were members of a Diocesan Religious congregation for men including priests and laymen of the Diocese of Kottayam who were ready to take the vows of chastity, poverty and obedience. The Diocesan Bishop was the founder and controlling authority of this 'religious congregation'. The vow of chastity did not involve any additional obligation because it was already implied in the vow of celibacy that was obligatory for all the catholic-ordained priests. In addition to this were the vows of poverty and obedience imposed on the Oblates of the Sacred Heart. (The word 'Oblates' comes, I understand, from the Latin word 'oblatus' and means 'the offered or the dedicated one'.) The obligation of this triple vow taken by a group of priests of the Diocese would bring them the halo of 'Religious' or of a higher level of detachment from the world and the worldly. But precisely because of that it would also bring to the founder Bishop the very comfortable and conspicuous advantage of the dedicated service of a group of priests whom he could more authoritatively order to service by virtue of their vow of obedience and with less expense by virtue of their vow of poverty. Only very late did I come to realize that there existed a tension of considerable intensity between the Bishop, who felt more empowered by virtue of those bonds upon the member priests and the members, who felt more tightly ordered to service under these bonds. I understand that this almost half-a-century-old tension grew and passed through critical stages involving appeals against the Bishop before the Papal Curia concerned and later litigations between the two sides over the rights of landed properties of the Congregation till the Congregation fought out and won greater independence from the all-controlling Episcopal authority through the intervention of the Papacy a few years ago. All this is very relevant here because it later turned out to be one of the decisive factors that helped me to come to know the religion of the Church and the Church authority from rather close quarters and triggered my peregrination through the dark dungeons to the dazzling dawn. But I shall come to the details later. I may also mention here that Fr Philip Visakhanthara, a man with a fair soul, was a member of the O.S.H. Congregation and almost a nightmare to the Bishop in the long struggle between the two sides.

To come back to the story of my Petit Seminary life. The two years spent in the Petit Seminary were indeed one of happy memory. Every morning, after half an hour of meditation, we had to attend mass or serve as an altar boy during mass. The ritual, performed in Syriac, lasted half an hour or more depending upon the priest. The pivotal part of the Mass is the 'words of consecration' uttered over the wafer and wine. They work the miracle of 'transubstantiation' – a highly theology-charged word. It means the change of the substance a highly philosophy-charged word – of the wafer and the wine into the body and blood of Jesus without in any way changing the 'accidents' – another highly philosophy-charged word- or physical and sense-perceptible characteristics such as shape, colour, taste and mass. The words are supposed to have been uttered by Jesus during the biblically reported event of the Last Supper. In English, the words are 'This is my body' and 'This is the chalice of my blood'. Its Syriac version, more or less transliterated, sounds thus: 'haanavoo ger puger' and 'haanavoo ger kasa de deem'. The rubrics prescribe that these words be uttered and completed with full concentration of attention and awareness on the correct articulation and meaning simultaneously. Often enough it has been highly amusing and awe inspiring to watch some priests, especially Fr Chackacheril and Fr Peter Vattaparambil, struggling to complete the simultaneous performance and repeating the parts, suspected to be improperly articulated, with almost hysteric gestures, finger movements and facial expressions. We admired their deep, honest conviction in this utterly dogmatic mystery formula. But I have never seen such strenuous efforts made by priests of later generations. On the contrary, I have witnessed some, still alive, who, tipsy under heavy drinks, ride along the ceremony of Mass as cool as cucumber.

I don't remember whether we had to pay anything for our Petit Seminary course. Fr Jacob Kalayil, Fr Peter Vattaparambil and Fr Cyriac Vattakalam have served as our Rectors during different periods. With respectful gratitude I recall Fr Philip Kamicheril, Fr Jacob Thottam, Fr Jacob Chackacheril etc handling various subjects on the syllabus. Fr Kamicheril alone had the luxury of owning a bicycle, a ladies model, for his moderately long trips. He used to call it his 'virgin cycle' because he never allowed another man to use his 'lady'! This was a small example of his deep sense of humour and hilarity. Food cooked and served by our slightly hunch-backed Pachychettan for breakfast, dinner, evening tea and supper was quite palatable. Before going to bed some time was spent listening to meditation points for the following morning, given usually by Fr Rector. Once a week, the evening study time was used for instruction class, often enough given by the Bishop, the Rt. Rev. Dr. Thomas Tharayil. Once during the instruction, he mentioned an aphorism to make us firm in our choice of the career. He said: 'Purpose once formed, death or victory!' I have never forgotten this vow, as later in my priestly service under his apostolic authority I felt that he lived his aphorism so thoroughly and vigorously that I had to bear its dead-weight. My experience with him also taught me that though it is a fairly good and useful adage, ordinary humans should practice it in life relaxing its vigour a bit with an opening for a second thought about the purpose once formed! An evening game of volley ball added to the joy of the memorable Petit Seminary Course, which ended in 1955.

# 5

# The Major Seminary: Struggles and Hurdles Faced

It was in 1955 that the illustrious Papal Seminary at Kandy in Sri Lanka was shifted to Poona (now Pune) and accessed to the De Nobili College of Theology run by the Jesuits. From time immemorial to me, the Papal Seminary, Kandy, claimed and commanded great prestige and honour. To be selected for admission to the Kandy Seminary for the major seminary course was regarded as a recognition of the candidates chosen for the purpose. Those who were fortunate enough to be educated and trained in Kandy Seminary were destined to hold honourable positions and great responsibilities. It being so, every single diocese in India, particularly in the thickly Catholic populated Kerala, wanted to send their best candidates to the Kandy seminary. Consequently hardly any diocese could get more than one admission each year. And admission was strictly on consideration of merit based on an entrance test in the knowledge of Latin, conducted directly by the Papal Seminary authorities. The 1955 year admission would be the privileged first batch of students of the Papal Seminary after its shift to Poona and amalgamation with the De Nobili College of Theology. After its amalgamation with the De Nobili, it was known as the Papal Athenaeum or University, but it has now come to be renamed as Jnana Deepam Vidhya Peet, Pune.

The announcement of the invitation from the Papal Seminary to take test for admission to the first batch of students in Poona Seminary was to us indeed news for celebration. There were eight in my batch in the second year of the Petit Seminary at S.H. Mount. And we took the test. We waited for the results with our hearts throbbing. And it came in due time. I stood first in the test and felt elated. All colleagues flocked to me to pat me on the back, head, shoulder and I don't remember where else, with the message of their cordial congratulations and, I suppose, with a pinch of acute but secret jealousy, naturally! But I never even imagined that this happy event was destined to trigger off my confrontation and struggle with my Bishop for whom the life-guiding principle was 'purpose once formed, death or victory'!

Needless to say, my mind and imagination were filled with dreams centered round the events related to my further studies at the Papal Seminary, Poona: the preferential treatment among my petit seminary colleagues, the dream of my first forty-four-hour virgin train trip to Poona, the four years of uninterrupted study in Poona, the home-coming for vacation after four years of absence and so on. In those years there was only one break or vacation, of two months, for the Papal Seminary students to go home. And that is after the four-year philosophy course and before the four-year theology course. My dream had grown to the extent of becoming an irresistible weakness.

Quite unexpectedly, His Excellency Bishop Tharayil called me. 'Abraham,' he said, 'Congratulations. Winner of the first rank in the Papal Seminary admission test'! 'I thank God for this grace and favour. I thank Your Lordship too for the opportunity,' was my very humble response. 'Wouldn't you like to go to Poona for your further studies?' he asked me. 'Very much. In fact I have no greater desire than that', I answered. 'Very good', and then he continued, 'A monthly contribution of Rs. 60 per student has to be paid to the Seminary for your expenses'. I felt a tremor somewhere within my heart. 'Will your father be able to pay the monthly seminary fee?', the Bishop enquired. I replied that it would be unthinkable for my father to find that much money every month, struggling as he was to make both ends meet. 'I too doubted that,' the Bishop said with deep understanding, in fact deeper than I could imagine. After a short pause he continued: 'Why don't you discuss the issue with your parish priest? Perhaps he could convene a general Parish Yogam at Piravom and he may persuade the Yogam to meet your seminary expenses as you are the first and only seminarian from Piravom'. That was an unexpected ray of hope of my dream coming true, and I felt deeply grateful to the Bishop. I rushed to Piravom and discussed the scheme suggested by the Bishop with the Vicar, one Fr Mathew Pralel, if my memory does not fail me. The very following Sunday he convened the Parish Yogam and explained the issue for their further reflections and responses. The final shape of the concluded Yogam deliberations were thus: as the first and only candidate from their parish, the parish would meet all my expenses for my continued priestly studies in St. Joseph's Major Seminary, Alwaye. It is for the Bishop and the diocese to meet my expenses for study at Poona, if the diocese wants Poona trained priests.

Rather disappointed but blaming nobody for the inability of my family to raise Rs. 60 a month, I returned to Kottayam to intimate the Bishop about the fate of the suggestion he had made. It was the beginning of April and already summer. The Bishop had moved to his summer villa in cool Peermedu, away from the heat of Kottayam. I rushed to his Mariagiri Villa in Peermedu and informed him of the outcome of my Piravom errand and of the decision arrived at in the Piravom Parish Yogam, including my painful decision to give up my Papal Seminary dreams. With a nod or two of his head forward and backward – what it really meant I could not divine – he said: 'So you have decided to give up your Poona dreams and go to Alwaye according to the wishes of your parishioners?' ending the statement in a high-rising tone. 'What other choice I have, I do not know,' I replied in a half-sobbing and broken tone. 'Are you going to serve as a priest under the authority of the Piravom parish or under me as your Bishop?' This time I felt his question carried an ominous import and felt another quake within me. 'Of course, Your Lordship is my Bishop and I am to serve under your authority,' I replied, again with deep humility mixed with uncertainty as to what next. 'Then listen to my advice. You join the O.S.H. Monastery and be ready to take the temporary vows. I will see to it that the Monastery meet your expenses for your studies in Poona. Go back and think over it and let me know your decision'. It was only then it dawned in my mind that he was to get me bound by the triple vow of chastity, poverty and obedience 'for the greater glory of God and for the service of the Church'. I left him and reached the bus-stop nearest the Bishop's summer villa for my return to Kottayam. Then His Lordship's driver, Pothenchettan, approached me and said: 'You are leaving without having even a cup of tea. Come, I'll make a cup of tea for you and after that you can take the next bus'. But my return-bus was already within sight and I thanked Pothenchettan cordially for his genuine kindness and concern and boarded the bus for Kottayam.

At Kottayam, I decided to meet our Vicar General, the authority next to the Bishop in the diocese, Mgr. Stephen Uralil, a Kandyan product. The elderly priest was fairly universally respected and honoured for his gentle approach to persons and their problems and his wise, understanding and fair opinions. After listening to the tragic story of my Papal Seminary dreams, Mgr. Uralil told me: 'I am sorry, son, to hear about what has happened to your Papal Seminary dreams. But, one thing I assure you: if any one in your batch goes to Poona this year, it will be you'. As he himself implied, his words were not of any considerable consolation or peace to me either.

I then approached the Superior of the O.S.H., Fr Jacob Mudakkalil, another popular and senior priest of the diocese who enjoyed the respect of the other priests of the diocese. On hearing the Bishop's advice to join the O.S.H. Monastery, Fr Mudakkalil told me: 'Son, if you have any genuine desire to join a monastery and pursue an ascetic life, please think of joining any other religious congregation, but not this one'! That remark was a summary though mild form of expression conveying a lot about the sordid condition and intense tension, as I have mentioned above, which existed between the Bishop and the diocesan congregation of the O.S.H., which the Bishop wanted to have at his command, bound by the bonds of vows.

I felt lonely as if in the midst of a turbulent sea: the high waves of the disappointed Papal Seminary dreams and the roaring waves of the foreboding thought implied in the Bishop's warning that my service is going to be not under the people of my parish, but under the authority of His Lordship, the Bishop. A few days of intense restlessness followed. And the major seminary course for me was to begin in June 1955. Suddenly a compromise formula dawned in my mind – to join the congregation of the O.S.H. That formula would open a two-layer high-way before me: To Poona for my further priestly studies in the Papal Seminary and later to the service as a priest under the Bishop's authority. I rushed to the Bishop, still cozy and comfortable in the cool enclosure of his Peermedu summer villa, and told him of my decision to join the O.S.H. Monastery. 'A wise decision that you have taken', the Bishop responded and congratulated me again for the decision. 'But, you know', he continued, 'according to the rules of the O.S.H. Congregation the members have to pay to the Monastery the portion of their patrimony, that is to say, the share of their fathers' wealth. And the minimum necessary amount is Rs. 500. Only then can I recommend your admission to the Monastic life and the payment of the seminary expenses from the Monastery. You go back home, discuss the matter about the patrimony with your father and let me know the result.'

Once again, dark clouds seemed to blot out my dream. I took the return bus to Kottayam. There was no point in discussing the matter with my poor struggling father. Even an amount of Rs. 50/- at one stretch would be beyond his capacity. So I wrote to the Bishop of the futility of discussing the problem with my father about raising for me a sum of Rs. 500 as my patrimony. But the Bishop quickly wrote back to me as the day of admission to Poona Seminary was fast approaching. His advice was: 'Go to your parish priest and request him to persuade the parish yogam to approve a help of Rs. 500 for you from the parish to enable you to join the congregation. After all, they had agreed to pay all your major seminary expenses at Alwaye'! Another peak in front of me to trek and I have to. So I rushed to my parish priest at Piravom. However the response of my parishioners was a summarily negative one. 'We want you to be a diocesan priest and in that case we will meet all your expenses. But we have no money to advance to enable you to join the diocesan congregation of the O.S.H.' All the possible paths in front of me having been closed, I turned to my Bishop with my final word: 'I am helpless in the matter of coming up with Rs. 500 as patrimony. I cannot pursue this matter any more.'

'If the parishioners of Piravom give you up, I will help you with a loan of Rs. 500', the Bishop said. 'Go to the Superior, Fr Mudakkalil and hand this letter to him and then you get ready for your journey to Poona.' It is relevant here to take special note of the words he used extending the help: 'with a loan of Rs. 500 that could be used as another lock or, shall I say, hook to clinch and complicate my bond with the O.S.H. congregation.

By now, it was almost the end of May. I think I was asked to take temporary vows of chastity, poverty and obedience and made a member of the congregation. I got a few cassocks stitched for my clerical vestition in Poona and on the evening of 29 May 1955 I boarded the Ernakulam-Bombay Express from Alwaye and left for Poona to join the Papal Seminary on the forenoon of the 31st, in time to start the next course of studies in June 1955. I reached the Papal Seminary, 'the Home of Love' as it has even now come to be affectionately and gratefully remembered by its alumni. During the train journey I had ample time to ponder over the Bishop's ominous aphorism: 'Purpose once formed, death or victory'. But death? Victory? Not yet. The story continues.

## In the Home of Love

The forenoon of 31 May, 1955. The Ernakulam-Bombay Express screeched to a halt at Poona Railway station. I got out with my trunk and stepped down to the platform. I looked like an Afro-American boy, after having been blasted by the coal-dust laden smoke emitted by the steam engine for about forty hours. I wonder how Brother Edathiparampil—later affectionately but humourously pet-named 'Mathaika' (Mathai Kathanar)—recognized me from a distance. He ran to me and took me by hand with a rather boisterous laughter, probably provoked by my carbon-smeared appearance. Brother Edathy, then a deacon and final year theology student, was the senior most student from the Kottayam Diocese. 'Let's go to our Home of Love', he said and took me in a taxi – or a *tonga* or cycle-rikshaw, I don't remember. 'Home of Love'. That is how the Kandy-Poona Papal Seminary was and is liked to be remembered by all its alumni, cherishing nostalgic memories about it. Even now my memories of my eight years of life in Papal Seminary, Poona are charged with heavy nostalgia.

Brother Edathiparampil took me to the Rector, Rev. Fr John Ancot. His face beamed a heavenly smile when he gave a pat on my dirty shoulder and said: 'Abraham, nice to see you join the Papal Seminary. Feel at home here'. 'Brother Mathew', he turned to Mathaika and said: 'Take Abraham to his novice-master, Brother Mathew Thottyil'. After entrusting me to the care of my novice-master, Mathaika went back to his room in the theologians' wing. The theology students' wing was separate from that of students of philosophy and ordinarily the two groups were not permitted to interact.

The novice master, Brother Mathew Thottyil, now Fr Mathew Thottyil of Kothamangalam Diocese, was then a final year philosophy student. He will readily forgive me if I am confusing his name with some one else's. The novice master was to us a guardian angel. By the by, the system of assigning the new comers in small groups of four or five as novices to one senior student as their novice master was a practice adopted by this 'Home of Love' to induct the timid, newly admitted ones like me into the family atmosphere with the utmost care. Each group is called a 'novice family'. The novice master is always around them like a hen watching over its chicks. He can always be approached for any and every need or doubt so that the new comers should not feel left to the darkness of any ambiguity or uncertainty. The novice masters are chosen on merits of their personal qualities. Under their care and guidance the neophytes soon get into the warmth and rhythm of the seminary life and are relieved of the feeling, if any, of being in unfamiliar waters and given the feel of being at home quickly.

My novice master took me to my room in the philosophy

wing and showed me the bath rooms at the end of the corridor. The rooms are arranged on either side of the long corridor with a break in the middle for open air. Ours were single rooms, furnished with a warm bed – to me it was even cozy – a well protective mosquito curtain, a table, a chair, and a light and fan. I took a shower bath - my first shower bath - then changed my dress and deposited my sooty clothes at the place assigned. The washed clothes were to be collected after a specific period from pigeon holes assigned to each student. My novice master was ready to take me to the dining room.

## In the Dining Hall

The dining table with its sumptuous spread for dinner (lunch as it is called now) was a pleasant surprise. A spicy soup followed by three delicious dishes, one invariably non-vegetarian to be taken with bread. After these items came boiled rice with three separate condiments and curds. Finally dessert – ordinarily fruits and occasionally ice cream—consisting of plantains, oranges, sweet limes or grapes. Half a dozen students are appointed as Refectory Servers on weekly turns. They help the diners with water and second helpings. I must have been a spectacle to those around me as I struggled with the cutlery, never having used a spoon, fork and knife. I had not been given any training as yet in the use of these and in the accepted practices of table manners. What a sumptuous dinner, I wondered, and all this arranged in my honour, I thought. My! I felt elated. But I was wrong. Later it was that I realized that the menu was that of the ordinary daily meals. Interested readers may imagine the menu items for special feast days. Fr Peter Po Montfort, the Seminary Procurator, was very keen to see the students well fed and taken good care of. Here I take the liberty of describing the daily food habits. Breakfast, usually served at 7 a.m. after Mass, consisted of one egg, one rice flour item such as a dosa or idli served with a suitable stew veg or non-veg, in addition to bread and butter. Coffee, milk and sugar are kept separately for each one to concoct according to each one's taste. Last item is a selection of fruits again. At 10 a.m., before going to classes coffee would be kept in the refectory ready for those who would have a cup of it. After class at 4 p.m. tea with bread butter and jam was kept ready for self-service. And finally for supper at 8 p.m. we were given three separate dishes with bread followed by fruits. Meat was forbidden on Fridays as per the third commandment of the Church.

After my first dinner I went back to my room. My mind was heavy with the dead weight of all the tension caused by the hectic rushes to and fro between Kottayam and Peermedu Mariagiri summer villa during April and May. It was a period of intense strain added to the tension between bulging hopes and choking despairs and dark uncertainties occurring like a see-saw. My novice master had advised me to be free with Fr Rector or any other Father of my choice as my Spiritual Father, to talk about any or all problems. Without further ado, I unburdened my self to Fr Rector and to Fr Antony Sabino – I chose Fr Sabino as my Spiritual Father because his Italian accented English was easier to me to follow than that of Fr Robert Bellarmine Crieme. Both of them were well experienced with religious life, being Jesuits. They had taken perpetual profession of the triple vow of Religious Orders. They were also well aware of the canon laws regulating the norms of the profession of religious vows. They as well as all other enlightened Catholics knew fully well that canon law prescribes absolute freedom on the part of the person wanting to choose Catholic priestly vocation or Religious ascetic life binding oneself with the triple vow. They also know that canon law pronounces the severest punishment of ipso facto excommunication from the Church on any one who compels any body to take up priestly vocation or profession of religious vows. Both Fr Rector and Fr Sabino separately advised me one and the same counsel: 'Son, you are now a student of the Papal Seminary for the next 8 year course of studies. Draw a thick curtain over all that happened during the last two months and close your mind against those events until you complete your studies and return to the diocese as a priest. Then it is left to your absolute freedom to continue or to terminate the religious profession you have temporarily made. And focus your attention upon the studies ahead of you'.

I took in their counsel whole-heartedly, felt relieved of the whole lot of load that was weighing me down. Fr Rector took me to the chapel and conducted the short ceremony of my clerical vestition, accompanied by a short service of prayer and blessing. I put on my cassock with a red sash around my waist. The red sash was a distinctive characteristic of the clerical attire of the Papal Seminary students. I set my mind on the next long years of study ahead of me.

# 6

# My Four-Year Course of Philosophy

Not long after the arrival of every new batch and before the classes began in full swing, newcomers were inducted formally into the community of the 'Home of Love'. It was an occasion for the seniors, including the Fathers, to have some fun and roar with laughter at the expense of the helpless newcomers. It was a kind of the Papal Seminary version of what goes on now a days in the name of ragging, against which the High Judiciary has issued severe strictures and injunctions. The modern practice of ragging is the highly decayed, degenerated and dehumanized form of it, a game of wild cruel enjoyment of the senior rowdies at the merciless expense of the victimized newcomers. The Papal Seminary version of it had an entirely different and ennobling spirit and atmosphere. It was an opportunity for the mischief-mongering seniors including our novice masters to burst into roars of laughter, of course at the expense of the novices, but without causing the least injury or pain of feeling of offence. The newcomers would never realize, until they were exposed on the day of the organized humour, that their seniors had been closely watching all the uncouth peculiarities and habits which in turn would be acted out on an elevated dais in front of the whole community, bringing forth waves of laughter. My heart was throbbing and drumming pud-pud against my side when it was my turn to be mimicked. The scene acted out was none other than that of my first dinner and the mess I made there with the use, for the first time in my life, of knife, spoon and fork, and the plate full of food in front of the hungry me. Those who were closely but unostentatiously watching me were wondering whether the fork in my hands rapidly moving from the one to the other, would enter through my nostrils! Another piece of my adventure that was staged out was my looking out of the chapel window with great strain at a booming plane and following its flight from the chapel pew at the peak of the liturgical worship!

**The Poona Pontifical University Community**

The Papal Seminary students of philosophy and theology courses formed one part of the two major groups of students forming the Papal Athenaeum or University community. Almost all the seminarians were from different catholic dioceses of India including the Latin and the Syrian dioceses of Kerala, with the exception of a few coming from Sri Lanka, Sikkim etc. The other major group was the group of the Jesuit scholastics living in De Nobili College. Both groups live well within the University campus. The Jesuit group was largely cosmopolitan in character, and most of them came from other continents such as Australia, America and Europe. There were also other small groups of students belonging to various other religious orders such as the S.V.D. or Societas Verbi Divini, O.I.C. or Order of Imitation of Christ and C.M.I. or Carmelites of Mary Immaculate etc. living in study houses established in the premises of the Athenaeum campus, and attending the University courses together. As such, the Papal Athenaeum Community was a university community of great magnitude and cosmopolitan in character. All the students attended the same classes offered by the University Faculty of Philosophy and that of Theology. The classes were conducted in class rooms, each arranged like a miniature theater, one next to the other as extension from the Central Library. The library was undoubtedly one of the largest in South Asia. I feel honoured and privileged to have had as my seminary mates such illustrious persons as the late Archbishop Alan De Lastic of Delhi, Valerian D'Souza of Poona, Patric Nair of Meerut, James Pazhayattil of Irinjalakuda, my own venerable classmate for eight years, the Most Reverend Joseph Mar Powathil, the worthy Syro-Malabar Archbishop (retired) of Chenganacherry etc.

My four year course of Philosophy was one of the happiest and most successful periods in my life. I heartily thank Almighty God for the opportunity to learn from eminent and dedicated professors of Philosophy such as Fr Gasper Koelman (Dean), Fr Richard V. De Smet, Fr Antony Sabino, Fr Robert Bellarmine Crieme and Fr Joseph Edamaram. Fr Edamaram was the only Malayalee, short, slightly hunch-backed and with a small round head sparsely covered with short soft fur, and a face with closely cut but sparse hair and a tuft of long beard dangling loosely from his under-chin like the bushy tail of a beautiful wild squirrel, which danced according to the rhythmic movements of his lower jaw. He was very particular that his students should clearly understand what he taught. He used to remark by way of a joke meant but a poke implied: 'The students understand well what I teach and they speak of me as a philosopher without depth. They don't understand what certain other professors teach and they speak of these latter ones as philosophers with depth'.

There were two distinct courses in Philosophy: one was the short course meant for those who were not exactly backward, but rather not interested in delving into philosophical levels and who came aspiring for priesthood late in life. After three years they would be promoted and pushed into theology without any degree. The other is the long course of four years consisting of the courses for degrees (B. Ph.) and post-graduate degrees (M.Ph.) in philosophy. Most of the students took the long course. The course of philosophy begins with the paper on Minor Logic. It deals with the principles of ratiocination or syllogistic reasoning. This is the fundamental equipment necessary to tread the field of philosophy. The course then spreads out into papers on Major Logic, Ontology or Metaphysics, Psychology both metaphysical and practical or experimental, Cosmology, Theodicy and Moral Philosophy or Natural Ethics. Classes, especially the advanced ones, were very energetic and interactive. Once while teaching Metaphysics, Fr De Smet put a question to Brother J. Without any pause, Brother J. began to answer—but in a flood of Latin words. Neither the other students, nor Fr De Smet nor I think even Brother J. himself understood what those words meant. 'Brother J.', Fr De Smet intervened and said: 'Start thinking before you start talking'! With due acknowledgement to Fr De Smet, I have several times given this tip to many of my own students in the colleges where I have served as a professor.

One of the most important and prestigious academic performances was the annual public disputation (Disputatio Publica as it was generally celebrated). It was held not only for philosophy, but for theology as well. The function was held in the large central auditorium, attended by the whole University Community, students as well as professors. On the elevated public dais were seated three students, the defendant in the middle, flanked by the first and the second opponents. It was the faculty concerned that chose the defendant and the opponents from the final year classes. Obviously the choice of the defendant fell on the one considered by the faculty as the best and the choice of the opponents on the second and the third best ones. The medium of the whole exercise was exclusively Latin. The defendant would highlight the theses chosen and set by the dean of the faculty concerned. The opponents in turn would attack his exposition and arguments adduced to prove the theses through counter arguments arrayed according to the strict principles of ratiocination. After about two hours of the arguments and the counters, it was time for all (T.P.O. or Tempus Pro Omnibus) the students as well as the staff to take up the rational attack against the defendant's position. And the defendant had the burden of defending his theses against attacks from any corner of the large attentive audience. The whole exercise was then concluded with a thunderous applause for the defendant as well as the opponents. When it came to my final year of philosophy, in 1959, I was chosen the defendant, an achievement which I recall with moderate pride and great gratitude to God.

In those days, the Faculty of Philosophy evaluated academic performance thus: a score below sixty per cent was considered failed, and sixty to sixtynine per cent was considered as pass. Seventy to seventynine per cent brought a pass in the second class, eighty to eightynine per cent secured a pass in the first class 'with praise' or 'Cum Laude', and ninety to ninetynine per cent was a first class with distinction 'with great Praise', or Magna Cum Laude. Finally, a score of 100 per cent was considered the highest rank with the 'Highest Praise' or Summa Cum Laude. Hardly any humans attain this grade.

## The Days of Festivity

One of the greatest festive days in this 'Home of Love' was no doubt Christmas, as it is also for the whole world. The food items of every festive day, particularly of Christmas are better left to the reader's imagination than described. In one word, the spread was simply grand. Yet, even the more enjoyable event was the community meeting that followed the dinner, bringing together both philosophy and theology sections. The chief guest of the day was, expectedly, Santa Claus, acted out by one of the students, usually the fattest one. Santa came with a gift for each, from the Rector to the chef. Together with the presents he would also dole out a prod to every one, some like the ones I got on our induction day. The prod each one received was sure to trigger a roar of laughter for the whole group including the one who receives it. To cite but one or two instances: prodding on Fr Sabino's alleged absent-mindedness, Santa Claus once said: 'Fr Sabino once stepped on to the verandah in front of his room, completely drenched in a heavy rain in spite of his umbrella, folded the umbrella, opened the door of his room, entered his room, placed the drenched umbrella in his chair and he went and stood in the corner of the room behind the door'. Congratulating the chef for his efficiency, Santa once said: 'Our chef shapes six cutlets simultaneously, two with his palms, two with his elbow folds, and two with his arm pits'. Again, poking on Fr Sabino's Italian dental-prone articulation of English linguistic sounds, Santa related an incident: 'Fr Sabino luckily escaped a slight bike accident caused by a buffalo that crossed his road without due respect to traffic rules. Morally indignant at this traffic rule violation, Fr Sabino stopped his bike, looked with raised eye-brows at the buffalo that was looking sympathetically at him from the other side of the road and shouted, `You, you stupidth Baffalo' and then on a second sudden thought continued his ride'.

Another memorable festive day was the 28th of December each year. This was Feast of the Holy Innocents, in memory of the children murdered by the Roman soldiers at the orders of King Herod in his vain attempt to get rid of infant Jesus, as narrated in the New Testament, a story that had its parallel in the Indian tale of the many children under two years killed by Poothana at the order of King Kamsa in his vain attempt to kill the infant Krishna. The day was set apart to honour and entertain the three youngest members of the 'Home of Love'. The youngest one was made the master of the Seminary for the day and commanded the entire order of the day. For that day the various officials were those he appointed for the duty. Even the Rector himself was under his command. The two other younger ones joined him to form an oligarchy and they ruled the roost! A sumptuous dinner equal to the Christmas dinner was arranged, and the youngest three were the distinguished and honoured guests. In addition to all these were the gifts of various kinds showered on them by nearly every other member of the student community. All I remember about the 28 December 1955 is that I was the second of the three youngest heroes of the day. I regret to have forgotten who the first and who the third were. I have treasured many of the gifts I received that day, especially the books in my moderately large home library. The other day while turning the pages of some of those books, I was reminded of one of my special friends, one Noel Senevaratne from Sri Lanka. By the by, 'particular friendships' were strictly forbidden as strictly as the 'rule of touch' was enforced as a precaution against certain 'unhealthy tendencies' that could possibly develop, human weakness being what it is!

Other days of festivity that remain vigorously in my memory were the nights of the last day of each year, on which we bid farewell to the year gone by and usher in the new. The night of 31 December 1955 was the first of the kind in my life.

### Games Indoor and Outdoor

Another factor that kept our seminary life healthy, vigorous and lively was the many games facilities available. The most popular game was basketball. There were separate courts for the philosophy and the theology sections. After classes and tea at 4 p.m. two hours up to 6 p.m. were set apart for games. A vigorous game of basketball followed by a shower provided the best atmosphere to serious intellectual work. Though I began to play basketball only in the Papal Seminary, very soon I became proficient and I was in fact basket ball captain for several years consecutively. I was also proficient in volleyball, badminton and table tennis. The only rival in the Seminary that I was scared to face in table tennis was one Patric D'Rosario. He was so fat that it would take time for him to complete a round about turn. But at the table tennis game he would turn round about at the speed of the rotation of the Earth. However I continued to foster the little skill in table tennis that I acquired in the Seminary until I was given the award for winning the first place in the table tennis in the annual day of sports and games organized by the Gymkhana of Karnatak University 1970, which was the final year of my M.A. English Literature studies in that university.

### Towards the End of the Philosophy Course

I took to my studies quite seriously and Providence rewarded my efforts with the satisfaction of a successful course. By the end of the first year, I think, I got the recognition of professors and class-mates as one of the bright students. When it came to the award of my B.Ph degree I got the recognition as one of the possibly top students in my batch. I got slightly above eighty per cent for all the academic exercises including the various project studies according to the requirements of each Paper or subject. In the final evaluation of my academic performances for B.Ph., I was awarded the degree in first class 'with Praise' (Cum Laude).

I began my academic voyage to the shore of the post-graduate degree of M.Ph. My sail to M.Ph. was far brighter and more successful than that to B.Ph. Most of my project studies fetched me 90 or above per cent of marks. And my project on the study of the Philosophy of the British philosopher

Bernard Bosanquet, done under my Metaphysics professor, Fr De Smet fetched me full marks and an encouraging pat on the shoulders from Fr De Smet.

There was a sharp difference of opinion between Fr De Smet and the Theodicy Professor, Fr Joseph Edamaram, regarding 'the Gratuity of the Beatific Vision'. The Beatific Vision, according to the Christian dogmatic faith, is believed to be the final vision of God granted to and attained by each person after his death. The attainment depends upon the holiness of his/her personal life according to the norms of the Christian Religion, the authority of which is assumed to be from God Himself. The Beatific Vision confers the ultimate bliss of Moksha or Sayoojya of each individual. Beatific Vision and the personal Moksha attained consequent to the faithful practices of the dogmatic religious creed and the other stuff produced by theological argumentation around this core religious faith are all matters pertaining to the areas of dogma where philosophy has no entrance. That the Beatific Vision is a 'gratuitous' gift of God is also a matter of sheer dogma of Christian faith, according to the theology of St. Paul. All Christians including Jesuit professors of philosophy are obliged to believe the same. But the point of difference of opinion between these two mighty philosopher Jesuits, Fr De Smet and Fr Edamaram, was around the irreconcilability about the 'natural desire for' and the 'gratuity' of Beatific Vision. Fr De Smet held that there is a 'natural desire for Beatific Vision' because bliss or happiness is the fulfillment of a desire and nothing, if undesired, can be said to fulfill and render bliss. Fr Edamaram strongly countered that any 'natural' desire for the Beatific Vision will destroy its 'gratuity' because God the author of Nature is bound by the rules of Nature – rules that are ultimately the expression of God's own Infinite Wisdom.

The point of this dispute became a matter of deep interest among the students. I wrote an article entitled 'The Gratuity of the Beatific Vision on the Balance?' with a big question mark at the end of the title. My article was fully supportive of Fr De Smet. And he got it published in a national theological periodical called *Indian Ecclesiastical Studies* (Vol. 3. July 1964 No. 3) and publicly recommended it in the classroom to other students for reference. That was the first ever article that got published in my name in such an illustrious periodical. Needless to say it was a boost to the recognition I had been getting as a student of philosophy. But the greatest boost up came when I was chosen as defendant in the 'Disputatio publica' of the year 1959, an enviable recognition indeed as I have indicated earlier. The days that followed my selection up to the day of the event were not without a good measure of anxiety and uncertainty. I was almost overwhelmed with greetings and good wishes from all my classmates, particularly from my good friend Silvester De Souza of Allahabad Diocese, if I remember well, and from my own Diocesan seniors Jacob Chollambel, Joseph Manappallil, Cyriac Koratyil, who were then theologians three years ahead of me and of course Joseph Karottukunnel, the senior-most diocesan and deacon doing his final year of theology. Finally the greatly awaited day of the Public Disputation 1959 dawned. The exercise started and it went off with a bang! I thanked God for the grand success which it turned out to be.

## Towards the Finale

The finale of my philosophy course was already on the horizon. As I looked forward to the day I would go home on vacation after being away for four years, my mind and heart were filled with nostalgia and emotions. My father and my other family members had never seen me vested in clerical dress. Soon they would see me so. Perhaps my Bishop might ask me to accompany him, as he had done several times during the Petit Seminary course, on an official visit of his to Piravom. There my family along with my parishioners might see me with the Bishop – the Bishop in his gaudy, purple-frilled, brilliantly white attire with a broad, glazing red sash and me in a thin, immaculate-white cassock with a narrow, say, two inches or more broad red sash, looking like a bishop-chick.

But there was a very important event to face before that. I had to take my final examination for my Master's Degree in Philosophy, M.Ph. It was not a written examination, but oral.

A board of four professors would confront me with theses comprising the whole syllabus prescribed for the four-year course. I had to defend and be ready with all the theses of the entire course not against the attack of student-opponents as in the 'Disputatio Publica', but against the four White Whales of the deep sea of philosophy. Yes, I had to face them and I decided to. The rest of the days ahead were days of hectic preparation for the examination.

On the evening before the eve of the examination, I went through the theses one after another. Major logic, alright. Metaphysics, Psychology, Cosmology, all allright. I looked at the theses on Ethics or Moral Philosophy and I began to lose my confidence. I read through the theses on Ethics one after another. Doubts increased, my confidence started to drain away and darkness began to spread all over my mind. I went over the theses of the other subjects. This time they were not all right, but all wrong! I felt lost. 'Lord, have you forsaken me?' I asked silently. No! I must regain my mental poise. I spent a little time in prayer in the chapel. I went back to bed with a mind still rather disturbed. But I got some restful sleep. Next morning after the morning chores, the Mass and breakfast, I returned to my revision of the theses for the examination. I opened the notes on Ethics and made a thorough revision. Ha! Light seemed to stream into my mind. Darkness and doubts seemed to vanish like clouds from the sky and the horizon of my mind appeared to clear up. I read through the Ethics theses. My confidence seemed to return. I went through all the theses of all the subjects slated for the examination the following morning. They seemed to be pretty well clear. I felt my mind getting more and more peaceful and the substance of the theses in front of me clearer and clearer. Oh, I thanked God. Within the last twenty four hours I learned one more lesson of immensely practical importance first hand: anxiety kills the mind and blacks out the light of intelligence. One should try to regain the calm and poise of the mind to get learning more efficient. I have several times quoted my experience to drive this lesson home to my own students and to rouse confidence in them before the days of their exams. I went to bed and had a restful sleep that night.

**The Final Exam for M.Ph.**

The day of my 'doom' dawned. In due time, I reached the exam dais. There sat the four White Whales of the deep sea of Philosophy: Fr De Smet, Fr Sabino, Fr Edamaram and, I think, Fr James McGinley, Professor of Ethics, each beaming a smile of welcome which seemed to corroborate my confidence.

The examination started. Each professor in turn asked me to expose and establish the thesis of their choice. After my exposition and explanation they began their attacks hurled at me through logically formulated syllogisms to disprove what I tried to establish. And I countered also in logically formulated syllogisms and showed the fallacy of their argumentation against my exposition. The more we advanced, the firmer my confidence seemed to grow. I remember one of the trickiest problems thrown at me by Fr Edamaram to lock me up. Combining the theses of the omniscience and immutability of God, related to Theodicy, with the freedom of man related to the Metaphysical Psychology, Fr Edamaram argued: 'The omniscient God knows all your future actions. The immutable God's knowledge cannot change. So the future actions of yours have to happen as God knows it from all eternity. Where then is man's freedom?' My answer was: 'Philosophy has not yet grown enough to solve all the mysteries in the universe. And it will certainly not solve the mystery of the irreconcilability between God's omniscience read with His immutability and man's freedom. God cannot create a square circle. It does not prove anything against God's omnipotence'. I think I saw another smile of satisfaction beaming from the four White Whales and heard a sound of applause from the audience. The table bell before the board of examiners rang and I came out of the hall. I remember Joseph Karottukunnel, my senior most diocesan, rushed towards me and said pressing me close to his side: 'Congratulations! You can expect a good result'. And the result was soon out. A first class with distinction 'With Great Praise' – Magna Cum Laude!

# 7

# The Spirituality in the 'Home of Love'

Life in the Seminary was filled with the bubbles of mirth, resonant with boisterous laughter provoked by the jokes shared with us by Fr Crieme – he visited us fairly regularly with a copy of the newspaper *The Indian Express* during the after-meal intervals to update us with contemporary important socio-political events. This mix of academic work and vigorous sports enleavened with laughter and jokes was just the surface. Below the surface was a solid layer of high spirituality that ultimately controlled the whole movement of the life in the seminary and no doubt it emanated from the exemplary lives of our professors and Fr Rector. But it was characterized by the age-old Christian other-worldly spirituality, oriented towards a heaven after death, as preached and taught even now. The main beams of this other-worldly spirituality structure are the understanding of the symbols of the Christian discipleship. And the symbols are, in Jesus' own words, 'Deny yourself, take up your cross and follow me'. Self-denial was understood as mortification of desires and thereby practice of asceticism. The Cross was understood as the symbol of all forms of sufferings, even self-imposed ones.

## A Comparison with the Indian Spirituality

One may fairly correctly maintain that this vision of the traditional Christian spirituality, rooted in the practice of asceticism through the curtailment or renunciation or mortification of all desires, is continuative of and profoundly influenced by the Hindu spirituality of the 'Universal self denial' or the 'Sarva Sanga Parithyagam' as the only path to the Hindu concept of Moksha or Sayoojya. The systematic practice of this asceticism of the 'Universal Self denial' ultimately achieves the purification of the individual soul or freedom and release from all desires. Desires are the source of suffering. Once purified of all the desires, the individual soul attains the status of the Pure Light, the 'Disinterested Witness' for its merger into the Absolute Light of God and thus achieves union with God or Moksha. The union of the individual soul with God is also the ultimate end or Moksha or Beatific Vision according to the Christian dogmatic faith as well. The only difference seems to be that, according to the former, the purified individual soul or the 'disinterested witness' merges into the unity and simplicity of the Absolute. 'Ekamevam, Adwideeyam, Aham Brahmasmi, Tatvamasi' [approximately translated as: Only one, No second, I am the Absolute, That you are], whereas according to the Christian concept of moksha, the purified soul gets into union with God in the Beatific Vision, gratuitously granted to it at the same time maintaining the immortal plurality of the individual souls. Only one more dogma is added to this: the belief that the bodies of these souls, interred, decayed and transformed into its elements, would resurrect, come back and join each its original soul to continue the new resurrected immortal individual life either in heaven enjoying the eternal bliss of the Beatific Vision, or in Hell in its eternal, inextinguishable flames. A highly wishful and imaginative piece!

That the systematic practice of self-denial, mortification of all desires and asceticism can endow man with almost invincible power of the mind is quite true and understandable. I remember to have read somewhere the story of a beggarly-looking ascetic. He publicly defied his king, a very arrogant man. The king's bodyguards picked him up and threw him down at the king's feet. 'Did you dare defy me, you, you miserable creature?' the enraged king asked him. 'Yes, I did' was the ascetic's cool and calm response. 'Don't you know that I have the power to kill you?' the king roared at him, brandishing his unsheathed sword. Pat came the ascetic's reply, 'Don't you know that I have the power to be killed by you?' What could the king's mighty military power do against his invincible spiritual power?

## Sex: The Infernal Villain?

The spirituality as practiced, taught and preached by the Jesuits of our Home of Love was strongly traditional. They endeavoured to practise and to train us to practise the maximum degree of asceticism and mortification of desires. There are three factors that serve as the sources of desires in us and create obstacles in the way of religious ideal of asceticism and self-purification. They are the world, the devil and worst of all the body, as traditional Christian spirituality drilled into us at our catechism classes. Those are the triple traditional enemies of the soul. The whole Christian life is thus a constant and hard strife against the temptations of these three enemies of the soul: Devil, the instigator to all desires and consequently to sins; the world with all its wealth and power to trigger off worldly desires and worst of all the body the greatest source of desires, the worst part of it being sex, the source of 'impure sins'! Sex being the worst and the most villainous one, very strict precautions were prescribed to keep the thug under control, check and chain. One of these checks was the Rule of Touch, prescribing that the maximum possible voluntary touch permitted in the Seminary was a hearty shake-hand from a respectable distance from each other. Another was the strict ban on 'Particular Friendship'. All other violations of divine commandments were sins, mortal or venial. But violation of the sixth commandment in any form—even the smallest and casual form of indulgence in sex—was an 'impure' mortal sin. In matters regarding indulgence in sex, there is no veniality but only mortality! That was the principle in moral theology, as we were taught by Fr Crieme. Seeing a person of the opposite sex may not be a sin. But looking at him/her could be a mortal sin! (seeing is unintentional, but looking is intentional). Unlike in the Hindu god-families, in the Christian dogmatic god-family of the Triunity, there is no touch or smell of any female element. The Father and the Son are no doubt masculine. At least they sound masculine. But what about the third member, the Holy Ghost? The third member always appears as a dove. No theology has given me any indication as to whether the third member of the Triune god-family is a male bird or a female bird. But in the Hindu mythologies and legends a Devan has always a Devi to share his life with and for a merry time. The most handsome and attractive figure of Krishna, believed to be the incarnation of Vishnu, was enviably surrounded by the most attractive Gopikas vying with one another to be at Krishna's service, just as Jesus himself had many women to follow and serve him.

At times this other wordly and anti-sex Chistian spirituality has made me wonder why God imposed on man such a curse and tantalizing scourge as sex. It took many more years for me to realize that sex could perhaps be thought of not as a curse, but as one of God's greatest gifts for man for which man could not be adequately grateful to God, gifts such as the sense of taste brings the joy of a variety of tastes, aesthetic sense brings the joy of enjoying the wonderful beauty in Nature etc.

In order to keep this 'villainous' and the 'impure' bodily desire under check and chain and to foster the religious practice of mortifications and asceticism, we were encouraged to practise small forms of self-inflicted modest bodily torture like kneeling on hard ground with both hands fully stretched out sidewise till the shoulder muscles ached and knees acutely pained, avoidance of at least a small part of the sweetest item of food etc. The gluttonous and voracious eater that I was, this last practice of asceticism was even more painful than the other measures. I was terribly scared of even a casual touch, however slight and casual, on certain most 'delicate and sensitive' part of the body. It would suffocate my mind with a swelling sense of 'impure sin'. But for all the human weakness there was the dogmatic remedy of the practice of weekly sacramental confession and earnest and enlightened spiritual guidance of my Spiritual Father to cleanse the 'impurities' of the mind and body. At the advice of my Spiritual Father, Fr Sabino, I used to wear metal chains two to three inches broad, rather tightly on the upper thigh and/or muscles just above the elbow. These chains were woven of small pieces of thin metal wires with their sharp barbed ends facing inside. Fr Sabino himself had taught the craft of making such a hard, unostentatious means of self-inflicted bodily torture to punish my villainous body for its mischievous impure urges. After enduring the pain of the pricks of the chain barbs for a tolerably considerable time, I would unfasten it for later use. In fact I had continued this practice for many more years as seminarian, and later as a priest until the end of 1960s – the period of my studies for M.A. English Literature, in the Karnatak University Dharwar. My subsequent personal reflections on the philosophy and theology I learned in the seminary and my being exposed to the study of aesthetics and literature had led me to begin to think and wonder whether God is that much jealous or religion that much sadistic. In fact in the early 1970s I wrote an article entitled 'Is God Jealous, Religion Sadistic?' It was published in the clergy monthly 'Vaidika Mitram' (Friend of the priest) published from Quilon by the young, energy-packed, daredevil Fr Christie Daniel.

**Cross, the Symbol of Jesus' Discipleship: A Re-Thinking**

By that time I had begun to think more on and understand the symbols of the discipleship of Jesus (Luke 9, 23-24) in a way, slightly deviant from traditional understanding. I began to think that 'Deny oneself' could mean the mortification of the extremely selfish 'I-attitude' and even of the communalistic 'we-attitude' to the exclusion of the 'You' and the 'they' attitude and the acceptance of the all-inclusive, universal 'we-attitude', leading to the sense of one's identity and solidarity with the rest of humanity. After all, Jesus called himself 'son of man', identifying himself and feeling solidarity with the whole humanity. Similarly, 'take up your Cross' could mean the supremely heavenly and beautifying cross of the two-fold relationship the soul of every individual is woven of: the vertical relationship with God, who is Truth, Justice and Love or the 'Moral Imperative' as German Philosopher Immanuel Kant describes God, and the horizontal relationship with the rest of the human community, fixed and hinged on the vertical one. This way of understanding the symbols of the Christian discipleship seemed to go well with the other words of Jesus who said: 'I have come that you may have life [not crosses of torture and sufferings] and have it more abundantly'. (John

10,10) and 'I came to establish the Kingdom of heaven (ruled by the principles of Truth, Justice and Love or the principles of the Moral imperative) here on earth' [Luke 12, 29-34] and not in the high-up above there somewhere after death and after the expected resurrection of the already interred and decayed bodies after ages to come, if it comes at all!

Yes, the spirituality that I found in the Seminary was identical with that of the traditional one taught and preached in the Churches in Kottayam and probably in all other churches over the entire world. The only difference was that the churches taught and preached this spirituality to the gullible followers while the Jesuit Fathers in the Seminary at least during the period of my life there practised, taught and preached this dogmatic spirituality in spite of their being also profound philosophers!

## A Heart-Rending Farewell

Fr Peter Po Montfort was our Fr Minister. He administered the external material and physical affairs of the Seminary life. Apparently aloof from the students and hardly intermingling with them, he was in fact deeply concerned for our food, comfort, accommodation, health and matters concerning games and other necessary facilities. We had heard it reported that once one of the Jesuit higher authorities, a regional Provincial, if I remember well, suggested to Fr Po to cut down the quantity of food supply to the students by way of introducing some kind of rationing system, because 'the students are eating in great quantity'. 'Are they?' Fr Po was reported to have answered: 'That's a good sign that they are healthy. They should be given even more food'! He was not in the habit of making any personal complaint if possible. However one day he approached Fr Rector with a complaint of some stomach pain. Later, Fr Rector told the students that the moment Fr Po made the complaint, he had come to the fearful conclusion that Fr Po's days were numbered. His assessment was very accurate. Fr Po was rushed to hospital in Poona. A preliminary investigation revealed that Fr Po was a cancer patient. An immediate operation was decided upon. Fr Po was subjected to an emergency operation. The revelation of the result of the operation was shocking to all except to Fr Rector, who had the lion's share of the shock earlier. The cancer had advanced far beyond any hope of cure and almost destroyed his alimentary system beyond any hope of recovery. The doctors closed the wound which they had cut open, put the stitches and discharged him from the hospital within a few days. What remained necessary for Fr Po was a tomb for his body to be interred after the imminent death. But the Seminary had no graveyard yet and it had to be sanctioned by the Poona Municipal authority. An application was filed before the authorities concerned for the sanction of a cemetery in the Athenaeum campus. But the authorities showed extreme reluctance to give the sanction applied for. Finally Fr Po himself drove down to the Municipal office and demanded sanction for a cemetery where he would have to be buried within days already numbered. The required sanction was immediately granted, and without any further delay Fr Po himself took the initiative to get a grave dug. He blessed his own tomb and then waited... waited for his last breath.

The philosophy post-graduate degree examination of all the students of my batch was completed and my colleagues from Kerala and myself were about to leave for our long awaited two-month long vacation to be spent at our homes. My colleagues Joseph Powathil and George Vavanikunnel from Chenganacherry, Joseph Martin and Paul Cruz from Quilon, John Kannankara and Samuel Thundyil from the Syro-Malankara Church, Trivandrum and Thiruvalla and I approached Fr Po to take leave of him for our much coveted and long-awaited vacation. Fr Po as usual exchanged pleasantries with us, wished us all well and prayed for God's blessings on us and then said: 'Go, my children, go home and spend the two-month vacation happily with your home members and come back for the course of theology to begin in June. On your return if I am still alive, we will meet each other. Otherwise, fare you well and God bless all of us'. With throbbing hearts and tears rolling down from the eyes of most of us, we bade him farewell. When we returned in June, Fr, Po was no more. We visited the tomb that had been blessed by the man whose body there remained interred. The words, we were told, as spoken about him by His Eminence Valerian Cardinal Gracias, then Arch-Bishop of Bombay, in tribute of Fr Po remain significant and indeletable in my memory. The Cardinal was reported to have said: 'Fr Po, when he lived, taught us how to live and when he died, taught us how to die.' On a pillar, near a circle there is a semi-circle 'PO'.

**Back Home on a Two-month Vacation**

Another about a forty-hour train journey from Poona. The Bombay-Ernakulam Express screeched to a halt at Alwaye. I picked my trunk, and stepped down to the platform, once again looking like a dark-skinned Afro-American adolescent. After a bath or thorough wash, I rushed to the bus stand and boarded the Kottayam-bound transport bus. I was back at my 'new' home of O.S.H. Monastery at S.H. Mount, although my imagination was filled with the image of my father and other members at home waiting to see me back, clad in cassock with a red sash!

Fr Superior and other Fathers and Brothers, Kakoo, Chacko, John etc. of the Monastery gave me a cordial welcome. By the Brothers of Monastery, I mean those men who became members of the Monastery and shared the Monastic life of asceticism, also bonded under the triple vow. They were not aspirants for priesthood. But they would live in the Monastery, most of them in charge of humdrum duties like supervision of the sacristy, of the refectory and kitchen, of the visitor's bell and reception room etc.

Meet the Bishop, of course, I did. I don't remember whether the meeting took place at the Bishop's palace or in the Monastery during one of his usual regular visits. He enquired about my studies and results. He expressed his satisfaction over the details, and congratulated me on my creditable academic performances. 'Now you can go and spend a couple of weeks at home. Get the traveling expenses from the Procurator of the Monastery. But, remember, you must be back in the Monastery in time for the renewal of the vows before you go back to Poona for Theology', the Bishop gave me leave. Without any further delay I started for home. I expected my father to await me with arms extended to hug me. And indeed he was there with his extended arms along with the other members about him. But I had a shock to see his extended hands taking the shape with two palms joined together and head bent and bowed before me, his third son, with an awesome reverence. He then greeted me with the words: 'Praised be Jesus Christ'. Only then did the realization dawned on me that the paraphernalia I was vested with, the cassock and the mini Episcopal red sash, had destroyed the natural, warm family atmosphere and replaced it with something unnaturally supernatural! To ease the awesome unnatural supernaturality of the atmosphere around me, I retold the story of Pope Pius X as Fr Crieme had shared with us. The Pope, after his coronation and installation as the Pope, visited his mother and extended his right hand, raising his palm a little towards his mother to make it easy for her to kiss his heavy, brilliantly shining pontifical ring. The story continues: the Pope's mother showed him her wedding ring and asked him to kiss it first. 'But for this ring', she told her son, Josepe Sarto, then Pope, in front of her, 'You would not have even been born'.

By the by, I had forgotten to mention that before I left for Poona in 1955, my second brother had got married. Naturally now, the number of the family members had increased. We exchanged the usual pleasantries. Naturally enough, they had a lot to ask me about my past four years of life away from them in entirely strange and different circumstances. I too had a lot to ask them and about the new arrivals into the family. But what I heard about them disturbed me considerably. One of my weaknesses was my being too much sensitive when it came to the atmosphere of my family. My father had already informed me through letters that my two brothers with their families had decided to live separately and that my elder brother had started living in another house that was somehow or other built for his separation and that my father was in the go-between! What made me upset and disturbed my already ultra-sensitive mind was that the atmosphere and peace of the family I left in 1955 had slightly worsened, and the decision for the two families to live separately was consequent upon this worsened family atmosphere. The family had also to face a loan taken for the construction of the new house. Well, I sought to console myself by reasoning that the practice of brothers moving to separate houses after their marriages was not anything unusual, but quite ordinary. But that did not soften the shock. It was not as slight and temporary as I thought. It had temporarily disappeared from my conscious mind. But it got deposited as a sediment in my subconscious mind to give me some trouble later.

The days I spent at home and with my other relatives seemed to pass faster than usual. The date of my return to Poona to start theology was approaching. I returned to the O.S.H. Monastery according to the instructions of the Bishop and the superior for the renewal of the temporary vows, Meanwhile I learnt that the relationship between the Bishop and the Oblates was getting more and more strained. The Bishop was to tighten his sovereignty over the Oblates by maintaining its status as a diocesan congregation with the reins of the threefold vow. And the Oblates were determined to extricate themselves from the Episcopal clutches and become more independent by attaining the status of a regular religious order directly under the Pope. Once that status was obtained, the bridles of the bonds of vows would fall off the Bishop's grip! I had no time to go deeper into the matter. The problem had been pushed down into my unconscious region through the wise advice and guidance of Fr Ancot and my Spiritual Father, Fr Sabino given in 1955. I attended the one-day recollection-cum-retreat conducted in preparation for the renewal of the vows. But the whole ceremony only served to push up the disturbance from the unconscious to the subconscious – one more sediment deposited along with the one got from home. I left Kottayam and boarded the Ernakulam-Bombay Express at Alwaye. The train screeched on all the while emitting carbon-packed smoke blowing over me and pushed me out on to the Poona station platform, once again as a dark Afro-American teenager this time.

# 8

# My Four-Year Course of Theology

It was with ever greater fervour that I prayed for divine guidance through my course of theology. Theology, I believed, was the most sacred and superior knowledge because it was the direct knowledge about the Triune God-Family. It was imparted and guided by God's own infallible authority with which God has invested the Pope, His Vicar here on Earth, and the hierarchy of priesthood in communion with the Pope. Then surely, the God who guided me along the path of the profane field of philosophy so successfully would certainly guide me in the sacred field of theology even more successfully. So I thought and I prayed and began my course of theology with much greater conscious dedication.

## The Light of Reason Blacked Out

'Philosophy ends where theology begins', we were told by Fr Joseph Neuner S.J., the reputed Dean of the Faculty of Theology, introducing us into the sacred theology. It was a clear clarion call to black out the light of reason before entering the mysterious field of dogmas. It was a direction to cling to and hold on the rod of the infallible doctrinal authority or the magisterium of the Church. It was an invitation to take the plunge for the thrilling expedition into the mysteries of the dogmas of the Christian Faith. It was an expedition into the profundities of the five-fold Christian Faith drilled into me from the very childhood through the first question in the Sunday catechism and conditioned and clinched by dint of the strict and regular repetitions of the same through rituals, liturgical prayers, and other religious practices.

The various subjects laid out in the syllabus of the course of theology were strictly in accordance with the order of the mysteries learned by heart in the first catechism class. For example, about the Mono God (de Deo Uno), about the Triune God (de Deo Triuno), about the Incarnation, about the scheme of the Father God for the Redemption of Mankind through the sacrifice of the Incarnate Son God, staged out through the tragic scenes - almost along the lines of the Greek Tragedies of Fate, the scenes of the Passion, Death by crucifixion, Resurrection and Ascension back to his seat on the right hand side of the Father-God in the Triune God-Family, about the Church, about the Sacraments, about the Priesthood transmitted through the traditional, uninterrupted ritual imposition of hands and structured in a perfectly symmetrical hierarchy, about the Eucharist, about the Canon Law, about Moral Theology, about the sacramentals and so on and so forth.

## The Prime Importance of the Hierarchy of Priesthood

The redemption drama of the sacrifice of the Son God for the atonement of the sins of the world, original and personal, has to be continued for all generations to come. This continuation is worked out through the Church Hierarchy of Priesthood. The continuation is to be executed through the still more mysterious Eucharistic sacrifice or Mass. Mass is one of the seven sacraments instituted by the Incarnate Son God. The sacraments are the only and necessary means for the believers to be redeemed. These sacraments can be administered only through the Priestly Hierarchy. Hence follows the prime importance and inevitability of this Hierarchy of the ritual priesthood. As the theological adage has it 'Out side the Church there is no salvation' (Extra ecclesiam nulla salus). This is the theology of the Catholic Church. However the number of these sacraments varies from denomination to denomination. It is the Holy Ghost, the third member of the God-Family, who chooses and anoints the priestly hierarchy and he does it only through the hierarchy. This process of choosing and anointing is called priestly ordination. And I was beginning to go through this course in preparation for this day of ordination and entrance into this hierarchy. In fact priesthood is laid out in a perfectly orderly and symmetrical hierarchy. At the peak is His Holiness the Pope, also known as the Supreme Pontifex. (This word, coming as it does from Latin, means Bridge-builder.) Coming down on the hierarchy in order are Their Eminences the Cardinals, Their Graces the Most Rev. Arch Bishops, Their Excellencies the Rt. Rev. Bishops, Their Lordships the Rt. Rev. Co-adjutor/Auxiliary Bishops, Their Reverences the Rt. Rev. Monsignors, Very Rev. Fathers, ordinary Rev. Fathers, almost Rev. Fathers and irreverend Fathers like poor me! The function of this hierarchy is to save ordinary mortal men from their sins and transport them from this valley of tears to the Triune God - Family high up above there somewhere for the enjoyment of the Beatific Vision of the Triune God-Family after death. The mortal men are saved from sin through the re-enactment of the Redemption drama in its mysterious miniature form of the Mass and through the administration of the sacraments. This salvation of the mortals from their sins is the exclusive monopoly of this Hierarchy.

The 'extra ecclesiam nulla salus' formula was a dogma drilled into my mind from my childhood till the days of theology and even after for many years of priestly ministry. Considering the inevitability and the extreme importance of the bridge building function of this priestly hierarchy, it can be considered as a super-duper escalator from the earth below to the heaven up above there somewhere. Even while being pushed through the mould of the course of dogmatic theology, I used to have the mischievous thought that if the bridge loses its connection or touch with either or both the shores, it could be of no use, nay, only a hindrance to the passage across the river. I begin to feel now that the exclusiveness and monopoly, claimed by this once-considered super-duper escalator, believed to be engineered and constructed by the Incarnate Son-God, do not carry any much weight. Almighty God, Who is Goodness itself and Love, could not have left the whole human race to the availability of this escalator as the only and exclusive passage open to their final destination. God-believing men, including those within the sheepfold of the ecclesiastical hierarchy have begun to feel that far too many steps on this hierarchical escalator are either dislodged or in dire need of serious repair, a thorough overhaul or even replacement because they have become dangerous or corroded by rust, for want of the lubrication through the oil of grace.

## Infallibility Getting Diluted

The light of reason having been blacked out of the mystery-packed field of dogmas, the only measure of security to go by was the blind man's rod of the teaching authority of the Church, claimed to have been invested with the divine attribute of 'infallibility' supported by the authority of biblical quotations, the authority of the great Fathers of the Church, the authority of the unbroken apostolic tradition etc. The density of the dogmatic faith in this divine attribute of infallibility had been solidified by the first Vatican Council. The council had defined this infallibility as a dogma of faith. It had defined that ex-cathedra pronouncements (pronouncements made by the supreme teaching authority) of the Popes are infallible, including the Pope of the same council, who, fully conscious of his, I don't say, arrogance, but authority, said: 'Who? The Church? I am the Church'! But since then the solidity has started to melt. For Example, it started to melt when the infallibility of the Pope was brought to be tied down to the collegiality of the Bishops by the second Vatican Council. To cite a concrete example, before the second Vatican Council, according to the infallible ecclesiastical teaching authority, the primary end of marriage was procreation. The mutual fulfillment of man and woman was only secondary and therefore subject to the needs and norms of the primary end. When it came to the second Vatican Council (by that time we had reached almost the end of our theology course), marriage came to have two ends of equal status: procreation and the mutual fulfillment of man and woman. The primary-secondary grade difference simply vanished, with conspicuously significant practical issues following the new stand. (About these issues, later.) And with 2010 when even the use of condoms came to be officially admitted as permissible, (later the stance was debated and given up) whatever be the strenuous attempts to explain the change away, the solidity of the dogma of the infallible teaching authority has, doubtless, become very dilute.

## Canon Law

Canon Law was one of the layouts of the syllabus for the theology course. The priestly hierarchy, claimed to have been jure divino instituted, next arrogates the 'divinely imposed duty' to take upon itself and to continue the 'redemptive mission of the Incarnate Son-God'. The Pope at the apex of this hierarchy is the incarnate God's vicar or the administrative deputy here on earth. It is naturally inevitable, they argue, that this priestly hierarchy be endowed with a legislative authority on a par with the divine. The enactments of this jure divino legislative authority are what are called Canon Law. The parity of the jure divino Church legislative authority with that of Almighty God Himself is itself another dogma of Faith. Its jurisdiction covers the entire life of each individual believer from sanctification by infant baptism to sanctification and confirmation of death through the administration of the last sacrament, called the 'extreme unction'. It can also enact laws for levying charges for all the 'redemptive services' of the hierarchy, a kind of toll, at times heavy indeed, for access to this necessary service of the escalator. The fifth commandment of the 'Holy Church', for example, imposes on every believer the toll of the tithes and a share of their wealth fixed by the competent authority on the hierarchy, namely the High Priest, in accordance with the need, and not greed, I wish, and in the context of the contemporary economic situation. The observance of the ten commandments of God is no more obligatory than that of the five commandments of the Church, just as the violation of any of the Church's commandments is no less mortal than violation of any of the commandments of God.

**Moral Theology**

This was yet another subject in our syllabus. While all reasonable humans have moral philosophy or natural ethics, those who live by religious dogmas and canon laws have moral theology. Let us note well, it is moral 'theology' and not moral philosophy. In moral philosophy the norm of morality is Nature, or natural laws, where the light of reason has a role. But in moral theology, it is the morality of religion. The norm of this morality is dogmatic religious practices and observances and performances of rituals as prescribed and ruled by canon laws. Its main thrust was the other worldly spirituality, based on the traditional understanding of the symbols of Christian discipleship: namely denying self and taking up the Cross. The Christian life came to be understood as a heroic call to ceaseless practice of asceticism and mortification of desires. It came to mean to wage an uncompromising war on the triple enemy of the soul: the world, the devil and, the greatest villain of all, the body with the additional curse that sex is! Succumbing to worldly desires is sin and succumbing to bodily desires, particularly related to sex is 'impure sin'. Prevention is better than cure. Attack is better than defense or counter attack. Strict measures of asceticism and acute self-inflicted bodily tortures are the tactics of attack rather than defense or counter attack. No wonder various forms of monastic systems started to sprout and flourish. God and life of union with God began to be sought in forests and dense, in ashrams and nunneries far away from the din and the fun and frolic of human civic and family life. No wonder monastic centres of asceticism and nunneries of various religious orders grew up like mushrooms and were filled with sanyasins and nuns renowned for great severe asceticism, mortification and self-inflicted bodily pains like rolling on fresh rose twigs cut and spread out on the floor in the place of beds. The Church's dogmatic authority declared many of them as saints in heaven, united with myriads of winged beautiful angels singing the perpetual and ceaseless hymn of 'Holy, Holy, Holy' to the Triune God Family. The Church has saints like Simon on the Pillar, who is reported to have spent hours and days on top of a pillar by way of scourging and oppressing the deadly enemy that his body was. Pilgrim centres and huge pilgrimages came to be established and organized. But the tragedy that meanwhile developed was that while religions took God to dense and forests and to Monasteries and nunneries and tried to please him there and to get into union with him in heaven after death, and while pilgrims and pilgrimages began to grow and over-grow, the world of human family and civic life has become terribly arid and devoid of any ethical values of Truth, Justice, Love or Grace or peace, searing under dishonesty, corrosive corruption, terrorism, quotation groups (groups ready to take contract for murdering persons), communal clashes and what not. Our media are full of stories of corruption of a magnitude causing tremors—the Rs. 176000 crore scam of the 2-G spectrum, the Rs. 20,0000 crore scam of ISRO spectrum, the Lavelin scam, the Idamalayar scam, just to cite a few instances. While ecclesiastical legislative authority imposes toll for the use of the escalator of priestly hierarchy, the civic legislative authority turns its machine to chop out chunks of civic freedom for sale in the corrupt political market. Religions grow, split and grow. Political parties grow, split and grow. Then these innumerable splinters enter into all kinds of alliances according to the need for the acquisition of power, just like the art of cuisine turns out food items through different combinations. Civic society has become a human crowd ready 'to pledge or barter even the Creator for money'. The world became worldly and the body became bodily. God gets shut up and locked behind the closed doors of the sanctum sanctorum or the Sreekovils and is let out on parole once or twice a year for the 'darsan' of the devotees according to the schedule fixed by the Priests and Pujaris. Humans have ceased to be the living temple of God. But they have become the living temple of the Mammon. Of course it took years of true and faithful observance of traditional spirituality and priestly service under the thick dark dogmatic beliefs for me to realize this new form of evolution or rather devolution under the face of the sky-ward looking other-worldly spirituality. This sky-ward looking other worldly spirituality drilled in to the followers by the 'jure divino' custodians of dogmas who follow a thoroughly downward looking life style, has bitingly been satirized by one of the Malayalee poets through a piercingly satiric poem, roughly translated thus: 'Die and go over this earth and God will throw open the gate of heaven, it is said, but nothing but intense suffering to the son of man here on earth, his birth place. Say if you can: is it said in the Gita, in the Bible, in the Quran, this ludicrously ridiculous holy scriptural nonsense?' If the tree is to be judged by its fruits, as Jesus said, it is high time one judged religion by the fruits it has produced. Jesus came to establish the Kingdom of God here on earth. But life on earth has become a veritable hell. Jesus came 'that you may have life and have it more abundantly'. But nothing but intense suffering fills life here on earth. In the early 1970s I was inspired to write articles like 'Is God Jealous, Religion Sadistic?', 'Is God to be sought in forests and dense?' I rather felt that God is to be sought in the thick of human civic and family life. I may be wrong in feeling a kind of moral indignation at the skyward looking spirituality which the gullible devotees are conditioned in by the sharply earthward looking guards and custodians of dogmas—the moral indignation that inspired me to write 'Time for Christianity to Look Forward'. Looking upward one finds the beautiful blue sky which in reality is only infinite space of emptiness, a mirage, but tumbles down over stones or falls into abysmal ditches. Looking downward, one finds marshes infected with deadly germs and pests. Looking forward, one meets the horizon where the earth and the sky meet, where the earthly and the heavenly meet. The horizon, showing the abundant life of rich green foliage is a symbol of the earthly meeting the heavenly, the human meeting the divine leading to the miracle of the incarnation of the divine in man which Jesus is and to life in all its abundance which he came to give to the world.

## Fr Miranda, Professor of Moral Theology

Fr Miranda was our Moral Theology Professor. He was indeed

a Jesuit 'Mirandus' (to be wondered at) for his forthright way of dealing with his subject, Moral Theology, particularly 'De Sexto'(about the Sixth Commandment – about sex). He taught us the traditional dogmatic principles governing the morality of sex. But he felt the least inhibited when he explained the physics and the chemistry of sex and showed himself extraordinarily imaginative and poetic. I remember the story he once related in the class, the story of a prince visiting his princess. Her residence was fronted by a lovely gentle garden. The prince slowly and leisurely made his way through the garden till he reached the door. He gently searched for the bell. Having felt his touch on the bell, he continued ringing it until the sweet music fully awakened the princess who was sleeping or rather dreamy of her prince. Then the door was opened for the prince to enter into her recess and they together enjoyed the extreme joy of this sweet visit. Lost in the cryptic character of the story, I was helped to understand its meaning by a senior Jesuit classmate of mine who gave me the clue of replacing the 'bell' with 'clitoris'. I relate this story here just to indicate that Fr Miranda, though he taught us the traditional theology of sex morality, was capable of seeing everything created by God as good and therefore as a divine gift to be accepted and enjoyed with deep gratitude to the Creator.

My expedition through the mystery-filled interiors of the dogmas which theology unfolded before me was one of groping in the Dark world of Faith, holding on to the blind man's guiding rod of the 'infallible teaching authority of the Church'. In this peregrination the light of reason had been blacked out from the very beginning. In addition to the rod of the infallible teaching authority were the biblical verses cited, the authority of the Fathers of the Church, the authority of the unbroken apostolic tradition etc. adduced as evidences to establish and clinch the mysteries of the faith formulae as pushed into my mind and learned by heart from the day of catechism. I took in a lot of it, stuffed the mind with undigested and indigestible materials. The indigestion caused by the indigestible dogmatic stuff that I swallowed in and the consequent discomfort and uncertainty of the mind added another kind of sediment to the other two which had already got stuck in my subconscious mind. The three together worked themselves into a form of disturbance of the mental peace. I began to experience a kind of state of mental anxiety almost to the verge of insomnia. In course of time I realized that this experience was one of the greatest blessings of God in disguise as it helped me to understand how the conscious and the subconscious levels of the mind interact and affect the working of the mind and create problems that can develop and become psycho-somatic. It also helped me to understand similar problems of many others under heavy mental strain and deeply vexed with uncertainty and anxiety. But more about it later.

## Progress in the Study of Theology

My formation in the traditional ritualistic religious practices and my firm belief in the so-called jure divino infallible teaching authority guided me in my study of theology and helped me to easily take in more and more mysterious stuff that was plentifully served in the theology classes. The oft-repeated din of the 'infallible magisterium' gave to my mind a sense of satisfaction that I was learning and that my course was successful. Only later did it dawn on me that it was in fact a satisfaction brought by belief in blindness rather than by any interior light. It was something like the overnight peace and calm sleep that imbibing large quantities of strong liquor brings to a mind deeply disturbed by serious and apparently insurmountable problems of life. Only the next morning will the poor victim of the large dose realize that all the problems that were disturbing him till the consumption of the liquor the previous evening have returned with their hood furiously spread and swaying back and forth, plus one additional problem: the fact of the consumption of the large doze the previous evening. The confidence and the apparent peace that my faith in the dogmatic authority of all the sources of evidence adduced to establish and clinch the dogmas seemed to simply vanish, when later hard-core experiences with these very dogmatic centres disillusioned me of all my faith in the jure divino infallible dogmatic teaching authority, self-assumed as the only escalator to heaven. These later experiences convinced me that the bridge had lost all its contact with both the shores and that the little light of reason that Almighty God has invested every mortal human with, was much safer guide in life against all kinds of exploitations under the thick shadows of dogmas and that it is a sin against God to extinguish that little internal light for any heaven reserved far above there somewhere and promised after death. All or almost all class tests, examinations and other academic performances fetched results with a first class. In due course, I was awarded my degree B.Th. and post-graduate degree M.Th. in theology.

When my batch's turn for the annual University academic performance of the 'Disputatio Publica' in theology arrived, I never expected to be assigned any significant role in it. However, though quite unexpectedly, I was selected to the team of the three to appear on the dais of the 'Disputatio Publica Theologica', but this time, very significantly indeed, I was selected not as defendant, but as the first opponent, a role which, I believe, God had reserved for me in the future too. The defendant was one of my close and affectionate friends, Brother Sylvester D'Souza, of the Allahabad Diocese. I don't remember who the other opponent was. Brother D'Souza had enough freedom to share any joke with me. 'Abraham', he told me on our way to the disputation hall, 'I'm afraid you will blast me off with your missiles'. 'Don't be afraid, Sylvester', I replied. 'You are well protected and secure within the bullet-proof walls of the 'jure divino' infallible magisterium.

# 9

# My Ordination and the First Mass

By ordination to priesthood I would get to the first and lowest place in the hierarchical escalator. But there were six other minor steps to get across to this lowest position in this escalator. They were: Tonsure, or a rite of admission to the clerical state by the clipping off of a tuft of hair from my head; Janitor or door keeper (of the Church, I presume) a promotion from tonsure accompanied by a ritual performance; Exorcist, or investiture of the priestly candidate with 'authority' to practice exorcism or command over the devils – a power I have never exercised nor wanted to exercise; Acolyte, or official authorization to assist a clergyman officiating any ritual practice, to ring the bell, to prepare the altar for the ritual – the work of an ordinary sexton or altar-boy, but officially authorized and sanctified for it by the imposition of hands; sub deacon or the next promotion or authorization to take minor parts in officiating any ritual performance, but bound by the vow of perpetual celibacy, and finally deacon, which is the last step to priesthood, authorizing the candidate for closer and more substantial participation in the performance of rituals.

Of these six preparatory steps to priesthood, the third step is highly used, or worse still, abused by priests in deluding the simple folk with claim of having mystical power to exorcise devils from persons and houses said to be haunted, to scold and forbid pests from entering agricultural fields and destroying farm produce, to order better yield from cultivation etc., and they make capital out of this power of exorcism! I remember an incident connected with one of my nearest ones which he himself related to me. The yield of his tapioca cultivation was not up to his expectation. To improve it he sought the help of his parish priest – a man who some how or other managed to maintain a luxurious and posh life-style. The Rev. Parish Priest went into his room inside the presbytery and brought out a bottle of 'holy' water. He produced a few mysterious sounds along with some cryptic gesticulations over the bottle of water. My poor near one with his mere L.P. School education had no way of ascertaining which linguistic sounds his parish priest was producing. On the contrary, he said, the sounds and gesticulations which the priest performed reminded him of fits shown by victims of epilepsy during the attack. The priest then solemnly handed the bottle of the 'holy' and 'holified' water to my relative and directed him to sprinkle it at the four corners or sides of his plot of cultivation and around his straw-thatched house. With bowed head he took the bottle with both hands and performed the rite over his tapioca field as prescribed. 'How much did you pay him for this performance?, I enquired of him. 'Oh! No. He did not ask me to pay any cash. But I presented him with a big bottle of strong and undiluted arrack,' he told me. 'And what was the effect of all these sacramentals upon your tapioca yield?' I continued my unobtrusively mischievous enquiry. 'OK, so, so. Not any considerable difference. Haven't you too learned this sacred performance?' he innocently asked me. 'No, I haven't learned, nor do I want to learn any such non-existent cryptic tricks to delude gullible people, like you. If any body had come to me with any such request, as you made to your parish priest, I would have asked him to till the ground deep enough, plant tapioca, water it in case of insufficient rain fall, clear the field of weeds in due course, supply proper manure in due time and wait for a better harvest'.

All these minor orders, ordinarily prescribed as preparatory steps having been completed, I prepared myself for my ordination. The priestly ordination date has been fixed to be conducted on the 3rd of October every year and the first Mass on the 4th. In October 1962, however, the second Vatican Council was to open in Rome, and all the reigning bishops were in Rome getting ready to attend the fourthcoming

Council. The only High Priest available in and around Poona was the auxiliary bishop of Bombay. The day of my ordination, 3 October, 1962, was perhaps the happiest day in my father's life, because one of his sons was going to be anointed and declared 'alter Christus' – Another Christ! That was the set up of the mind of every ordinary catholic faithful. A priest is 'another Christ', obviously because he is supposed to re-enact Christ's 'redemptive drama of the Sacrifice on the Cross' in its mysterious, mystical miniature form known as Mass. My father's third son was going to be another Christ and perform this sacrifice of Mass on the day following! He had already arrived in Poona with a few of my relatives, including one of my dearest and nearest cousins, Santhamma, then an aspirant in Jesus and Mary Convent, Poona and now Rev. Sr. Christine R.J.M., in the same congregation. To be ordained along with me were my classmates, including my worthy colleague Joseph Powathil, now Most Rev. Dr Joseph Powathil, Archbishop (retired) of Chenganacherry. After the ordination ceremony, all those who officiated and attended it were to kiss the 'anointed palms' of the newly ordained. When it came to my father's chance to kiss my 'newly anointed' hands, I could only imagine what the level of emotion swelling in his paternal heart must have been. Unfortunately he had no wedding ring on any of his fingers. In fact his hands, very rough due to callus, caused by the daily hard manual labour, were really anointed, I thought, with the sweat of hard work. He kissed my 'anointed hands', still emitting the smell of olive oil, and then hugged me tightly with an intensity of satisfaction. This satisfaction must have been what God must have reserved for him for all the 'redemptive hard-core sacrifices' he made for redeeming his three motherless children from abject want and privations – I describe our lot as abject want and privation in contrast with the standards of modern life.

The next morning, for the first time, I 're-enacted' the Redemptive drama of the Incarnate Son-God in the form of my First Mass. That day I offered it as my greatest gift and act of thanksgiving to Almighty God for His providential guidance up to that day. From the next day onwards, every Mass I said fetched a handsome amount as stipend, or toll for the escalatory service I just started, not for me but for the Procurator of the O.S.H. Monastery of which I was a member. I had been bonded by the vow of poverty which prohibited me from having any income or receiving any money from any source for personal use other than from Fr Procurator for any of my needs sanctioned and approved by due authority. All I had to do was to perform the ritual of the Mass for the 'intention' of the Superior of the Monastery. He would exchange this intention with the intention of the pious faithful who would pay the stipend. The stipend or toll is fixed according to the tax-pay rules issued through canon laws from time to time.

## A Blessing in Disguise

It had all begun towards the end of 1959 or early 1960. A state of anxiety and uncertainty started disturbing the calm of my mind. The focus of my mind's attention began to split towards three different directions: one centred round my home, another centred round my bondage with the O.S.H. Monastery and the third centred round my conscious struggle to get intellectually accommodated to the indigestible stuff taken in daily in over-doses in the name of dogmas and dogmatic authority.

News came from home that my father had divided his property into two between my two brothers. He lived with them in convenient turns. I have already mentioned that when it came to my family, my mind became highly sensitive. The sensitive mind then began to indulge in wild imaginations over a disturbed home, consequent upon some break off in the family relationship. Then came the news that my elder brother had sold his portion and gone to Rajakad in the High Ranges in search of better prospects. A little later my eldest brother too took the same route and went to settle in the same Rajakad village territory. These were pieces of news shocking and disturbing enough to my highly sensitive mind, far away from home surroundings, to indulge in imaginations of all sorts of calamities. It needs experience to realize how much damage such a state of uncertain, unnecessary imaginative and sensitive mind can invite and cause mental restlessness.

The second source which distracted and split the centre of my mental concentration was my bondage to the vows related to the O.S.H. Monastery. Of course the advice of my former Rector, Fr Ancot and my Spiritual Father, Fr Sabino and Fr Crieme had pushed the uncomfortable thought to the back of my mind. But it was silently fermenting and now and then belching up into my consciousness, consuming considerable part of my mental energy. Truly enough, the spiritual advice received assured me of my absolute and even canonically protected freedom of terminating this bondage of temporary vows by simply refusing to renew it at my will. But then the powerful yeast of the Bishop's threat was aggravating the unhealthy fermentation – the threat directed against me in 1955 when, back from my fruitless errand to my home parish at Piravom, the Bishop, ominously asked: 'Are you going to serve as a priest under them or under me your Bishop?' Besides, I had also known something about the man in him, for whom 'decision once taken, it was a matter of death or victory'!

Added to these was the burden of the intake of dogmatic theses built upon the dogmatic authority of biblical citations, the dogmatic authority of the infallible magisterium, the dogmatic authority of the unbroken apostolic tradition and finally the dogmatic authority of the Fathers of the Church. Trying very hard to digest the indigestible stuff of these dogmatic theses, my mind began to feel very tired. When the mental energy level falls low, it is recharged by switching of the mains, that is, by sleep. But there lay the rub. There started a kind of my technical problem: my main refused to get switched off. I went to bed and waited for sleep. But sleep kept on evading me. I could not sleep. The more anxiously I awaited this much sought after sleep, the further away did it seem to be. I seemed to be caught up in a vicious circle. The more anxious I was to get sleep, the more distant it remained. The greater the delay to get sleep, the greater the anxiety to get it! A kind of heat seemed to blow up from the lower back of my head and spread upward. I don't remember if sleep ever stole in unobtrusively and suddenly vanished before I could feel any comfort thereof. I used to get up from bed and pray. I used to walk up to the chapel and spend some time there and return to bed only to relapse into the anxiety even more keenly. Once the morning bell at 5 a.m. rang, I would get out of bed for the morning chores. While engaged in the daily routines, the centre for the sleep-anxiety got switched off and I went about with my studies and other engagements. But when it came to bed time at about 10 p.m. the anxiety to sleep got me entangled in the vicious circle again.

Quite a number of days went by. I began to worry about the future. A kind of uncertainty about completing my priestly studies began to grip me. Once I approached Fr Ancot – he was then no more the Rector, but Spiritual Father – and shared with him my worries and problems, particularly about my anxiety over completing the studies and becoming a priest. 'Leave it all to Almighty God, my son', he replied. 'As for your anxiety about reaching up to priesthood, rest assured: if one in your batch would be ordained, you are sure to be, Go in peace'. Go in peace indeed I did. Fr Ancot's encouraging words fetched me extra peace and strength to face the situation. Meanwhile I came across the book I got as a present on 28 December 1955, the day of the feast of the Holy Innocents: *Achieving Peace of Heart* by Narciso Irala. The book is still in my personal collection of books. It is a book about a man who got him shot through his head during the second world war, (if I remember well). He survived the fatal wound, although he could not enjoy the luxury of sleep for the rest of his life. I read an incident related therein – I read it nearly fifty years ago. A man highly worried over his insomnia and anxious to get at least a short sleep, was advised to go on a long picnic to some distant healthy, favourable resort. His trip experiences including highly exciting scenes and sights would switch off his anxiety centre and cool down his mind and dispose it for a peaceful and restful sleep.

After a long exciting and indeed pretty expensive trip he reached his resort, hired a posh room, took a comfortable and clean bath, had his dinner ordered earlier than usual, ate it quickly and lay down in his cozy bed waiting the sweet, stealthy entrance of his mistress sleep into his room. But the arrival of the expected guest, sleep, appeared to be very delayed. His anxiety centre got switched on. Adding fuel to fire, he heard loud snoring from an adjacent room. He was at the peak of his mounting anxiety and disappointment. He wriggled restlessly in his bed, turned on his right, then on his left, profusely perspiring. 'Damn it all!' he cursed himself and his adviser, while still rolling in his bed. He had nothing to do but to wait for the dawn and then pack up and go back, he decided. The snore from the next room still continued in a perfect rhythm. Suddenly something caught his attention: the perfect rhythm of the sound of snoring. He listened to the rhythm: one…two…one…two...one…two. When the centre of attention to the rhythm was switched on, he did not realize that the centre of his anxiety for sleep got switched off…. He did not know when he fell asleep. When he woke up the next morning his neighbour had finished his breakfast, packed and gone!

Life is such that moments of anxiety may come to catch men unaware. Even now I experience moments of anxiety, avoidable or even unavoidable, for various unexpected or imagined reasons and consequently fall into the usual vicious circle. But I then apply the lesson I learned from the incident I have related above. I listen to the rhythm of the gentle snoring of my wife under my right arm. After reading *Achieving Peace of Heart*, I thought: 'If Narciso Irala showed that man could live and work without sleep, I could as well, even if I am denied the luxury of a restful sleep. I would accept it if that is God's design for me'. That was the beginning of the cure of my insomnia, because the intensity of my anxiety for sleep was reduced. The period of insomnia was for me an experience of anguish. But I thank God for it because it was the path of obtaining an authentic insight about a life of suffering caused by worries, avoidable or unavoidable, and also into the intimate interaction between the mind and the body. It was indeed a blessing in disguise and a piece of first-hand knowledge about the various disturbances of the mind and how they affect man's mental peace and cause psychosomatic after-effects. I felt myself equipped with this precious lesson when later in my ministry I came across several persons having problems very similar to mine.

## A Great but Irremediable Regret

Just as 'vocation' to priesthood from Catholic families was considered an unusually great prestige and a symbol of status in society, 'vocation' to nunhood was considered equally prestigious. No wonder that my decision to take up the 'consecrated and sacred life of celibate priest' became an irresistible persuasion to two of my nearest and dearest sisters. I have already mentioned Santhamma, now Sr. Christine R.J.M (Religious of Jesus and Mary) holding very high position in the Order. The other is Pennamma, now Sr. Fabian also of Jesus and Mary Convent. She has been sent to Bolivia where she now holds high position of administrative authority over the Order there. It was not without a great measure of pride that I thought of them as heroic and dedicated souls to take cue from me and sacrifice themselves to please God through a life of 'struggle against the triple enemy of the soul: the World, the Devil and the Body'. I felt proud of their courageous decision to serve and please God through a life of asceticism and renunciation until I began to think years later that God is not jealous nor is religion sadistic, until the later years of my life-experiences and reflections on and understanding of the symbols of Jesus' discipleship brought about a revolutionary attitude towards God-given life. Life here on earth is meant to live out fully in accordance with the principles contained in the symbols of Jesus' discipleship: the vertical and the horizontal relationships. Further, Jesus came that 'You may have life and have it more abundantly'. I continued to feel proud of my cousins until a new understanding dawned on me about Jesus' concept of self-denial and of the Cross of the two-dimensional relationship. With the dawn of this new awareness, I began to feel a kind of guilt that I was the cause for depriving them of their God-given right to live and to live more abundantly. My regret does not imply in any way that they regret their decision taken nearly fifty years ago. On the contrary, following their conviction in the traditional way of looking at true Christian life as a constant struggle against the 'triple enemy' of the soul and therefore feeling a kind of fulfillment in the very act of self-renunciation and emptying of life, they may not have any regret over the choice they made of their life. Nay, they may feel righteous for being in the right track of 'spiritual life' and have regrets about the way I strayed away from the way of the Cross. However I feel guilty and regret having been the cause of depriving them of their God-given life, although there is hardly anything left for me to do by way of atonement except to rely upon Jesus prayer: 'Forgive them, Father, for they know not what they do' (Luke 23, 24). My regret remains irremediable.

### Bidding Farewell to the 'Home of Love'

The four-year course of theology that I started in June 1959 came to its finale by March 1963. I took my final examination in March and got my post graduate degree M.Th. in theology with creditable success though I had to chew and swallow a heap of indigestible dogmas like chewing straw. It was time for me to bid farewell to the Papal Seminary. A Home of Love indeed it was to me. I had completed two of the three different types of life experiences described by Fr Vishakhanthara, as mentioned earlier. He had said: 'Before you join the seminary, you are natural. In the seminary you are super natural. Once out of the Seminary when you come to take orders from your Bishop, you will begin to feel unnatural'. It was time for me to begin to face this third phase.

I packed up the little things and a small collection of books, thanked all the dear Fathers and got their blessings and, by the end of March or early April 1963, I am not very certain which, I left Poona for my next phase of the unnatural struggle. By that time my brothers had given up their settlement in Rajakad and returned to where they are settled now, the prospects they sought there being not as prosperous as they had expected. As soon as I got back to Kottayam, I came to the Bishop's House. Of course I was welcome back. I was then instructed to go to the Monastery of O.S.H., meet Fr Superior and others. And the Bishop granted me a few days' leave to go around visiting my family and other near and dear ones. They were all eager to see me back 'consecrated' as 'Another Christ', to kiss my 'anointed' hands and to see me celebrate Mass, for almost all of them, my First Mass. The 'First Mass solemn celebration' was conducted in my then home parish, St. Antony's Church, Marika. Almost all my relatives and friends had been invited and had come for the function. At the end of the sanctioned period of leave I returned to Kottayam to begin my peregrination through the Dark Dungeons.

## My Priestly Struggle Begins

The struggle of my priestly service began with my first official assignment: I was given the charge of the Catholic Mission Press and Depot as its assistant manager and of the editor of the Diocesan Week 'Apna Desh' and the Diocesan Sacred Heart Monthly. I was also appointed as assistant vicar of the Cathedral Church, attached to the Bishop's House, where I was to reside. As assistant to the cathedral vicar, I didn't have any grave duties, but to hear confessions, visit the patients in the Kottyam Medical College Hospital (now the district government hospital) close by the cathedral and to render priestly services to those who asked for it, services like baptism, extreme unction etc. I was given to baptize those infants brought to the cathedral by poor parents traveling in buses or walking. Those brought by parents in gaudy dresses and wearing rich ornaments and driven in cars of their own were baptized by the Very Rev. Vicar directly.

## An Unforgettable Experience

My duty as chaplain, visiting and interacting with the patients in the hospital wards, was one of very valuable and rich experiences and gave me immense satisfaction. My visiting time was from 4 to 6 p.m. I visited patients, mainly those admitted in the general wards. While talking to a rather old but healthy looking, smiling patient, I was requested by him to administer – that is the word to be used in this context, according to the theological parlance—the sacrament of extreme unction, usually known as the 'Last Sacrament'. According to the principles of theology of sacraments we had been taught in the seminary, extreme unction is to be administered only just before or during the death pang, it being the last push to Heaven above, from the escalator service of the priestly hierarchy.

'What!' I exclaimed to the still smiling old man. 'You, in such good shape, cheer and health, you're asking for the last sacraments? No, not time yet. I'm not going to give you the last sacrament now'. 'But, Father', he pleaded, 'I'm more ill and weak than you assess me from my appearance. I think it is time for it when I can consciously respond to it and I want it'. I didn't argue with him any more. I immediately went back to the cathedral vestry, took the last-sacrament kit, returned to the hospital and administered the last sacrament. 'Thank you, Father,' he said, 'and continue to pray for me'. I breathed a little prayer over him and went away. Next day while taking my lunch at the Bishop's House dining table I was given the message that the man I had anointed the previous evening in the hospital was sinking. I swallowed the rest of the food on my plate in a few gulps, got up, washed my fingers and rushed to the hospital. The old man was struggling for breath. I recollected myself a moment and then made a sign of the cross over him uttering the words of absolution: 'I absolve you from all your sins [if any] in the name of the Father and of the Son and of the Holy Spirit'. That was the last official visa to heaven which I issued in the name of and by the power I was invested with, as I then believed, from the embassy of the jure divino priestly hierarchy, headed by the Pope hailed as Christ's Vicar or God's Ambassador here on earth. I then breathed a little prayer formula, usually whispered in the ears of the dying. I thought the poor dying man was repeating the prayer after me. When I saw his lips become still and eyeballs slightly protruded, I turned to the dead-man's son standing close by attempting to allay his grief and to condole with him when he said: 'I have never heard my father say a word of complaint about himself'. Suddenly I recollected what the old man told me the previous evening: 'Father, I'm more ill and weak than you assess from my appearance.'

### A Leap from Death-Bed to Life

There was another experience even more memorable and richly rewarding I came across in my ministry as the hospital chaplain. It was my encounter with a middle aged woman patient under treatment but in a very serious condition. It all happened towards the middle of the 1960s. I can't remember the exact date. I was out in the hospital on my routine evening visit to the hospital meeting and talking to patients. Around 4 p.m., I entered the female general ward.

'Good evening Father'. 'Good evening, sister', the duty nurse and I exchanged our usual greetings.

'Father, please try to meet the patient in bed No. 3', the nurse told me. 'The patient is highly tensed up, unable to relax or sleep. Medicines administered do not seem to take any effect. The patient is in a critical stage. And the doctors seem to have lost all hope of restoring her back to health'.

'My God!' The words escaped from my mouth as by a reflex response.

'The patient is in extreme mental and physical agony', the nurse continued. 'She had an infection in one of her eyes which had eventually to be removed. But now the infection has spread to the other one and in fact seems to spread all over'.

Slowly I approached bed number 3. My heart beat seemed to take abnormal speed. Uncertain as I was as to what the encounter would lead to, I tried to gather up all my courage. In the bed was a pale, emaciated lady, about 40 years old, groaning and mumbling, turning and rolling in bed this way and that. It was very clear that her restless and stressful mind was under the tight grip of some trauma. That a feeling of utter hopelessness and depression was pulling her springs of energy down could be seen reflected on her contorted face. It seemed to have been wasp-stung all over. It bore a look of bitter complaint, mixed with intense rage. Who is she complaining against? Against God? Against the world? Against the doctors? I was uncertain. An angry look at me: that was what she welcomed me with. The lady saw me approaching her bed. She seemed to show an attitude of absolute indifference, almost intolerance to this another nuisance, as she must have thought of me. I slowly approached her, with a mind dark and groping in uncertainty. I saw her turn her face to the side opposite to me. The muscles of her face seemed to be stretched with a conspicuous frown on her eye brows. I thought as if I could read the words written on her face: 'Oh! Now for the priestly advice! The one last thing needed for the consummation!' Gathering all my mental poise and presence of mind, and silently muttering a little prayer from my innermost recesses for God's guidance, I came closer to the bed as if I were approaching a time-bomb, set to explode within seconds.

'How are you, Auntie?' I began in a very low and as gentle a voice as possible. Turning her head a little towards me she had another piercing look at me.

'Can't you see me and understand for yourself how well I am? Should I elaborate it for you?' The words struck me like a huge ball of fire from a lightning. I stood there, stunned.

'I don't know much about you, Auntie', I started getting a bit apologetic. 'I would like to know more, if you don't mind telling me more about yourself'. I tried to recapture all my lost mental poise.

'Then you may know that I am on the verge of death which can befall me any time', she began repeating what the nurse had told me all about her condition. 'The demon of death is at the door, bent on taking me with him any moment,' she concluded.

My mind seemed to fumble, not knowing what and how to respond next. I saw her one eye wet and drops rolled down into her ear. 'Oh, God!' The words seemed to resonate deep down somewhere in my mind. From my innermost profundity I called on the Almighty silently, but consciously and earnestly.

And then I asked her: 'So, Auntie, are you sure you are going to die soon?' My sound seemed to tremble with fear and anxiety.

'Ay, so the doctors say', she said. 'What else am I to expect to befall me? To recover and to come back to life hale and healthy? I am not that foolish as to expect to live much longer.'

'Then, are you prepared to face death calmly?' I asked. Pat came the retort: 'Thanks for your priestly advice to make me prepare to die! Father, it is easy for you to advise me to prepare me for death. After my death who is there to look after my motherless children? Who is there for a help to my husband? Who is there to look after my family?'

A thick darkness of uncertainty covered up my mind. 'What solution do I have to offer to her agonizing problem?' my mind murmured to me from within. 'Oh God!' I silently called on Him again in my mind. Mustering all my courage once again I continued, 'So, you expect to die soon, don't you?'

'What else am I to expect?'

'If you die, who is there to look after your children?' I suddenly turned the tables on her.

'Ha, that's my problem'

'Who will look after your husband and family?' I threw the question back to her.

'I don't know who', she replied.

'So then, you cannot do anything more for your children and family, can you?'

'No. I can do nothing more for them!'

'Now that you have come to the very flat rock bottom of your ability, will you favourably respond to a request I have to make?'

'Tell me what it is and I'll be positive, if I can.'

'Then, shall I suggest one thing to you, Auntie?', I said tentatively. 'Yes, you may', she responded.

'Don't you believe in God, under whose providential care we all are?'

'I do, Father', she answered

'Why don't you then entrust your children, husband and family into the protective care of Almighty God?' 'What shall I do for that?' She seemed to be a little more attentive to my words. 'Then, please repeat after me the prayer, won't you?' 'I shall', she readily agreed and began to repeat after me: 'My God, I'm on the point of death and I'm unable to do anything further. I entrust my children into your protective hands. I entrust my husband and family into your protective care. Be you a refuge in their helplessness and be you their Lord and Provider'.

At the end of this little prayer she looked at me. I could see a slightly greater degree of gentleness in that look. 'Is it sincerely and with all your heart and willingness that you entrusted your husband, children and home to the protective hands of divine Providence?' 'Yes, indeed, Father' was her response.

'Then, Auntie', I continued. 'There is one more thing you can do for your dear ones at home'. 'Tell me what and I'm prepared to do whatever I'm capable of doing'.

'When you lived, you taught them how to live. Now that you are prepared to face death, it is for you to teach them how to face death peacefully and serenely', I repeated the words of Cardinal Gracias spoken in tribute to late Fr Po Montfort.

'Tell me what and how I shall do for that'. I felt as if she made an attempt at a very gentle smile. I continued: 'Even in the midst of pains that seem to be acute and unbearable, you should try to put on a gentle smile like this. I know that it is difficult to attempt to smile in such painful moments. But, Auntie, you should do it. When the doctor comes for his rounds, when the nurse comes to administer injections or medicines, when your husband and children come to visit you, try to welcome them with a smile as gentle as this, will you?' 'I shall try', she assured me. 'What next to do I shall tell you when I return to you tomorrow,' I said, and left. On the following day at 4 p.m. I reached the female general ward and approached bed no. 3. As she watched me approaching, there appeared a real though gentle smile on her face. 'What is this Father going to say next', I imagined her to say to herself in her mind.

'Auntie, who is there to take care of your husband and children?', I enquired of her with a slightly mischievous and poking smile.

'Why, the Almighty and merciful God. I have entrusted all my dear ones to His providential care', she answered.

'Then, are you ready to welcome and face death as calmly as possible?' 'I'm ready, Father'. 'Now, when your husband and children come to visit you next time, you should put on the same smile'. 'I promise you, Father. I'll try'.

After that I came off. As I looked back, I saw the lady's gaze following me as far as she could.

Nearly a week and a half later, on my routine visit to the hospital, I reached the female general ward, bed no. 3. There in the bed was another patient. 'Sister', I enquired of the duty nurse, 'what news about our Auntie?'

'Yesterday, she was discharged from the hospital'. 'To which world did she go?' 'To her home at Kidangoor by car together with her husband and children'.

If any of the readers happens to visit Kidangoor and comes across a one-eyed old, smiling lady somewhere there, just ask her whether she had ever been an inpatient in the Kottayam district medical college hospital in the mid-1960s.

## An Extreme Conservative

My first assignment was not directly connected with any pastoral or parish ministry as such. However, I used to be invited by other priests of the diocese in charge of various parishes to give messages and officiate in solemn services of rituals connected with the parish festive days. Drilled and conditioned from infancy as I was in the traditional ascetic other-worldly spirituality of the renunciation of the world, the worldly and the bodily as satanic, my blood was hot with conservatism. Once Fr Thomas Valloppally, a close friend and colleague of mine, then parish priest at the Knanaya Catholic Syro-Malabar church, Cherpunkal, invited me to give a message at the conclusion of the solemn procession and ritual functions connected with the parish patronal feast on the eve of the day of the feast, and to celebrate the solemn High Mass in the morning of the feast day. My message at the conclusion of the evening functions was attended by a mammoth gathering. By the time the evening functions ended, it was nearly 10 p.m. There followed a magnificent performance of 'Kathaprasangam' – a very popular art form consisting of story-telling interspersed with rhythmic music and comic songs and humorous anecdotes capable of provoking the audience to uproarious laughter. Almost three hours passed unaware! Next day we priests got ready for the solemn High Mass, me as the main celebrant. But the church was almost empty of the faithful. Naturally, after the previous night's programme up to about 2 a.m. the people could not care to attend the ritual worship with its most irritating High Mass sung in Syriac melody. I thought of the people's neglect of the Sunday obligations as consequential to the stealthy infiltration of the worldly and the bodily into the other-worldly spirituality and stoic austerity that should be characteristic of authentic catholic spirituality. The traditionalist and conservative ascetic Christian in me got roused. My moral indignation spilled out in the form of an article entitled: 'Beware of Under-Currents', condemning the secret infiltration of the 'this worldly' like cancerous infection into the Christian Catholic religion. The article, published in Deepika, one of the most popular Catholic dailies in Kerala, in the edition dated Thursday 13 February 1964, triggered off a very vigorous and heated controversy over 'Arts Programmes in Church Festivities' for months until Joseph Cardinal Parekattil, then Archbishop of Ernakulam, issued a pastoral circular banning all 'Arts programmes and worldly shows' in church festivities and indirectly vindicating my moral indignation and intense fervour for the traditional orthodox other-worldly spirituality generated by the inveterate, infallible dogmas propagated and drilled into us by the church. The heated controversy, triggered off by my conservative orthodoxy, having subsided, my friend Fr Valloppally once met me casually and with a nudge on my thorax with his fist said: 'You, fellow, you almost ruined me with your damn article'. In fact he was far ahead of me in realizing the emptiness and the meaninglessness of the dogma-generated other-worldly spirituality.

# 10

## The Rite Mania: My First 'No'

As editor of the diocesan weekly *Apna Desh* I was brought into a great deal of involvement in another heated controversy, triggered off by the 'Restoration of the Pristine Purity of the Syro-Malabar Rite'. The restoration was officially declared on 3 July 1962. Its main agenda, as was vehemently argued out by its protagonists under the leadership of the learned Fr Placid, the then spokesperson and consultant of the Syro-Malabar Church in the Oriental Congregation of Vatican Curia, and under the patronage of the then Prefect of the Oriental Congregation, Cardinal Tisserant, was to purify the Syro-Malabar oriental rite from all its 'contaminations' contracted from its contact and co-existence with the Latin Rite through the Portugese missionaries: in one word: 'De-Latinization' of the Oriental Syro-Malabar Rite. I could never understand that the Latin Rite used in the West including the Vatican is such a dirty villain as to ravish the Syro-Malabar Oriental Rite and violate its 'pristine purity'. However, the pre-restored and 'Latin contaminated' rite had been in use among the Syro-Malabar Catholics for centuries and had become part and parcel of their religious heritage, sentiments and practice. The pre-restored rite was one they had lived and grown with. They were intellectually aware and broad-minded enough to look upon all rites including Latin rite as all right to grow in the love of God and man. They had no particular agenda or petty personal ambitions for titles and higher positions in the escalator hierarchy with the concomitant insignias and embellishments. And consequently they had no reason to contract any allergy against the co-existence with and consequent mutual influences and mutations on different rites, particularly against Latin rite. In fact, they felt deeply offended in their religious sentiments and ritual practices by the deformities inflicted upon their ritual practices by the promoters of the 'pristine purity' of an antiquated foreign liturgical form imported from Edessa or Mesopotamia. To them the features of this 'restored pristine purity' were something weird and repulsive. For example, the 'pristine purity' maniacs eliminated the crucified figure of Jesus from the cross. The two horizontal ends and the upper vertical end of the cross were chiseled and shaped into the shape of club of the playing cards, with the dove-god of the god-family sticking headlong on the top end club, as if in its head long landing from all the heights from heaven far above its head got stuck up irretrievably. Archbishop Powathil who 'worships rite rather then God', calls it St. Thomas Cross and expends his life and energy for the promotion and installation of this cross without the crucified figure of Jesus in front of every church and on every altar. Again, bending the vertebrae or the spinal column forward with the joint palms brought together with fingers intertwined and folded and shaped into a fist as a sign of veneration in the place of the traditional genuflection with the palms joined together as a lotus bud was not felt by the Syro Malabar Catholics at large as an exercise worth the labour when considered from the point of view of any spiritual benefit accruing from it. Yet another feature is the sign of the cross made from the right shoulder to the left instead of the traditional left to right. It would be a waste of time pointing out more specimens of the restored 'pristine purity'.

For the laymen it was the deformities, introduced in the name of 'restored pristine purity', that ravished their centuries old rite of worship and violated its purity and dignity and shape acquired from its co-existence and interactions with and influenced by the western Latin Rite. The Edessian rite maniacs could not feel with these enlightened laymen because they had their eyes fixed on the prospects of other higher ecclesiastical status and titles like Archbishop, Major Archbishop, Patriarch etc., with the concomitant insignias and colourful and grotesque embellishments. They of course had generated theology to support their petty personal ambitions. And 'where theology begins, philosophy ends' is the principle of theology! The fanatic champions of this 'restored pristine purity of Rite' went into hectic operation demolishing the altars and facades of churches and re-moulding them to install the 'club' crosses without the Christ figure. The enlightened, unbiased section of the lay-believers who failed to make any sense out of all these exercises and to find any relevance of all these rite reforms to grow in the love of God and man – the sum and substance of Jesus' message – were disturbed and felt their sense of religious sentiments outraged. They began to get organized under the lay leadership of eminent lay-men such as Chev. Joseph Pettah of Trichur.

Somehow or the other, I sympathized with the laymen's line of argument. My own Bishop, Dr Thomas Tharayil, too, was not much enthusiastic about the boisterously celebrated 'Rite Restoration'. He himself was still using the 'Latin-contaminated' and pre-restored Syro-Malabar rite. He had given me special permission to use it at my choice, although the priests ordained after 3 July 1962 had no choice other than using the restored rite. I wrote articles and commentaries in *Apna Desh* on the events related to the rite controversy that was rocking the Syro-Malabar church, supporting the very reasonable line of arguments taken up by the very elite of the lay-believers. Fortunately I found silent approval and indirect appreciation accorded by my own Bishop to the line of thought I had followed in my articles. The laymen's movement began to gather momentum, popularity and speed. They submitted a strongly and reasonably worded and forcefully argued memorandum of petition to the then Apostolic Internuncio pointing out the irrelevance of and the unnecessary disturbance caused by and the energy wasted for the bootless 'rite restoration mania'. The memorandum was signed by such dignitaries and persons of the rank and level of Judges, Chevaliers, Professors, Advocates, Educators and other professionals of high rank, erudition and practical wisdom and experience. [The whole text of the Memorandum and the list of the signatories are found published in Kerala Times, 26 July 1964, page 3]. All this infuriated the rite maniacs, who vented their wrath with the cudgel of the dogma-based magisterium and dogma-generated theological stuff and used all other modes of abuse against the laity. It was at this stage that I wrote an article supporting the laymen and showed it to the then Vicar General, Mgr. Cyriac Mattathil, and the then Chancellor Kuriokose Kunnacherry, who was to later retire as an Archbishop, for their Approval. With their green signal I published it in the *Apna Desh* as its editorial. In addition to this, Chev. Joseph Pettah printed the article in the form of a booklet entitled 'Commentary on Laymen's Memorandum and Counter Arguments' under my own name and distributed copies of it among the Bishops of the Second Vatican Council then in session. In the article, I argued that the laymen sought enlightenment and not suppression. The enthusiasts of the 'pristine purity of rite' had a duty to meet the laymen at the same level of argument, to meet ideas with ideas and not with rods and clubs. The laymen's erudite views as argued and highlighted in the representation submitted to the Prelates of the Syro-Malabar Church by Chev. Pettah in the form of a booklet entitled 'The Future of the Syro-Malabar Church' demand rational arguments and not dogmatic threats.

### My First 'No' to the 'Jure Divino' Authority

The article, coming as it did as editorial of a diocesan official organ, naturally caused a stir and irritated the rite maniacs. And these in turn must have nudged my Bishop who once, while having his dinner at his lone dining table upstairs, summoned me and asked: 'You wrote a few articles in *Apna Desh* in support of the Laymen's views and protests against the recent rite restoration, didn't you?' 'Yes' I answered. 'How many of them?' 'Some four or five if I remember well' I replied. 'Fine. And they must have been well argued out', he said pampering me a little and then continued: 'Now I want you to write as many articles fully supporting the rite restoration movement. I know you are clever enough to handle it properly'.

I was aghast at the Bishop's; I should not say nasty but diplomatic suggestion. 'My Lord', I expostulated, 'Am I to understand you really mean to order me to write articles supporting ideas contrary to my conscience and conviction?' 'Of course I do mean that you write as many articles to the opposite side, and I know you can do it'. 'No, I'm sorry, I can not', I said with a slight emphasis on 'Not'. And I continued: 'I had shown the articles to the V.G. and to the Chancellor for their information and approval. Still, if you think I have gone wrong in my views and if you show me what, where and how I have gone wrong, I am prepared to admit where I have gone wrong and make public apology. But write as many articles to the contrary, supporting ideas against my conviction and conscience, I cannot'.

I don't know whether he was taken aghast at my point-blank refusal of his order. But suddenly it came to my mind that the guiding principle of my Bishop was 'purpose once formed, death or victory'. At any rate, that was my first deliberate and definitive 'No' to the 'Infallible ecclesiastical magisterium' of Holy Mother the Church, shared by my Bishop as well.

The Rite Mania Racks and Wrecks the SMC, US

What is described above is a brief account of the condition of the Syro-Malabar Church (SMC) in Kerala in the mid 1960s and afterwards. The wave of the belligerent controversy and rite war-cry triggered off by the rite restoration on 3 July 1962 continued its violent course almost till the end of the century, causing rumblings and quavers within the Church in Kerala and has, to some extent, subsided. But, as I was scribbling the above described part of the story of my struggles, sitting at the residence of my son Jeslie at Okemos, Lansing, in Michigan, I got a call, quite unexpectedly, from Dr James Kottoor, one of my very intimate, resourceful and knowledgeable friends, then (early March 2011) in Chicago on a visit to his daughter. The call was a god-send to me as eventually it led me to a world of information about the SMC in USA, about the two belligerent factions of the same spitting venom on each other through their respective webs the http://syromalabarvoice.blogspot.com and the http://syromalabarfaith.blogspot.com, and about the Telephone Conference, initiated by well-meaning leaders like Mr T.J. Koovalloor (reachable at *tjkoovalloor@live.com*), Mr Mathew Abraham N.J. etc. as an effort at reconciliation and restoration of peace and about the India Peace Initiative (IPI) formed in the wake of the dastardly murder of the one Christian minister in Islamabad for expressing his difference of opinion on the proposed 'Bill of Blasphemy Law'.

I got a number of messages from the internet downloaded from the SMC voice blogspot and faith blogspot and a large number of e-mails from Mr Kuvalloor's Telephone Conference Conclusions and from Dr James Kottoor (jameskottoor@gmail.com) dated 3 March 2011 on Syro-Malabar Church in the U.S., dated 8 March, 9 March and 10 March. These messages throw ample light on what they scornfully describe as 'Palli Krishi'(Church cultivation) and 'dollar koithu'(dollar harvest), on the Coppell St. Alphonsa's Church built at a fantastic cost of two million dollars and dedicated not under the graceful divine protection, but under the armed police protection. All these in the name of 'the pristine purity of Rite', and of the Edessa imported St. Thomas Cross without the crucified figure of Jesus! In the SMC American parlance, this Cross without Jesus is pet-named as 'claver cross' or even 'B.J.P. Cross'. I was taken aback at this latter pet name and sought its explanation from my American friends. They easily cleared me of my confusion by explaining that B.J.P. Cross means Bishop Joseph Powathil Cross!

This rite mania played havoc in Kerala as it wounded sentiments, and shattered the peace and fellowship of the enlightened Kerala SMC lay fraternity in the last part of the 20th century. It created divisions among the laity. The factions spat venom at each other and were busy in mud-slinging. It created a belligerent atmosphere in several parishes, led to the waste of money and energy in demolishing existing churches in order to reshape them so as to install what the SMC US now calls the 'claver cross' or 'B.J.P. Cross'. But now the destructive and divisive wave of the rite mania has shifted to the richest cities of the US. The demon seems to have severely haunted the SMC US community, causing mutually conflicting factions under the internet IDs voice.blogspot and faith.blogspot. They engage in an exchange of venom. The demon seems to have entered under the garb of 'catering to the spiritual needs of the SMC US immigrants *in their own rite*'. It needs broad visions of persons like Dr James Kottoor to think that 'any rite is all right to pray'. But the 'catering business' turned into 'Palli Krishi' and 'Dollar Koithu'. When the rite demon works for Mammon, the picture becomes complete. The catering business has gone to the extent of attempting to murder possible candidates for the coveted hierarchical promotion such as Archbishop Jacob Thumkuzhy of Trichur through acid-mixed wine at Mass!

After all the heat and war cry over the 'pristine purity of Rite', we must ask ourselves what we have gained on the path of 'establishing God's kingdom here on earth'. Cui bono? Whose what interest has it served except perhaps pampering the petty private personal ambitions for titles and concomitant insignias and paraphernalia? To apply the test proposed by Jesus to judge the tree by its fruit, what fruit has it produced in our value-drained and colossally corrupt socio-political life, in the field of inter-religious amity, except adding fuel to fire, and intensifying the already disturbed social life? My response to all these disturbances and rumblings in the SMC US was given in the shape of an article 'The Rite Mania Racks and Wrecks the SMC in US' sent to Mr Koovalloor for consideration of all those concerned, if they thought it worth.

I suggested that it is time for God-believing enlightened people like the SMC US immigrants to think a little in depth and go into the facts. After all, reason is God-given while Faith is given and drilled in from our infancy in dogmatic formulae by the Church, supposedly by 'divine right' authority. It is therefore an equally religious duty to use our God-given reason precisely because it is God-given and therefore a religious responsibility, to exercise our reason. Consequently, leaving the responsibility of thinking and of being led by the light of reason to a super-hierarchy, whatever divine right authority they arrogate, and taking the attitude of 'pray, pay and obey' is dereliction of God-imposed obligation and therefore sinful. If any one of the priestly rank asks a God-believing person 'Who are you to think when we are here?' the priests should have the guts born of religious enlightenment to answer back; 'God is not in anybody's long pocket'. Jesus defined the fundamental tenet of his message in the form of two relationships or two commandments: the vertical relationship of man's love of God, the Moral Imperative, and the horizontal relationship of man's socio-civic responsibilities, in other words, love of one's neighbour, fixed on the former. In this cross of the two-fold relationship Jesus summarizes all the laws and prophets and he never mentions any rituals, much less of any 'pristine purity of rite'. The God-believing community should exhibit adulthood in matters religious as well. Should they gullibly pamper petty narrow-visioned personal ambitions and worship of the Mammon at the expense of their own peace, security, fellowship and prosperity? They should have the insight to see where they are led to by the dogma-based church hierarchy which arrogates the monopoly of the jure divino escalatory service to heaven and the right to fix the payment of toll for this service. They should not be content with being perpetual, praying, paying and obeying infants under the perpetual tutelage of the self-arrogated escalatory masters. When persons of petty ambitions, worshipping rite and communalistic diversities rather than God, sit at the helm of affairs, and gullible perpetual minors are ready to pay, pray, and obey, derelicting their duty of exercising their gift of God-given reason, events like the Coppell Church dedication are inevitable.

Relating to the movement of 'India Peace Initiative', I felt that nothing is more optimistic, relevant and wholesome than this in this era of inter-religious rivalries, enmities, communal clashes, fundamentalist terrorism, jihads, counter attacks of religious fanaticism etc. But one should remember that the very fundamental basis of such inter-religious rivalries and clashes is the blind faith in the dogmatic creed formulae preached to, and drilled into us, from our infancy by priests and pujaris. These creeds are different for different religions and mutually contradictory, and are responsible for the multiplicity of the mushroom growth of religions. Under the circumstances I think that attempts for inter-religious amity under the banner of any one particular dogmatic religion, even Christian, are a contradiction in operation and very unlikely to bear fruit. I feel that Natural Human Morality ruled by God, the Moral Imperative is Religion with a capital 'R'. I think it is this Religion that Jesus preached through his two-fold and all-inclusive commandment. Jesus' Religion is this Cross of the two-fold relationship, which is universal for all. It should be owned that God is not Christian, nor Hindu nor Islam, but the Universal Moral Imperative. Christianity is a product of the church leaders and the Roman Emperors in unholy political alliance in synods and is now synonymous with 'Churchianity'. When the German theologian Holger Kersten said: 'Jesus' message has been distorted beyond recognition', he meant this degeneration of Jesus' message into the dogma-pestered churchianity. I would humbly suggest to my friends working towards India Peace Initiative to think a little deeper with Kersten and see if a rethinking over the dogma-pestered mushroom religions is a need of the times or not.

# 11

# Break Off from O.S.H.: My Second 'No'

The struggle that led me to my second 'No' to the 'jure divino' dogmatic authority was in connection with my effort to extricate myself from the 'Diocesan Religious Congregation' which my Bishop had organized for the 'priestly sanctification' of its members. The real purpose was to net a group of priests bound by the vow of obedience, by virtue of which they could easily be ordered about, and bound by the vow of poverty by virtue of which they need to be given no remuneration or emolument except sufficient quantity of fodder. I have already pointed out briefly the story of my being netted by my Bishop. Now please allow the living records to re-tell and confirm this story.

My Bishop detected two weaknesses in me: my surging desire to complete my priestly studies in the Papal Seminary and the inability of my father, struggling as he was to make the family's both ends meet, to meet my seminary expenses. His Excellency my Bishop decided to hook me with these two weaknesses and net me into his O.S.H. Monastery. The saintly Fr Peter Vattaparambil wrote to me, from Cherukara church, on 4 February 1955: 'Enclosed please find a cheque of Rs. 65. Don't be bothered about getting a benefactor. I shall be your support. May God help me to help you in all your needs,' adding 'Be a humble and saintly seminarian'.

Informing me of the not so favourable a response from my home-parish yogam, the Vicar Fr Mathew Pralel wrote to me on 23 February 1955, 'On being informed of this (the parish yogam's response) the Bishop has replied as follows: 'If the boy joins the Mount, he will get all help". Fr Pralel also added: 'It would be better for you to seek the Bishop's advice and abide by it'. I suspected the Bishop to have been in touch with him suggesting to him to advice me so. The Bishop's letter to him dated 17 April 1955 confirmed my suspicion. The letter carried 'Good news for seminarist Abraham of your Parish. He is selected for admission at Kandy Seminary (now shifted to Poona) also by merits of his marks. That means he is a clever chap.

'As per the new Kandy Seminary rule, each new student will have to pay Rs. 60 per mensem....I know Abraham won't be able to pay it. But I may be able to find out a benefactor for him and S.H. Mount Monastery may be got to pay something for him, *provided he likes to join the congregation.*

'Considering his future, Kandy is certainly preferable to Alwaye. Look at the providence of God for him'!

At the end of the petit seminary course, before leaving for home on vacation, I had been confronted by the Bishop directly on this point. On submitting my unwillingness to join the O.S.H. he had threatened me with rejection from priestly studies, as he 'seriously doubted' the genuineness of my vocation, adding: 'I'll let you know if you are to proceed to the major seminary'. It was then that our Vicar General, Mgr. Stephen Uralil, seeing me coming out of the Bishop's room with tears rolling out of my eyes, assured me that if one in my batch went to the major seminary, it would be myself. (Good Mgr. Uralil, having been turned out of the Vicar General's post, left the diocese the following year and died heart broken in a religious house in Hyderabad.)

The lurking fear of my utter dependence upon the Bishop's mercy and the irresistible attraction of the prospects of going to the Papal Seminary almost vanquished me. Through my letter dated 7 May 1955 I surrendered to the Bishop's decision: 'But if you think otherwise that it is good that I join the S.H. Monastery, I submit myself to your holy will [thirumanas]'. Pat came the Bishop's quick reply dated 10 May sent c/o Fr Pralel: '...I believe the best thing for you will be to join the Diocesan Congregation of the O.S.H.' adding what he believed to be the secret of success in life: 'Purpose once formed, death or victory'. It took years of my later priestly experience to realize how far low he would stoop to put into practice this 'motto' relying on his self-arrogated dogmatic and therefore unquestionable authority. One can only pity the condition of priests and nuns and laymen under such authority. No wonder a 'Diocesan Priest' wrote in New Leader dated 9 May 1974: 'The prevailing canon law provides the Bishops with all sorts of props to keep an absolute sway over the priests under them. There is no independent judiciary in the church. The executive body itself is entrusted with judicial powers....Consequently priests are in effect slaves of the Bishops subjected to their whims....A priest cannot develop his personality and talents unless he curries favour with his bishop through fair or foul means'.

The irony of my situation was that in the same letter of 10 May the Bishop continued: 'Now you tell me some people are ready to help you if you become a secular priest.... Now you must get from home and with the help of those who are willing to help you Rs. 500 to be given at once to the Superior of the O.S.H. Monastery so that the congregation may see to the rest of your expenses.... Your father in the Lord'! In a p.s. he also added: 'I have no objection to the Piravom Church giving a sum towards your patrimony without any obligation'.

Again I approached the parish council with this letter but to no avail. Thereupon through my letter dated 12 May I informed the Bishop of my helplessness to raise Rs. 500. In his reply, again sent c/o Fr Pralel, he insisted on my procuring Rs. 500 from somewhere, adding a double threat: 'or else I shall find it difficult to send him to Poona. If he cannot have the patrimony, how can I send him to Alwaye even?' Apparently he conveniently forgot that his suggestion for my joining the O.S.H. meant to be a solution to my financial strain.

Having exhausted even my last resort I wrote to the Bishop on 12 May: 'All my relatives and friends refuse to help me if I join the congregation. Relying upon your over-flowing paternal affection, I take your advice. As for raising Rs. 500 towards patrimony, I am helpless. My father has already a loan of Rs. 600 or more to pay back. I should be grateful to know your holy will, regarding my vestition and details of my journey to Poona'. I was then made to sign a legally and canonically worded document dated 24 May 1955, which he drafted as my application for admission to O.S.H. With that I packed off to Poona.

## The Octopus Grip Being Tightened

On 24 November 1960, the Bishop wrote a common letter addressed to Brothers Thomas Peedikayil O.S.H., Cyriac Peringelil O.S.H. Kuiakose Thazhathottathil O.S.H. and Abraham Vellamthadathil O.S.H. He informed us: 'I received a communication from the Holy See to the effect that the New Rules may be enforced on the Oblates of the Sacred Heart of the Diocese, for a definite period for a trial (ad experimentum) and after that period, the New Rules, with modifications if any, may be sent to Rome for approval....After getting your individual replies (that you agree to the above) on or before 1 December next I shall inform you further steps in the matter'.

I knew nothing about either the 'old rules' or 'the new ', according to which I was to take my profession, nor had I made any novitiate. However on 27 November 1960 I replied to the above agreeing to make my profession, adding 'I had no opportunity to come to know the type of religious life the congregation enabled its members to have and to study its rules'. Subsequently on 25 March 1961 I was required to make my first religious profession of vows according to a formula drafted by the Bishop: I, Abraham Vellamthadathil, in the presence of the Bl. Virgin Mary and all other saints of the heavenly court...do hereby bind myself with a vow to Almighty God for the space of one year to obey you, my Lord as well as your successors in the see of Kottayam in all that shall be enjoined on me'.

## I Wanted to Speak Out

Meanwhile I began to feel my nerves shattered. I was brought to the brink of a nervous breakdown and to suffer from insomnia. I wanted peace. On 29 May 1962, during my retreat for sub-diaconate, I wrote to Fr Superior explaining my mental tension and concluding with my decision to leave the congregation. I feared delay to reveal it might put my sense of honesty in the dock. But my then Spiritual Father, Fr John Ancot advised me to withhold the letter and to go ahead with my ordination to major orders and to postpone the settlement of the problem by two years of experience with the O.S.H. life. I would be absolutely free to renew the temporary vows or not. I took his advice to heart.

On my return from Poona after my priestly ordination, I got my first appointment order dated April 18, 1963, appointing me as Spiritual Father of the Petit Seminary, and almost half a dozen charges were assigned to me with my stay fixed in the S.H. Mount Monastery. On 20 February 1964, I was given still another charge, as convener of the Diocesan Liturgical Committee formed as per No. 45 of the Constitution on Sacred Liturgy published on 4 December 1963, the closing date of the 11th session of Vatican II.

### The O.S.H. Community in Rub with the Bishop

The life of the O.S.H. Community grew steadily restless and unhappy. In 1964 V. Rev. Fr Placid C.M.I. was sent from Rome as canonical visitor in answer to an appeal made to Rome by the Superior and the Community. In an interview with Fr Placid, I explained the story of my 'religious vocation'. 'Your problem is simple,' Fr Placid diagnosed my condition. 'You were forced into the congregation. Hence you have the right and absolute freedom to leave it and find peace'. He also promised help against possible oppressive measures. In Fr Placid's letter from Collegio di S. Giosefat, Roma, dated 4 November 1964, he wrote: 'I carefully read your long letter and have understood the whole situation....I will recommend you to be on Vadavathoor [Seminary] staff. But will the Bishop spare your service in the Diocese?.... To join another diocese there is the need for excardination which I think will not be given easily. In this also I will try to do what I can....'

Meanwhile my father had to be hospitalized. Finding no way of paying the hospital bill on discharge, I appealed to the Bishop and to the Superior for help. But I was told that a person under religious vows of poverty had no obligation to take care of his family needs. However, in a subsequent letter dated 29 November 1964 the Bishop wrote: 'About your father, I am sorry for what happened. My idea was that you did not refer to me for some reduction or help from the hospital which could have been easily done by a chit. Never mind.'

## My Decision to Speak Out

I mustered all my courage and made an attempt to inform the Bishop of my reluctance to continue my membership in the congregation and consequently to renew my temporary vows. The Bishop advised me to try for one more year after which I could leave if I still felt like leaving and I obeyed. Subsequently through my letters dated14 March and 16 March I definitively made it clear that I did not intend to renew the temporary vow. 'For the last almost three years,' I explained, 'I very sincerely tried to be happy with this life, but never found a moment of peace and happiness....All I could find in this religious community, with the exception of one or two, is that so many individual interests and aspirations are tied together in the form of a 'religious life' by some external bond which is fear and uncertainty in some, and ambition and expectations in others....I feel that the prevalent spirit of this life will only help to change the genuine aspirations and priestly desires into hypocrisy'.

I was then given order No. 98B/65 dated May 15, 1965 giving me five more charges and shifting my residence to the Bishop's house.

To my letters dated 14th and 16th March, I got the Bishop's reply dated 16 May. After a tirade of admonitions and latent threats he added: 'So my advice to you is to rectify your conscience and find happiness without which you will be a failure even outside the Society. I now recall so many examples of eminent men gone astray by your mode of argumentation'.

The first paragraph exhibits a paper tiger. It says: 'You must be now happy that you followed my advice and took the vow [on 18-3-1965] unlike some others who refused to take the vow, who are told by the Apostolic Internuncio that they made a mistake in not taking the vow and that they are allowed to take vow on the 18th and that he would grant sanation for the break caused by their refusal to take the vow'. In my subsequent letter I persisted: 'I discussed in detail the problem of my peace of conscience with my Spiritual Father.... I was advised by him, by V. Rev. Fr Placid and Fr Claude Krishnamurthy that for my peace and spiritual progress I should leave the congregation'.

In my subsequent letter to the Superior dated 15 January 1966 I clearly told him: 'With reference to your oral intimation about the profession of perpetual vows.... I write to inform you that I am persuaded not to take the perpetual vow on account of reasons pertaining to my conscience'.

In reply, the Superior, Fr Thomas Kaniamyalil, wrote to me on 19 January: 'Those who took vows according to the new constitution and completed five years *are not permitted not to renew the vows*.... The vows taken before an authority approved by the holy Church are made 'foro interno' and hence reasons, even if 'conscientious', for not renewing them should be made known or give an application in triplicate written in English with reasons for leave of the Holy See not to renew the temporary'. Poor Fr Kaniamyalil. Formerly a Jacobite priest who got reunited with the Knanaya Catholic community, he might not have been aware of the absurdity of his letter. But the Bishop who dictated the content could not be excused for ignoring the absurdity contained in the letter. The letter was accompanied with a copy of 'Decretun Sacrae Congregationis Pro Ecclesia Orientali De societate Oblatorum. S. Cordis Apud Kottayam' (Decree of the Sacred Congregation for the Oriental Church about the Society of the Oblates of Sacred Heart at Kottayam) dated 13 January 1966. I wonder whether Fr Kaniyamyalil could read and understand even one word of this Roman Decree couched in classical Ciceronian style Latin!

To this I replied on 21 January quoting the Bishop's own

words uttered in course of an instruction imparted to the Oblates on 'The Priest Sanctification Day', 4 June 1964: 'We should join the existing order with its own rules....If it does not suit us, we should not commit ourselves to it. There is no compulsion. I feel this advice pointedly applies itself to me'. Fr Superior's reply to this was a long harangue on religious profession as 'means of sanctification through ascetic life of sacrificing oneself to God and obtaining grace' and what not. So he concluded: 'prefer your application for perpetual vows or application in English in triplicate with reasons for sanction from Rome for release from Rome'. Poor Fr Kaniamyalil lent himself to serve as a faithful stenographer of the Bishop.

Pat came order No. 16B/66 from Most Rev. Dr Thomas Tharayil, dated 11 February 1966 repeating the message of the Superior, power-packed within apostolic Episcopal authority, but slightly mitigating the vigour of the sanctifying effect of the *vow* of obedience to *promise* of obedience and prefacing it with a double threat of paper tiger: 'Very Rev. Fr Superior is awaiting reply from His Excellency the Apostolic Internuncio as to what may be done in your case...' and a reference to the 'Decree' mentioned above. Then comes the mitigation of the vigour and cutting down the dosage of this 'medicine' of priestly sanctification: the 'Decretum states that the members who prefer to take *promise* in stead of *vow* of obedience may be allowed to do so.

'You are therefore requested to submit to me your application to take either vow or promise of obedience...either perpetually or temporarily....With cordial blessings to Rev. Fr Abraham Vellamthadathil, O.S.H., Catholic Bishop's House, Kottayam', from the Bishop's room upstairs, to my room down stairs. My request to be heard by the Bishop was turned down and I was asked to submit my reply in writing. Accordingly my written submission dated 25 February 1966 repeated once again my conscientious difficulties to continue membership in the Monastery, concluding: 'I am now about to complete the term of the five years of probation Period. From the experience of this period of life as a member of this society, I am persuaded that this life does not in any way help me to be happy or maintain peace of my conscience. I am therefore convinced that, knowing this, if I were to take the perpetual vows, I would be acting gravely against my conscience'.

The Bishop's next letter, even dated, expressed his willingness to hear me, but required me 'to bring this letter and the one of February 11th and Fr Superior's dated 25-1-'66 and the 'Decretum' from Rome'. Hence I provided myself with copies of these documents for my file. The letter then expatiated: 'The gravity of the letter (Decree) from Rome would require me *to get permission from Rome to let you off*, even after the expiry of the period of vows on 18 March 1966 for the following reasons for which satisfactory explanations will have to be given to Rome'. Reasons to confirm absolute nonsense! The rabbit I caught had three horns! This paper tiger was absolutely out of place because after the expiry of the period of temporary profession I would automatically be out of the cage and extricated from the 'religious net' by virtue of all the canons and church traditions and practices and ordinary man's common sense. And the Bishop had no need 'to seek permission from Rome to let me off'.

In the fourth paragraph of this letter he continues: 'What do you gain by becoming a secular priest – You, I say, who would not have become a priest if you did not join the Oblates, or at least not have gone to Poona.' The cat is out of the bag! I remembered how prudent and insightful Fr Ancot S.J. was when he advised me as far back as 1961 to proceed with my studies and ordination and take my final decision after a couple of years of experience as a priest member of the Society. The Bishop showed himself addict to his working principle: 'Purpose once formed, death or victory'.

The fifth paragraph contained a deadly threat: 'You'll be thoroughly misunderstood, if you became a secular priest and remained in the diocese, though you make the required patrimony and get out of the Monastery'. As a remedy and possible self-protection against this my forecast doom in the Diocese he suggested: 'If you get out of the Monastery, the best thing will be to get out of the Diocese too (and no patrimony may be then required)'. But this forecast route of escape was over shadowed by the next sentence: 'But will you find a benevolent Bishop to take you, knowing the above situation?' He had another prop which the canon law equips the Bishops with, namely the clutch of 'excardination'. (The permission given by a Bishop to dehinge a priest from his diocese and to join another.)

The very next day, i.e. 26 February 1966 the Bishop conveyed to me his 'spiritual advice' in the form of a 'self-reflected' prayer of self-sacrifice: 'In the final analysis, it comes to this: what has not our Lord done for me out of love and what should not I do for love of Him? You decide with a balanced mind. If I were you, I would courageously decide to go ahead, come what may, trusting in the Lord. Sufficientia nostra ex Deo est'! [Our sufficiency is from God]

On 15 March 1966 the Bishop addressed a common letter to five of us members: Frs. Chemmarappally, Peringelil, Thazhathottam, Edat and Vellamthadathil showing once again the paper tiger of the 'Decree from Rome' and asking us 'to submit your reasons why you refuse to conform to the 'Decree from Rome''. Once again, which Rome can issue what decree to oblige anybody to take religious vows, I wondered. Then comes the threat repeated: 'If you do not want to be members of this society, which is of secular priests of the diocese, I fail to see why you should remain at all in the diocese as secular priests'. I too failed to see why all the other secular priests in the diocese had not or do not become members of this society of secular priests of the diocese! Nowhere in all my studies of theology or canon law have I come across the notion that secular priests are members of any society ruled by constitutions and bound by religious vows. 'So it is a question of finding a benevolent bishop to take you', the letter repeats the threat of expulsion from the diocese and concludes: 'My idea is to send you to your parish till further decision is made. And the decision will take time'. The idea is clear: a kind of home arrest, confining us to our parish presbytery.

To this I responded on 17 March 1966: 'The decree from Rome could expect me to submit my application for profession of perpetual vows [before 18 March, the day of expiry of the temporary vows] if and *only if* I wished to be a member of this society of O.S.H.' To the Bishop's contention in the same letter regarding the 'Decree'' 'first obey, next complaint' is the order', I submitted that there is no question of any disobedience, since no decree of any authority on earth can in any way compel me to make religious profession. I concluded my appeal with a request to reconsider his intention to send me to my parish suspending me from all priestly ministry. The Bishop simply returned my response with a note to 'do in the light of what I told you five'.

So I uttered my second definitive 'No' on 18 March 1966 when the temporary vows taken earlier expired. I decided not to prolong or indulge in this exercise of wasteful, meaningless exchange of Episcopal orders and priestly 'cravings on bended knees for the paternal kindness' of any Excellency any more. I decided to assert the absolute freedom I have of refusing to be bound by any religious profession of vows any more, come what may. So I wrote to the Bishop on 18 March 1966: 'As per reasons I have already explained to Your Excellency so many times before...I request to be relieved from this monastery'.

The Bishop then took his last weapon, hitherto kept hidden. My letter dated 13 April 1966 was returned by the Bishop with a note on it dated 15 April: 'If you wish to continue in the diocese, give in writing your willingness to return the amount spent by the society for your studies'.

### Attempts to Rescue my Priestly life and Peace

I was well aware of the future prospects of the rub with the dogmatic, apostolic, Episcopal power of this Most Rev. Bishop Tharayil, who ruled by the principle; 'Purpose once formed death or victory'. I knew that the octopus grip would only be tightened to strangle me, if I am weak enough under this grip. The highly conservative traditional dogmatic catholic in me still had the upper hand over the human in me. I clung to save my priestly service in spite of my family members, my father and my two brothers prompting me to cast away this cassock of priestly slavery. With the help and direction of Very Rev. Fr

Victor O.C.D. the then Provincial of the Kottayam Province of the Latin Carmelites and later Apostolic Administrator and Bishop in Kuwait, I wrote to Bishop Daniel Liston of the missionary diocese of Mauritius on 3 April, 1966, explaining in detail all the steps of my long struggle to extricate myself from the bucket of the 'Diocesan Congregation'. I offered my priestly service in his diocese. This I did in the wake of my Bishop's repeated threats. Besides, on 9 April 1966 he again wrote to me: 'If you wish to leave the diocese, I do not object to that also'.

I got Bishop Daniel Liston's very encouraging reply dated 19 April stating: 'I have pleasure in informing you that the diocesan council has favourably considered your kind offer to come to work in Mauritius and has asked me to go ahead with the necessary negotiations or arrangements.

'Of course my first duty is to communicate with your Bishop – I shall do so immediately and as soon as I have received his reply, will decide what is to be done'. This was a ray of hope to save my priestly ministry, but a hope overshadowed with my fear as to the response of my Bishop. My fear was not unfounded. In his order No. 71B/66, dated 26 April '66, the Bishop shifted my residence from the Bishop's house back to the S.H. Monastery with the additional charge of Malloosery chapel and of teaching in the Novitiate House of Nattassery convent and in the petit seminary at S.H. Mount, 'without prejudice to his present work' assigned earlier. These duties were apparently overwhelming enough for a man. But in my case they were only on paper. In reality I was required to do none of these duties. He had a hidden agenda. He was taking steps to keep me in the Monastery free of all duties to compel me to attend a course of training of the O.S.H. or Novitiate under Fr Claude Krishnamurthy S.J. to prepare the Oblates for the final profession of vows according to the 'New Rules' which he had framed and got approved by Rome. I readily obeyed. In my report dated 20 May 1966 accepting the new duties I informed him of my correspondence with Bishop Liston of Mauritius with an earnest request to bless my leaving for Mauritius with the necessary permission and paternal blessings and kind recommendation. I also informed him of my readiness to pay the balance, if any, of the expenditure incurred by the Monastery for my studies. 'I only request a little time as I have no means of my own to pay back the debt now'.

On 25 July 1966 Bishop Liston wrote from Port Louis to Bishop Tharayil for his leave of my working in Mauritius. While I was still at the Bishop's house also acting as his secretary, he made me type out his reply to Bishop Daniel Liston dated 14-10-'66 in which this (al) Most Rev. Bishop Tharayil had no qualm of conscience to write: *'Fr Abraham Vellamhadathil has now decided not to work in your diocese* on account of many reasons, specially of the language and climatic difficulties, though he made an attempt to brush up his French learned in the Seminary which is not enough to carry on the ministry efficiently'. This was another of the crudest shocks to me, because just the previous day I had insisted on going to work in Mauritius and before typing out the letter, I had protested against this naked lie. Yet this 'jure divino' catholic Bishop had no scruples in affixing his signature to this awful falsehood.

In yet another attempt to save my priestly life from being strangled here I wrote to the Rt. Rev. Victor O.C.D. again. In my letter dated 23 April 1966 I requested him 'to kindly give me incardination into your diocese and guidance and protection to my priestly life'. To this too I got no favourable reply, whether due to any behind-the-screen understanding between the two 'jure divino' Bishops or not, I am not certain.

In my letter to the Apostolic Internuncio, New Delhi, Most Rev. Dr James Ronald Knox dated 4 July 1966 I explained: 'The spirituality and peace of my priestly life is being cruelly tried under my Bishop almost beyond my ability to endure it further. He would neither show me kindness and allow me a humble life of peaceful priestly service in the diocese, nor let me go to find protection and guidance for my priestly ministry under another Bishop....I feel I am cruelly denied justice and fair treatment at his hands'. This appeal too for rescue fell on deaf ears and turned into a cry in the wilderness. A similar appeal dated 10 July 1966 was addressed to Gustavo Cardinal Testa

Pro-Prefect of the Sacred Congregation for the Oriental Church explaining all my hazards and craving for intervention. Its fate too was not any different from that of the earlier ones.

## The O.S.H. Imbroglio Continues

To the Bishop's oral instruction to give fresh application with 'reasons' to quit the monastery, and to submit Mass Balance sheet, I responded through my letter dated 26 May 1966. I submitted another 'fresh' application with reasons to quit the O.S.H. society. Mass balance sheet up to 18 March 1966 was also submitted on 28 May, because I said Mass from that day onwards retaining the Mass stipend as it was mine own since 18 March.

Behind the Bishop's order No. 71B/66 dated 26 April 1966 shifting my residence to the S.H. Monastery there was a hidden agenda. On 18 July the Bishop commenced a one year period of formation for the Oblates under Rev. Fr Claude Krishnamurthy. His purpose in shifting my residence to the Monastery was to compel me to attend the programme in view of the final and perpetual profession of vows. I submitted through my letter dated 18 July 1966: 'I don't intend to attend the course of formation ... since I don't intend to continue membership in the Monastery....I am here [in the Monastery]without any work....It is up to your Excellency to make use of my priestly life or not'. Again on the following day I wrote another letter through the Superior Fr Thomas Edathiparampil providing a number of informations called for. I included: 'I am prepared to return whatever I am obliged to restitute to the Monastery, but with request to allow a little more time'.

On 20 July after the Bishop's 9.30 p.m. instruction to the members of the monastery taking the one year formation, His Excellency came to my room seething with anger, his face red and muscles distorted. He found me writing [an article for the S.H. Monthly]. 'Are you writing for your gRRub?, he burst out, the 'r' sound of 'grub' resonating like a roar. 'I suspend you from saying Mass tomorrow'. He slammed my door and went to his suite. The entry in my 'Diarium Missarum' [Record of accounts of Masses received and exonerated] for the 21st of July 1966 reads even now: 'Suspensus a sacris for asking to be relieved of the Monastery'. I believe that my Bishop thereby stood ipso facto excommunicated by virtue of canon law which pronounces ipso facto excommunication upon those who compel any one in any way to take religious vows or priestly ordination, and with the Bishop the whole diocese under his jurisdiction.

### Ordered to House Arrest

On the very next day the Bishop through his order No. 108B/66 dated 22 July 1966 directed me to stay in my home parish St. Antony's Presbytery, Marika, and prohibited me to do any priestly ministry in any other church either within or outside the Diocese. Further he demanded to have two acres of property got registered in my name 'since your brother told me that the property in view is almost barren and the yield almost nothing'.

Further, 'During your stay at Marika, you will do well to make the amount of Rs. 3000 due from you to the Society of the O.S.H. which was spent by the society for your sundry expenses during the last 11 years....As soon as you have got ready the registered document and the required document, please inform me and I will ask you to go over.'

I think it is the first time in the history of all the Catholic religious communities that a member, whether leaving the religious community on his own or dismissed, was asked to pay back the expenses incurred on his behalf.

On the day of my suspension after informing Fr Superior, I went to seek the advice of His Grace Archbishop Mathew Kavukatt of Chenganacherry. But on the way I was called back by Bishop Tharayil and he forbade me to leave the compound of the Monastery without his permission!

On the 22nd he wanted me to sign a letter he drafted, addressed to the Apostolic Internuncio, New Delhi and requesting him to dispense me from my 'free and voluntary' profession taken for five years and hand it over to him in triplicate. Naturally I refused to sign it as it was contrary to facts.

Meanwhile he had sent for my brother, a below-average farmer with only primary school education. In spite of my earnest request to spare him the shock and the scandal when told of my being suspended, the Bishop told him that I stood suspended and I was mad and defiantly rebellious and disobedient and asked my brother to take me home to Marika.

In another petition addressed to Gustavo Cardinal Testa dated 24 July 1966, I submitted all the details that led to my suspension and house arrest. As for the re-payment of Rs. 3000, supposed to have been spent for my studies from Monastery, I pleaded with the Cardinal that I was pressed hard, specially for financial difficulties, as I have not been able to save anything since I was working in the diocese without any remuneration and saying Mass for the Superior's intentions for about three years until 18 March 1966. As usual I got no response from this eminent cardinal either.

I thought Bishop Victor S. Miguel, Apostolic Administrator of Kuwait was in the know of the cruel treatment meted out to me by this Bishop of 'jure divino' apostolic authority. In a letter to him dated Marika, 24 July 1966, I requested him 'to kindly help me and do the needed to extricate me from these extremely straining situations and to get me incardinated in another diocese'.

On 28 July I wrote to my Excellent Bishop Tharayil stating: 'I have property worth Rs. 1500. I shall procure a sum of Rs. 500 to be deposited in the bank to complete Rs. 2000 required as patrimony as per your direction.

'As for Rs. 3000 I am asked to re-pay to the Monastery, please consider that I have been saying Masses for the Superior's intentions for the last three years and more until 18 March 1966 and serving the diocese all this while' without any emolument.

### Letters of Sympathy and Concern

Meanwhile I had several letters from some priests and nuns

within the diocese, expressing moral indignation at this Episcopal senseless arbitrariness and conveying sentiments of sympathy and feeling of concern. For example, Fr Joseph Mekkara in his letter dated 30 July wrote: 'God forgive the Bishop for all the cruel injustice meted out to you.... It is almost unendurable for me to watch this injustice and do nothing about it'. Good old Fr Philip Kamicherry from Vianney Home Caritas, Kottayam, wrote to me on 12 August 1966: 'I am not surprised at the reply of the Bishop....Inform the Internuncio about the contents of the letter you received from the Bishop of Mauritius....Fr Cheruserry is also of the same opinion....Under the circumstances, is it not the duty of the Superiors to leave no stone unturned to bring the matter to an amicable settlement?... Don't get dejected in any way. Carry on life there quietly and peacefully. Everything will come to a happy end.'

Even nuns from convents wrote to me letters loaded with intensely emotional affection expressing their solidarity with me and ready to allay my sorrow by sharing it to any extent. For example, a letter from V+J, Kottayam dated 13 August [name withheld for obvious reasons] reads: 'That day you gave me the story, covered up and in mitigated words, of your being tortured. But when I came to know the story in its naked form, it broke my heart. You never deserved such an inhuman treatment. Your hardships are mine too. It breaks my heart to think that I have not done anything to share your sorrow and thereby to allay it. My constant worry is about you....Anybody who knows anything about you will not put any blame on you....'

Fr Jacob Kalayil in his letter, St. Martha's Hospital, Bangalore - 2, dated 19 August 1966 wrote: 'Hope things will straighten up as God wills without much troubles for you. 'Diligentibus Deum omnia cooperantur ad bonum' [To those who love God, everything turns out for good]....I am enclosing a cheque for Rs. 200 for forty three Masses 'ad intentionem dantis..' [for the intention of the giver].

**The Curtain Falls**

'Please don't worry about the distant future….Be brave and happy', Fr Krishnamurthy wrote to me from S.H. Monastery on 17 August '66. It was like the morning star indicative of the distant dawn after this first long peregrination through dark arduous dungeon around the S.H. Monastery.

Soon I got the Bishop's Order No. 123B/66 dated August 18, 1966, asking me to produce and submit registry document of required patrimony, P.P.F [Priest Provident Fund] membership receipt and document of settlement of account with the Monastery related to my seminary study expenses and repayment of Rs. 500 'given by me as you wanted to join the monastery of the Oblates' in 1955 before leaving for Poona.

The following day in my reply dated 19 August '66, expressing my inability to procure the required patrimony of two acres of property and to pay Rs. 650 for membership in the P.P.F., as per its rule, I submitted: 'As for the amount of Rs. 3000 demanded to be returned to the Monastery, I am prepared to return the balance, if any, after deducting the stipend of Masses I have been saying 'ad intentionem Superioris' up to 18 March 1966. I shall pay it through installments to be fixed by the benevolent Fr Superior and the council'. The Bishop returned this letter with the note dated 20-8-'66: 'The patrimony is for your future safety and so I do not insist….You have to pay only Rs. 5 to join the P.P.F. It is a question of meeting Fr Peter Uralil at once. Re. accounts with the Monastery, do meet Fr Superior.'

Accordingly I wrote to Fr Superior on 23 August: 'Your Reverence is aware that I have been serving the diocese all this while without any remuneration and saying Mass 'ad intentionem Superioris' until last March', and requested him to settle the dues with the Monastery taking into consideration the stipend of Masses accredited to the Monastery. 'If I am obliged to make still further restitution, please specify the quantum with details and I am prepared to restitute whatever I am obliged to'.

Superior Fr Thomas Edathiparampil's reply dated 30 August '66 says: 'Your seminary expense incurred by the Monastery amounts to Rs. 3169.35 and is to be restituted. Your Mass stipend cannot be compounded with the seminary expenses. The amount may be restituted in annual installments of Rs. 1000 in three years'. In my response dated 2 September '66 sent to the Bishop, I pointed out the unfairness of the Superior's stand as I was working for the diocese all this while from 1963 to 1966 without any emolument except food and boarding. My food expenses could not be considered as expenses met by the Monastery. The Bishop returned the letter with the Monastery principle: 'quidquid monachus acquirit, monasterium acquirit' [Whatever the monk acquires, the Monastery acquires], communicated to me orally and directed me to abide by the advice of Fr Krishnamurthy. In my next letter dated 3 September written to Fr Superior in the light of Fr Krishnamurthy's advice and seen and approved by him, I agreed to pay back the amount of Rs. 3000. 'Since His Lordship our Bishop in view of my past service to the diocese, has promised to help me to pay the amount back to you'. I request Your Reverence to return the Patrimony amount of Rs. 500 as you have promised as per your letter dated 30 August '66'.

Strangely enough the Bishop refused to be appeased with my offer for not accepting the liability unconditionally, the condition being the Bishop's promise of help to repay the amount. At this stage one of the senior most and most respected priests of the diocese, Fr Joseph Kandarappally intervened. In his letter dated 11-9-'66 he wrote to me: 'I have typed out the three copies of the letter to be signed and submitted by you. Since you want to close the matter and get yourself relieved of the great burden and high tension in which now you are suffering, you sign the three copies [as required by the Bishop] and close the matter and give the same to V. Rev. Fr Superior (for his counter sign) this evening before you go without waiting for formalities and technicalities'. He then drafted for me two letters one after another, both of which were rejected by the Bishop because the letter contained relevant 'facts' of the whole saga played out hitherto. Instead,

I was asked to sign a letter in triplicate which the Bishop had himself drafted.

I then made my third and final appeal to Gustavo Cardinal Testa dated 12 September '66 explaining the 'intensified and prolonged hardships from His Lordship my Bishop', repeating my request 'on bended knees' for intervention. As usual it too fetched no response.

I wrote to Fr Abraham Pulikoottil for his help to get an appointment for a meeting with the Internuncio. In his reply, St. Michael's High School, Gurgaon dated September 26, '66, he wrote: 'By your coming to Delhi and meeting the Internuncio, not much fruit will come out of it....When Bishop Tharayil comes to Delhi for the C.B.C.I. meeting in the second week of October, perhaps he may speak to him about you, I suppose. So wait and see for a few more weeks. In the meantime let us hope that the good Lord will help you in this crisis and that everything will be fine. I was sorry to know all these your difficulties. But never lose courage. God will protect you in all your trials'.

The Bishop's next order No. 127B/66 dated September 22, 1966, came to remind me 'to submit the documents called for without further delay' Accordingly I wrote to Fr Superior to countersign my acceptance of the liability made as per Fr Kandarappallil's advice and to give it to the Bishop. Superior Fr Edathiparampil, perhaps in his capacity as Bishop's stenographer, rejected my request to countersign on ground that it was not in proper form for 'not mentioning the number and date of the Bishop's two orders'. Hence I sent my formal unconditional acceptance of the liability as per letter dated S.H. Mount, 3 September '66: 'I, Fr Abraham Vellamthadathil, hereby agree to refund the amount of Rs. 3000 spent by the Society of the Oblates of the Sacred Heart for my studies in three equal installments, in three years' time as per the decision of the Superior and the Council of the O.S.H dated 30-8-66 and approved by His Lordship the Bishop dated 3-9-1966 in accordance with two curia letters No. 108B/66 dated July 22, 1966 and No. 123B/66 dated August 18, 1966. Sd/- Fr Abraham Vellamthadathil and 'Accepted' Sd/- by Fr T. Edathiparampil.

Appeased and self-complacent, the Most Rev. Bishop Tharayil condescended to issue his 'bene placitum', his magnanimous license of re-entry into the heaven-ward escalator service of the holy apostolic hierarchy as per legally and canonically worded order No. 131B/66 dated October 1, 1966: 'Under the above circumstances, as per letter from the Apostolic Internuncio (No. 27536 dated 12 August, 1966) cited above, and in accordance with the canon 190/2. and Can. 191/ n. 2 of the M.P. 'Postquam', I hereby dispense you from your temporary profession [invalid because taken under compulsion] with effect from today and declare that you cease to be a member of the Society of O.S.H. also with effect from today'!

My former seminary moral theology professor and Spiritual Father, Fr R.B. Crieme in his letter dated Chenganacherry, 25-10-1966 noted: '... May God help you in your great trial. *It is obvious that you are not bound by any vow.* Canon law says clearly that after the temporary vows have expired, a religious may freely leave the congregation and the decree mentioned by the Bishop does not change anything to this. Your conditional profession is invalid by the non-verification of the condition [of freedom of profession].

'I do not see why the Bishop wants any more proof of your lack of vocation than your refusal to renew your vows. One has to give a proof of vocation, and not of non-vocation....

'Do all you can to get out of the diocese? But I am afraid the Bishop will not release you until you have paid the last farthing! Let us pray much.

'If the Bishop is ready to release you, you might apply To Bishop A. Mathias of Chikmangalore. I am ready to recommend you....

'God bless you, my dear son, and may His Grace help you to bear generously your trials. Relief will come, you may be sure...only have patience'.

One needs to be surprised only if these words of this godly-man did not generate tears of joy and consolation. These words reminded me of Fr Visakhanthara's words said to me in 1955: 'Before you join the seminary you feel natural. In the Seminary you feel supernatural. Once ordained you come in contact with the Bishop you begin to feel unnatural'.

The curtain was thus pulled down over this sordid melodrama. I feel ashamed of myself for having written one more letter to the Apostolic Internuncio dated 10-10-1966 explaining all the relevant facts connected with this melodrama and the extreme financial strain I was struggling under, concluding: 'I therefore request that the patrimony amount of Rs. 500 be returned to me to enable me to regain footing in this present circumstances. His Lordship refuses to return the amount [though the Superior agreed to return to the member on leaving the society as is the practice], claiming that the amount was lent to me by him, whereas the truth is that he had donated it to me in 1955, knowing that I had no means to procure this amount as patrimony. This fact has been explicitly mentioned in my application for admission submitted on 24-5-1955. The application was dictated by His Lordship himself'.

As usual I got no response to this appeal either. The Bishop successfully stuck to his principle: 'Purpose once formed, death or victory'. Whether it was death or victory is yet to be seen. But for the present, my hard-core traditional conservative faith in the monopolistic heaven-ward escalatory service of the Catholic Apostolic Hierarchy, arrogating divine-right authority, received a terrible shake-up and I was left with the doubt: 'Is this escalatory service for which heavy toll is arbitrarily levied leading the beguiled faithful to heaven or to hell?'

I closed this phase of my struggle under the dead weight of dogmatic faiths with a letter addressed to Bishop Daniel Liston, Eveque de Port Louis, Mauritius in an attempt to get me cleared of misunderstanding if any on his part, caused by the mischievous or shall I say, villainous letter of Bishop Tharayil dated 14-10-'66, stating: 'Fr Abraham Vellamthadathil has now decided not to work in your diocese', lest Bishop Liston should think of me as capricious. It was followed by another letter dated 23 December '66, as I felt myself bound to ask his pardon for having hidden those facts related to my relationship with Bishop Tharayil, with copies of the three appeals I sent to higher authorities as proof for those facts. 'I hid those facts not out of duplicity but out of reluctance' to reveal those sordid details. Bishop Liston's reply was highly consoling: 'Don't worry about what has happened – forget the whole thing and if the opportunity ever again offers, will see what is best to be done'.

A few years later, Fr Crieme in his letter from the Papal Seminary Poona dated 4-1-1970, wrote to me: 'I appreciate your difficulties. I know and realize well the strain that is on you owing to the little sympathy you get from your Bishop….I shall go to Mauritius in April or May and I can speak to the Bishop there….But it will be a delicate point. The Bishop may not be willing to let you go. He is a difficult customer. I wonder whether it is his health that makes him like that'.

I also had sent my fifth appeal to the Internuncio on 28-10-'66 for intervention, concluding it thus: 'If this last appeal also brings me no reply in due time, I shall be forced to conclude that I have been abandoned by my higher ecclesiastical authorities' and it too fetched me no response. Now, I thank God, I escaped this supposed heaven-ward escalator which only rotates round and round like the giant wheel of circus companies. When I wrote this last letter, I had not yet realized that my struggle had not reached its nadir yet. Struggles worse than this were yet to follow.

# 12

# As a Diocesan Priest

## Mariagiri High School Peermedu

My first appointment as a diocesan priest was at Peermedu. The Bishop's order No. 140B/66 dated 22 November '66 was issued appointing me assistant warden, Mariagiri English Medium Residential High School Hostel in place of Rev. Fr Jacob Chollambel. My duty was 'to maintain proper and up-to-date accounts of the hostel and school...and send monthly balance sheet to the undersigned'. In reality I was also to have the entire charge of the Mariagiri Educational Institution, although the good old Fr Thomas Choolaparampil was the headmaster officially. As a retired high school headmaster and therefore officially qualified as per the requirements of the departmental rules of staff qualification, he had to be officially in charge. I knew that hard times would follow if the balance sheet ended with a debit balance. And as was to be expected hard times did follow. Let me summarize it quoting a few lines from my reply dated 14 January 1967 to Fr Thomas Tharayil to his letter from Nirmala Nagar, Belgaum, dated 15 December 1966, most heartily inviting me to join the missionary diocese of Belgaum. I wrote: 'The recent problem I had to face was the financial problem of this school and hostel....The average monthly expense for the hostel and the school comes to a minimum of Rs. 1200. But I was not given money to manage here. I had therefore recourse to borrowing with the hope that at the end of the month, after seeing the balance sheet, His Lordship will help me to clear arrears and deficit balance. But he refused to examine the balance sheet and clear the deficit, thereby putting me at an awkward position before my creditors. I am therefore struggling to realize the deficit balance of last month and then request His Lordship to relieve me from this office. What else am I to do, I do not know. On revealing this difficulty to Fr Cyriac Vattakalam, I was advised by him to refuse to go back to Peermedu'. The headmaster, Fr T. Choolaparampil too sent a rather hot letter to the Manager, Corporate Educational Agency of Schools, Kottayam Diocese, Fr Joseph Karottukunnel dated 15 January 1967 in which he wrote: '...In the light of the above facts, does not your remark...appear pointless? Please don't pass easy and cheap judgement.

'...Any way, I may repeat that the deficit balance shown in the balance sheet is really due to Fr Vellamthadathil'. Once again, I feared, I was beginning to have another feeling of unnatural hellishness brewing up all around me. I leave the rest of the Peermedu story to anybody's imagination in the light of the following quotation from Fr Choolaparampil's letter dated 31 January 1967 to Fr Karottukunnel. Fr Karottukunnel was then a prospective candidate in contest with the Diocesan Chancellor Rev. Dr Kuriakose Kunnacherry for the vacancy of a co-adjutor bishop, already in the horizon and therefore working with the ruling Bishop in co-operation from 'close quarters'. Fr Choolaparampil wrote: 'I am sorry to point out that actually your letter is incomplete (and not Fr Vellamthadathil's balance sheet) since you have not indicated the source for funds to defray the expenses of the things to be ordered for. It is strange that even after knowing the financial stringency those in charge here are driven to, you are *directed* (emphasis added) to write such a letter. May I suppose that I am not expected to run the school at my own expense....

'I suppose you have not forgotten what *we both* discussed with the Bishop regarding the deficit balance of last month and how the Bishop directed you to get Rs. 300 from Mgr. Mattathil to enable Fr Vellamthadathil to cover the deficit of the previous month in part. In the light of the above, how do you dare to say that I owe Rs. 300 to Mgr. Mattathil? I do not understand the implication of such letters and the attitude behind....'

In another letter to the Bishop dated 3 February 1967, Fr Choolaparampil wrote: 'In the light of the above, may I point out that unless financial aid is given from there, I am afraid the Institution may not run much further time'.

Quite a number of sizzling exchanges took place between Fr. Karottukunnel and Fr Choolaparampil. The latter in his letter to Fr Karottukunnel dated 10 February 1967 wrote: 'The deficit amount was nothing but due to Fr Vellamthadathil, but was refused to him. I took the trouble to come over there and discuss about it only because....I found the plight of the one in charge who could not and cannot proceed without money to run the Institution. I suppose you have no misunderstanding about it....'

I put a full stop to this Peermedu affair with my letter to the Vicar General, Mgr. Mattathil, dated 10 February 1967 with these remarks: 'A couple of days ago I rushed down to the Bishop's House with the balance sheet...to explain the plight we here are driven to due to shortage of money....I was not even shown the courtesy to be heard and given the chance to explain myself....The word was sent to me that I need not be taken to see His Lordship, without however making it clear either where else I should have gone to explain the difficulties we face here....If I have still come away back to Peermedu to take up the cross of this unbearable burden, my motive cannot fairly be interpreted as weakness, but as loyalty to duty imposed by the order....I shall not be here to see what may happen here from next Saturday onwards, unless other arrangements are made to enable me to continue the work.'

In his letter to Fr Choolaparampil dated 4 February 1967, Fr Karottukunnel, pointing out the four days difference between the date of a previous letter and the post mark date, had called into question the honesty saying: 'I know full well that is a great lot of honesty in some people's view point and I have nothing more to say'. In my reply to this dated 11 February 1967, I paraded just a handful of bare facts related to him and concluded: 'Of course you would not like me to relate these events with the standard of honesty, but you would perhaps have me call them adjustments. So let them be. But may I point out that we may do well not to speak much of anybody's honesty, or dishonesty. For, then we may have many more things to say. I am afraid what we all miserably lack is a spirit of brotherly understanding cooperation and genuine help whenever and wherever it is required, even if it would cost us some inconvenience or curtail any of our vested interests'.

## A Dream Cut Short

Fr Thomas Tharayil from Nirmala Nagar, Belgaum wrote to me on 30 January 1967: 'I would like that you meet my uncle (Fr Jacob Tharayil O.S.H.) and Mgr. Mattathil [to both of them he had also sent personal confidential letters] as early as possible and speak for yourself and request them to help you to get permission from Bishop Tharayil *at least for a few years time* to be away from the diocese for the peace of your mind and satisfaction of your conscience. Please see that this matter is not let out to anybody except these two'. He also wrote an even dated letter to Mgr. Mattathil explaining the extreme need of more priestly service in Belgaum. Let me quote: 'While prayerfully I was resigned to the will of God, I received a letter and an application from Fr Vellamthadathil, expressing his desire to join this diocese. I do take as a supply directly from Jesus....'

But perhaps God's ways are inscrutable and different from ours; for, Fr Thomas's letter dated February 9, 1967 informed me that his Bishop on his way back from Goa on the 7th after the funeral of one of the priests, was killed on the spot when his car, which he was himself driving, collided with a truck. 'Due to the demise of the Bishop, your affair might proceed slowly. However don't be discouraged'. Years after this when I write this in the light of all the struggles I had and after the delightful Dawn in my life I would like to look upon this as another blessing of God in disguise.

## My First Pastoral Assignment

My letter to the Vicar General, Mgr. Mattathil, dated 10 February 1967 had its immediate aftermath in the shape of a 'pastoral' order – Order No. 26B/67 dated 15 March 1967, appointing me as vicar of St. Theresa's Church, Memury, with effect from 19

[Palm Sunday]. 'Pastoral' orders are issued in exercise of the 'Apostolic Episcopal Pastoral Authority', reportedly to have been directly imparted by Jesus as recorded in Jn. 21, 16-17 'Feed my Lamb' and 'Feed my sheep'. I fear some Bishops misread it as 'Feed on my lamb and feed on my sheep'. In my case, Bishop Tharayil exercised the 'Apostolic Pastoral Authority' to show me the door from my Peermedu duties, appointing me as vicar at Memury and replacing Fr Joseph Kalapurackal. The order further directed me to vacate the place (Peermedu, I presumed) on the 16th and take charge of Memury Parish before 19 March! When masters order their slaves about, they consult and consider only their own convenience and not that of the slaves. It was only on the previous evening that I came off to Peermedu from the Bishop's House after meeting the Bishop. Naturally the order to leave the station and to take charge of a parish with the space of twenty four hours was indeed a bolt from the blue, considering the implication and insurmountable practical problems involved. So on 16 March I wrote in reply: 'Ever since my ordination up to now I have been either in the Petit Seminary with the O.S.H. Community or at the Bishop's House, or in the boarding of the Peermedu school, but living always with a community. It is the first time I am ordered to go to a parish as vicar, and I am given only two days to prepare for my departure from here and to take charge of a new parish. I shall easily be understood that it will be impossible for me to commence my stay in a new place without the minimum necessary preparations and bare minimum of outfits like bed, pieces of furniture, kitchen utensils etc. and a person to help in the kitchen.

'Hence I request to be given leave at least till Easter (26 March) with the hope that I may be able to secure the minimum requirements for commencing my stay and a person to help'.

For the first time I found my Bishop relaxing a little his principle: 'Purpose once formed, death or victory'! His secretary Fr Jacob Kollaparampil was directed to write to me on 18 – 3 – '67 allowing me leave till Wednesday following: 'Fr Kalapurackal's servant is of the locality and he may be available for you. If not, the trustees will see to your messing for some days. You can take the necessary things and know what furniture is there in the presbytery so that you may transport things which are not available there'.

And so I began a priestly service that was hitherto unfamiliar to me. I tried to love and to serve the simple, affectionate and highly cooperative parishioners there as cordially and sincerely as possible and to my great mental peace and sense of fulfillment. The nearly one year of 'pastoral service' in Memury was largely an uneventful one. However I remember one event that may be mentioned because of its practical relevance. One of my elderly friends, a man of some leadership quality and widely known in the locality as a knowledgeable man of common sense, living very close to the presbytery, used to spend several evenings with me in friendly chat. Once during his usual chat, he took up the subject of his recently married son. He told me: 'If I were to ask my son whom he loved more, his mother or his recently wedded wife and if he were to answer that he loved his mother more than his young wife, I wouldn't believe him'. 'Friend', I replied, 'never ever ask your son such an unwise question. You are trying to compare your son's filial love with his conjugal love. The two are incomparable. You can compare the length of a yardstick with the length of another stick. But you cannot compare the length of the yardstick with the weight of another'. He thought for a moment and then I think he thanked me for the clarification. I recall with respect and gratitude the trustees and Jose the sexton boy for their whole-hearted and devoted cooperation.

Meanwhile, my move to join the Missionary Diocese of Belgaum had not come to a standstill with the untimely and accidental death of Bishop Coutinho. Rt. Rev. Augusto Cabral, who took over the diocese as Vicar Capitular, wrote to me on 4 March 1967 to know 'whether your offer stands after the abrupt end of our beloved Bishop'. If so, he would take up the matter because 'certainly our diocese is in need of good priests...and although I am a Vicar Capitular, I feel that if I prepare the field in this matter to the new Bishop, he will only applaud my endevour'. Fr Thomas Tharayil too wrote to me on 27 March advising me to approach the Bishop here and discuss the matter with 'caution'. 'If His Lordship has any objection, express to him that for the sake of your soul and peace of mind, you may be permitted for a few years at least as a change'. In my reply to the Rt. Rev. Augusto Cabral dated 29 March 1967 I iterated my desire: 'I hasten to reply that I still do persist in my great desire to join that diocese....I therefore await further directions and pray to God that the procedure may take favourable course and reach a successful destination'. As advised by Fr Thomas Tharayil, I wrote a very 'cautious' letter on 3 May 1967 requesting my Bishop Thomas Tharayil to consider my request for a change of place and atmosphere of my priestly ministry at least for a period of time as 'this is a question that touches very much my priestly life and consequently my own soul and therefore is sufficiently serious'. The Bishop's response dated 17 May to my repeated request for permission to join Belgaum diocese was to find peace faithfully doing the duties 'assigned to him by his Bishop, who represents Christ for him.... Try to find peace of soul by prayer and deep attachment to the will of God'.

Yes, when I look back, this advice in the light of my present experiences under 'representatives of Christ' like my Bishop, Most Rev. Dr Thomas Tharayil, I am persuaded to believe that there was God's holy will and design even in this advice because had I taken up my priestly life under other 'representatives' of Christ, I would have continued my peregrination in the darkness of the dogmatic dungeons and would never have come out of it to come to the delightful dawn. Any how, once more I wrote to him on 1 July 1967 enumerating the very bitter experiences I had to suffer at his hands to establish that the peace of one's mind is not only subjective but very much dependent on objective events and circumstances. I wrote: 'Evidently these are very objective circumstances of my priestly life, where I cannot find peace as long as these circumstances continue. I did not mention all these facts in my previous letter first because they were known to you and secondly because of the delicacy in having to remind you of them afresh....I don't intend to go on any further this kind of useless correspondence.... I wish to give a final and definitive word to the favourable move to my second attempt for seeking protection for my priestly life'. The Bishop's response was his letter dated Caritas, 25 September, 1967 consoling me with some usual spiritual clichés among whom was: 'Let your ambition be, as priest, to please God, by doing His holy will, *always manifested through your superiors*. (emphasis added) Please give up your ambition for study or change of work or change of diocese...the life and work are now set for you by the providence of God and by your free choice at ordination to priesthood'! This Episcopal spiritual counsel only made me doubt whether my free choice at ordination to priesthood in the Catholic Church was a source of blessing or of curse and slavery.

## A New Co-adjutor Announced

It was towards mid January 1968 that the announcement of the appointment of the then diocesan chancellor, Rev. Dr Kuriakose Kunnacherry as Co-adjutor Bishop was made. It was a bit of relief to me because he was in the know of every thing about my struggles faced hitherto, and with him I was in consultation on all my points and process and he was supporting me – at least that was the impression I got – in my desire to join another diocese. He assured me now that my persistent desire would favourably be considered. In the light of this assurance I wrote to the Bishop of Mauritius reminding him of his promise of 8-11-'66: 'If the opportunity ever again offers, we will see what is best to be done'.

## The Event That Changed the Course

It took place on 24 February 1968 – the Episcopal consecration of Dr Kunnacherry as the Co-adjutor. The solemn and grandiose event, held in the S.H. Mount Football Stadium brought about anu-turn in my attitude. Up to the eve of that event, I was insistent on leaving the diocese. 'But on that august morning', I wrote to the Bishop on 1 March 1968, 'some how or other I was persuaded to commit myself entirely to and put myself completely at Your Excellency's disposal. If it pleases Your Excellency to allow me to leave the diocese, I will gladly accept the permission and leave. On the other hand if Your

Excellency continues in your decision not to let me leave the diocese, I am equally glad to abide by that decision'. In fact I had entered the ground of the consecration ceremony with another petition to be given to the Cardinal, officiating the function and got an appointment to meet him. 'But during the impressive ceremony, I was persuaded to withhold the letter and to leave the matter entirely to the good pleasure of Your Excellency'. I made an apology for the remark I had made in a fret of temperamental outburst in one of my earlier letter: 'Your Excellency may consider me a priest lost to the diocese'.

Pat came the Bishop's letter dated 2 March 1968: 'My dear Fr Abraham Vellamthadathil [adding in his own hand], my son', expressing his great delight. Then he added: 'It is the work of Providence as you say, and I thank God for it'. I fully endorsed this observation though neither he nor I understood then the dramatic irony of this divine intervention. The dramatic irony, I feel now, is the fact that I should have walked a little more along the hard and narrow path under his own 'divine right apostolic authority' in order that I learn and feel the more intensely the darkness of the dogmatic dungeons to appreciate and enjoy the delight of the dazzling dawn to come. Only later did I realize that I had to tread more along the narrow and thorny paths to reach the path of God-given light. 'Well', the letter continued, 'since you leave the matter to me, I must inform you that I am so happy to have you in our diocese.

'In your present disposition, I am willing to tell you: work for admission for M.A. in English if you like to study for it from next June'. (He must have thought it too much of a favour to me to send me abroad for higher studies.) In fact on my return from Poona after my seminary studies, I had told the Bishop that, if left to my choice, my first preference would be the ministry of teaching. I preferred it to any other ministry because this would put me in touch with the world of the youth where ever fresh intellectual enterprises would be met with.

# 13

# P.G. Studies in the Karnataka University

In fact since as far back as February 1966, I had been searching for the best place for my post graduate studies with my PhL. degree from Poona Papal Athenaeum recognised by secular universities as equivalent to a bachelor's degree. I had been advised by the Dean of Philosophy, Fr Koelman, through his letter dated 14 March 1966 that Poona University would easily admit me to M.A. in philosophy with the recommendation of Fathers like Fr De Smet, or Fr Joseph De Marneffe. 'Now these Fathers do not recommend simply anyone who has passed. However, in your case, I am convinced there would be no difficulty since you are known to them'. However, Fr Koelman made a very wise suggestion to me to try for my P.G. Studies in the Karnataka University Dharwar. 'In Dharwar, according to the information given by Professor Meneses, the senior most Professor Emeritus, is directly appointed by the U.G.C., New Delhi: 'If you have the Licentiate in Philosophy of the Poona Athenaeum, you are, according to the present practice, eligible for admission to M.A. in any subject of your choice, though not any of the science subjects....Can there be anything more clear and favourable?...'Any subject of your choice!' These are Prof Meneses' own words'. However, applicants like us for P.G. admission had to take an entrance test related to the subject of our choice and conducted by the University. It was probably in view of this entrance test that Fr Koelman had warned me that applicants should have made some extra reading on the subject of their choice.

I decided to go in for M.A. English Literature. I was relieved of my charge of Memury parish with effect from 1 May 1968 to enable me to go 'to Poona for interview in connection with admission to Poona University for M.A. course'. I began reading up English Literature in view of the university entrance test to be taken in the first week of July 1968. By the first week of June I left for Poona where I was sure of accommodation in my alma mater till my entrance test and where I could more intensely prepare myself for the test.

## Hurdles in my Life's Race

On the way in the train I felt an ache somewhere in my abdomen. I continued my journey as the pain also continued to progress. When I reached the Papal Seminary, the pain had grown acute. Under the care and influence of my professors I was rushed to the Military Command Hospital Poona and got admitted there on 11 June. The cause of my abdominal pain was quickly diagnosed as indirect inguinal hernia (LT). The nearest convenient date was fixed for operation. At about 9 p.m. on the eve of the operation, the surgeon who was to conduct the operation the following day, a Lieutenant Colonel who was Associate Professor of Surgery, Armed Forces Medical College, if I am not mistaken, came to visit me in my bed and found me reading. 'Aren't you worried and tense about the operation tomorrow?' he asked me. 'Why should I; it is you who are going to conduct the operation', I answered. 'Ah, you…' he continued with a gentle smile, 'But you need rest. Better stop reading now and try to have a good sleep'. I closed my book, said a short mental prayer and went to bed. I thought of my father and brothers at home. But as I had decided not to inform them of my operation they may be in sound sleep. Let them, and I too enjoyed a calm sound sleep.

Next morning I remember to have been taken to the theatre and told to count One.. Two.. Three.. I don't remember how many numbers I counted. When I regained my consciousness it was near 4 p.m. I felt something heavy upon my abdominal region. I asked the nurse standing by my side what it was.

'Bandage? Have no worry; just bandage over the wound', she replied. It was only on the eighteenth day morning after the operation that I was permitted to sit up with my legs dangling from the side of the bed and to walk up to the toilet.

I was discharged on 5 July 1968. The discharge sheet carries the medical instructions: 'No heavy weight bearing or cycling for six months. Suspensory bandage to wear for one month'.

The very next day I left Poona for Dharwar and reached Karnataka University only to be told that the entrance test for the 1968 admission had been conducted two days before! I felt darkness in my mind and darkness all around. Whom to approach and what to say? Oh! God, where should I turn? Tell me....! Suddenly I remembered what Fr Koelman had written to me about Prof Meneses, how helpful he was to many students then studying there. I hunted out and met Prof Meneses – a venerable old saintly incarnation of gentleness and helpfulness, I thought. I explained to him all that had happened to me since I left Kottayam for Poona in the first week of June. After a short thought-immersed pause Prof Meneses examined my qualifying certificate and the mark list of my P.G. Philosophy degree issued by the Papal Athenaeum, Poona and said: 'I think you deserve a special consideration. Come and meet me tomorrow at 10 a.m.'. He himself arranged for my accommodation that night, I don't remember exactly where.

The next day, at 10 a.m. I reached Prof Meneses' residence. 'I consulted the Registrar and the Controller of Exams and we have decided to conduct a special entrance test for you alone today,' he said. Was it Prof Meneses himself who spoke to me or the Grace of God incarnate, I wondered in the recess of my mind? I took the University entrance test held for me alone and very soon got the result too. 'You have passed the test and have been declared qualified for admission to M.A. Literature course this year,' he said. Eventually the formalities for admission and for hostel accommodation were completed. It is hard to believe that a University will conduct an entrance test for just one applicant alone. And yet it can happen when authority anointed with grace rules the campus. Prof Meneses was not a person who received ritual priesthood through the imposition of Episcopal hands as Valerian Cardinal Gracias, then Archbishop of Bombay, had mistakenly taken him to be, but a person who had received the royal priesthood through the anointing with the grace of God. I remember a humorous incident which Prof Meneses shared with us in the class later. He said: 'Cardinal Gracias once addressed a letter to me as 'Rev. Fr Meneses'. Poor Cardinal did not know that I was the irreverent father of three children and grandfather of four'! Yes, Prof Meneses had the Karnataka University conduct an entrance test solely to assess my qualification as an applicant for M.A. English. And I thank God, I did not fail him in his assessment as I stood first in the final university exams of 1970 in the aggregate marks of the six compulsory Papers. Having taken phonetics and English grammar as my optionals, I was pushed back to the second position by a lady student who had chosen Old and Middle English as her optionals.

The two years I spent in Dharwar was a period of great satisfaction and happiness. During the second year I was appointed editor of the University Periodical called *Ghymkhana*. I have also been given an award for my work as *Ghymkhana* editor in addition to the award of 'Winner in Table Tennis' (singles, 1970.) The fellowship of all my colleagues, a group of very handsome young men and a group of extremely beautiful young ladies added to the joy of our studentship there. Particularly among the latter was the lovely Mary Satyavathy on account of whom the jolly good guys of other batches of students of other departments too felt greatly jealous of our class because 'Sathyavathy is not in our class. You, guys, ask her to join our class so that we also may enjoy her graceful presence'. She reminds me of Homer's description of Helen's grace and beauty in *Ilyad*: 'Even old men could not help having a look at her'. If Mary Sathyavathy ever happens to read these lines, I request her to take them as a sincere compliment from one of her old, admiring colleagues.

Another memorable event was that I was included in the Karnataka University Contingent that took part in the Commonwealth Youth Festival held in New Delhi in October

1969. Its inauguration by the newly elected President of India, Mr V.V. Giri, was in fact his first official function after his swearing in ceremony. Our contingent staged the first and the last scenes from *King Lear,* me playing the roll of King Lear and quite successfully too, I was told by competent persons after the performance.

One of my problems I had to face was the expenses for my studies and lodging there. The only source I had was the Mass stipend. As was the custom with the priest students there I too said my daily Mass in my living room. I got the Mass stipend from my priest friends back in the diocese. In fact I wrote to the Bishop for help. He answered favourably through his letter dated 7 August 1968 congratulating me for securing admission for M.A. in Dharwar and enclosing a cheque for Rs. 500 'for your immediate needs, hoping to adjust the same some how later on'. During the course of my studies there some of my brother priests were kind enough to help me with small loans to be paid back 'according to convenience' and sent me Mass intentions with stipend. Fr Luke Pathyil, for instance, in his letter dated Kaipuzha, 27 – 10 –'69 wrote: 'I wish I could be richer to help all those good souls who are in need'. Only one thing aggrieved me: the denial of Priest Provident Fund (P.P.F.) subsidy to me by the Director Board because of the Board's strict interpretation of the 'spirit' of the otherwise clearly framed rules. More about it later.

## P.G. Course at Dharwar Completed

Our final examination of the second year M.A. Course was conducted during the last week of April and the first two weeks of May. And I took my M.A. Degree with First Rank in the six compulsory papers, but the Second Rank when computed with the marks of optional subjects, as mentioned above, and I left Dharwar thanking God Almighty and my professors, particularly Prof Meneses and returned to Kottayam for my second, even more fierce phase of struggle with my 'divine right' dogmatic Church Authority, now exercised by two Bishops.

# 14

# The Second, Even Fiercer, Phase of My Struggle

## P.P.F. Benefits Denied

I started my teaching ministry as Lecturer in English in St. Stephen's College at Uzhavoor on probation for one year from 1 July 1970 to 31 May 1971 as per the appointment order issued by the manager, Mgr. Cyriac Mattathil, dated 1 July 1970 on the Government fixed salary scale of Rs. 300–20-400 – 25-600 plus D.A. Rs. 146. Ten weeks later, on 17 September, 1970 I received another appointment order No. 77B/70 BIS dated 30 June 1970 from Bishop Tharayil to the same effect but fixing my share of my salary to Rs. 100 per mensem. 'The rest of the amount as per aquittance roll salary will be his monthly contribution to the Education Fund of the Diocese, as agreed'. Who agreed what and when I was absolutely unaware of. It was the Bishop's usual sort of 'unilateral agreements', something similar to the signed blank cheques got from customers by the blade company managers. I was also given the additional charge as Assistant Warden at the college hostel for men.

A few months elapsed. I signed the aquittance roll for the salary as per the scale given by the government every month, but I got only Rs. 100. The rest was taken by the Bishop for the 'Diocesan Education Fund' as my 'contribution' fixed by the Bishop. Meanwhile I had to pay back the loan I had taken from some of my priest friends. With a motor bike to maintain, I was able to make no savings from my monthly remuneration of Rs. 100. I then remembered that I had been hospitalized in Poona for 27 days. As per the P.P.F. rules, I had the right to claim my Mass stipend and remuneration for these days from PPF. I applied for these benefits but was refused, according to the 'unanimous decision of the general body', because the rules were wrongly worded and not clear and it had to be interpreted according to the 'spirit' of PPF.

The expert legal opinion of advocate Mr Joseph Malieckal and his neighbour and retired judge, Mr P.D. Thomman, taken at the Bishop's suggestion, said that the word and the spirit of the P.P.F. rules were in my favour and I had a right for the P.P.F. benefits for the period of my hospitalization. The Bishop then advised the P.P.F. Board to dispose my application according to rules. By now the issue became the question of prestige and the president of the Board wrote to the Bishop on 1 September 1970: 'To carry out Your Lordship's suggestion would ultimately make the general body members fools and idiots and Fr Vellamthadathil could glory [sic]that he was able to win his point by making us all fools'. The issue was thoroughly discussed and debated in the general body meeting held on 12 September 1970. The defeated Bishop candidate, Fr Joseph Karottukunnel, opined that the general body was the supreme authority to decide matters and the opinion was taken for the end of the discussion, after amending the rule 18(a) thus to suit the majority's 'spirit': 'When a member is not one who is working in an establishment of this diocese or outside the diocese with remuneration, and is not saying Mass, he shall be given from the society a subsidy equal to the aggregate subsidy'. Many like Fr, Jacob Valel and Zacharias Vellanal amidst shouts of protests and shame, got up and protested saying that might was hushing up right. Senior priests like Fr Jacob Kalayil urged me to have recourse to legal remedy. [Eventually after the election of the Co-adjutor, Fr Joseph Karottukunnel relinquished priesthood, married a nun and left for US where a few years later he suffered an untimely death. R.I.P.]

On 17 September I wrote to the Bishop pointing out the irony that even according to the amended rule, my claim stood justified and sought his permission to take my claim to a law court for a legal decision. In his reply dated 23 September 1970 he of course denied me permission for any legal procedure and advised me thus: 'Let us agree to disagree and follow the advice of St. Augustine, 'In essentialibus unitas, in dubiis lebertas, in omnibus caritas'. [In essentials, unity; in doubts, freedom; in all things, love] Keep smiling'! Pressed by the rule of natural honesty and decency to pay back the loan taken for my P.G. education at Dharwar, I could not go on smiling. Relying on which of his information from where, I don't know, the Bishop went to the extent of denying the occurrence of any such 'shouts of protests and shame' at the general body meeting. In a subsequent letter dated 25 September 1970 I wrote to the Bishop: '...I was a fool to have expected anything just or fair from a majority of priests. The incident has but served as an eye opener'.

I approached the Co-adjutor Excellency for intervention, but in vain. 'We are going to ratify [the Board's] decision' was his response. The senior Excellency then cooked up a sophisticated compromise formula, arranging to give me Rs. 90 for the 27 days of my hospitalization 'as a special case'. But I refused to accept any large amount of 'alms' and said: 'All I want is to know whether I have any legal claim'. Strange indeed was his response to this: "Why should we fight for principle? What you need is some money....Does it matter whether it be given as per legal claim or concession?" I came off refusing to accept concession and to stand by principle.

## Repayment of P.G. Study Loan

A little later I requested him to help me from the diocesan Education Fund to repay the loan of Rs. 2750 taken for my PG studies. 'How do you expect me to repay your loans? You have to pay it yourself. After all for others I give only Rs. 100.' 'But' I replied, 'the others were sent to America for their studies where they could make money and not spend'. Back came the Bishop's 'spiritual advice': 'If they went to America and you to Dharwar, don't you know that it was all the arrangements of divine Providence?' I came off disappointed, wondering what the relevance of the Diocesan Education Fund was into which all my monthly salary, given by the government, is absorbed after the pittance of Rs. 100. I made it very clear to the Bishop through my letter dated 2 September 1970 that 'my intention was not to somehow or other get some money, but to ascertain the truth of the guarantee and security promised in the PPF rules'.

Soon I was pressed hard to return immediately Rs. 1300 and I approached the Bishop for help in this urgency. In reply I received a short note dated 9-2-1970 offering me parish charge of Pius X Church with vicar's remuneration along with my college duties, staying in the presbytery there. 'Old Fr M. Chollambel and people will be very happy as you are active and young. Pro te etiam aliquid plus. [You too get something additional]' This apparently generous offer [to work more to earn more] was something like jumping from the frying pan into the fire because staying in the presbytery without electricity connection, daily travel to college and back and providing the minimum necessary furnishings and kitchen utensils and a person to cook meals: all these would involve prohibitively heavy expenses and the net result was: 'Pro te aliquid plus oneris quam muneris' [you too get an additional burden, not earning]. So in my reply dated 12 December 1970 I submitted: 'However this arrangement is not going to help me to repay the urgently required part of loan of Rs. 1300. If you find it difficult to make any other arrangement, I should be happy and satisfied if you will sanction an advance from the college for this amount. I could pay it back slowly'. In reply I got a thorough oral scolding in addition to the order to pay back the annual installment of money I owed to the diocese through the O.S.H. Monastery.

I then appealed to the Co-adjutor Excellency on 11 February 1971 to kindly use his influence and mediate and informed him that if I got no favourable response, 'I must think out what I can do to pay the loan back to the Bishop. I hope to call on Your Lordship on Saturday the 16th in the morning'.

Meanwhile my probationary period having expired on 30 May 1971, I continued my duties in the college. On 8 September

1971 I received the Order No. 7/Rec/71-72 appointing me on permanent basis on a pay scale amounting up to Rs. 725. But I continued to get Rs. 100 as usual. Pressure to make the repayment of my education loan began to mount. So I wrote to the Bishop on 30-6-'71: 'It is more than a year since I came back after completing my studies and began teaching. Last year I was asked to repay the loan. But on my request they obliged me with a delay of one more year. Now I have no excuse to delay repayment of this loan any further' So I appealed once more for an advance from the college. The advance could be recovered from the monthly allowance of Rs. 100, I agreed. But no advance was made available.

## Wielding the Rod of the 'Apostolic' Authority

The college ministerial staff had sent a complaint to the University. Mr P.P. Jose Pallikunnel and I were required to work for a conciliation talk with the complainants separately and informally and arrive at an amicable settlement with them. Mr Jose and I in close consultation and collaboration with the Principal and the forane vicar Fr Joseph Puthenpura completed the attempt and reached the Bishop's House on 6-10-'71 with the report of the efforts at a settlement with the attenders. The effort involved several rounds of talks. But the Bishop's treatment meted out to both of us was highly insulting. I expressed our sentiment in my letter dated 7 October '71: 'You did not even bother to take a look into the paper first and then scold us for the 'stupidity' the efforts might have appeared to you. We were required to tell you how Jose and myself met the college ministerial staff separately and then informally in the college. As usual you then told us that we should have done exactly the other way! That, I suppose, is the way of sanctification available to us priests...bonded by the vow of obedience to their Bishops. But I wonder whether such ways of sanctification are much edifying or intelligible to laymen. A priest, I am to understand, is supposed to have no right to respect or recognition because he has taken the vow of obedience to his Bishop. They have only to obey. They can therefore lawfully be insulted, buffeted or what not! But I don't think a layman deserves any such treatment, nor, I am afraid, will they take it well...(Mr Jose and I) don't remember to have done anything criminal except that in all good faith we did what we could have done according to the directions you gave us. And yet, if we met with such treatment, I think I should say in the words of St. Paul: 'After all these, say that you are but unprofitable servants'. I thank you very much, my Lord'. The satire in my words, if any though unintended, seemed to have piqued the Bishop who sent me a small message dated 12 October 1971: 'Fr Ab. Vellam, my son. I got your L. which was unwanted. Pride goes before a fall. Vidi satanam cadentem de coelo. [I saw Satan falling from heaven]. Pray and be humble and do *your* duty. With blessings + T.T.'

To this I responded on 14 October thus: 'Your 'vidi satanam cadentem de coelo' upset me much. As is usual with me in moments of such distress I went to our Lord in the Bl. Eucharist for peace. Very soon He helped me regain my peace with the thought: 'My son, don't you remember that I called St. Peter 'Satan' and Judas 'friend'?' And Your Lordship represents him to me'.

## Honouring me with Onerous Promotion

It was May 1972. The Bishop issued order No. 62B/72 dated 1 May 1972, appointing me as warden in full responsibility for discipline, Mess, accounts, monthly and annual balance sheets according to the principles of the Finance Act 1970. Fr Luke Puthiakunnel, Lecturer in Physics, was appointed as Assistant. When comparing the departmental work of both of us, Fr Puthiakunnel had much more leisure time than I had. So I requested to entrust the Assistant Warden with the full charge of Mess and accounts, or appoint me as Assistant Warden. But the reply I received through the Secretary Fr Karottukunnel as per letter dated 5 June 1972 was to the effect that the sacrosanct order was immutable and that 'the Catholic students, the future laity of the Church, must be fed with the Word of God (doctrine of the Church)'. Was it an indirect warning that the Church's stand should be treated as the Word of God? I immediately replied, iterating my previous request to divide the responsibilities between the two wardens as 'I find it impossible to cope with the whole work in the hostel according to the present arrangements, at the same time doing justice to my teaching work in the college'.

There was a long period of closure of the hostel due to the struggle between the Private college managements and the Government on the issue of the direct payment of salary. The hostel students submitted a memorandum dated 10 January 1973 requesting reduction of hostel rent during the period of the closure. The Bishop replied to this memorandum as per his letter dated 20 January 19'73 shifting the responsibility of the decision to the Principal of the college. But the Principal declined to play any role in this issue.

## Disowning the Responsibility of PPF Benefit

As I have mentioned earlier, before the 'Direct Payment Scheme' was introduced I was given only a pittance of Rs. 100, and the rest of my salary was withheld as 'Contribution' to the 'Diocesan Education Fund'. My request for a loan from this Education Fund to pay back the loan I had taken for my P.G. Studies was turned down, although I had agreed to forgo even the monthly share of Rs. 100 till the full recovery of the loan. I had then applied for the PPF Benefit due for the period of my hospitalization in Poona in 1968. But the PPF Board declined my application on some imaginary lame excuses which the Bishop found proper to approve. My attempt to get my PPF benefits through legal procedure was denied permission by the Bishop. In his letter to Fr Joseph Puthenpura dated 20 January 1973 returning my two earlier letters about the hostel students' memorandum and the Bishop's shifting the responsibility of the decision upon the Principal, the Bishop indicated that he had no role in the matter of the PPF operation with the remark: 'I wonder why (Fr Vellamthadathil) writes all that to me'. In reply to this I wrote to him on 25 January 1973: 'You seem to suggest that you have nothing to do with my PPF Problem....If it is so, I wonder why you ratified their decision and denied me permission to question their decision in a court of law and why you have asked me to write to you about it at all. However, since you have asked for it, I present the case as briefly as I can.

'The PPF rules say: 'when a member is not holding an office with remuneration and is not saying Mass, he shall be given from the society a subsidy equal to the aggregate subsidy (both Mass stipend and monthly allowances included) given at that time by the Diocese to the priests of the Diocese who are in office and are able to say Mass'. In my case when I was admitted in the hospital in Poona in 1968 I was a member, not holding an office with remuneration and was not saying Mass. Yet, I was denied the subsidy guaranteed by the PPF rules as given above'. It is this denial of what is due to me which the Bishop earlier ratified and now asks 'Why he writes all that to me' as if he has no role in the PPF operation.

Meanwhile, on 28 March 1973, Fr Joseph Kandarapallil wrote to all the priest teachers inviting us to meet the priest senate at the Uzhavoor presbytery for an 'amicable settlement' between the Bishop's 'unilateral fixation of the voluntary contribution of the Priest-teachers to the Diocesan Education Fund, the whole issue being an aftermath of the Government scheme for 'Direct Payment of Salary'. I replied to him saying that the principle of priest-solidarity motivating the effort for the 'amicable settlement' should have been applied in my issue with the PPF. 'As long as this is not done, I shall have to consider myself written off by my priest-fraternity', I added.

### 'Bishop's House Not a Hotel'

On 27 April 1973, on my way to Uzhavoor from Trivandrum, coming from the Summer Institute of English conducted by the Kerala University for English teachers as part of a FIP (Faculty Improvement Programme) I reached the Bishop's House at 9 p.m. and spent the night there, and proceeded to Trivandrum the following morning to join the FIP. As soon as I reached the Bishop's House I was summoned by the Bishop who administered on me a severely insulting reprimand for spending the previous night at the Bishop's house, saying Mass in the morning at the Cathedral and taking breakfast from the Bishop's refectory, 'as if it were a hotel'. Immediately I left the Bishop's house with a heavy heart deeply wounded by this insult, spent the night at S.H. Mount and left for Trivandrum the following early morning. On 8 May, I wrote to the Bishop reminding him of the event of the accursed eve of 28th April which sat heavy upon my heart. 'That day I came to you as summoned by you. Let me assure you that I was not disappointed at the treatment you meted out to me. My past experiences have taught me to expect nothing different in kind from that treatment....I hadn't thought it that improper on the part of a priest to have spent a night, said Mass and eaten a breakfast in his Bishop's house....I should say that I was rather misled by what you yourself told me about a year ago when you called me to the Bishop's house to get me do extra work as a lecturer to fill in the place vacated by the resignation of Mr C.J. Thomas Cheruthanny. That day before you asked me to take extra hours in the college, you very paternally scolded me for not coming to the Bishop's house often enough, for not taking any meal from there etc. on ground, as you yourself gave me to understand, that a Bishop's house is not any one man's private property, but the property of the community. These two communications of yours seem to be contradictory. Both cannot be true at the same time. I should therefore be very grateful to be instructed as to which of these two counsels of yours I am to take seriously.

'When a priest is insulted by his Bishop, is he to feel himself the holier because insulted by the Bishop? May be. Or perhaps, if my being insulted affords any personal satisfaction to any person other than myself, I should feel flattered for being called upon to render such a service on my part'.

To this my rather taunting lines I got a reply from Fr Jacob Chollambel, written as directed by the Bishop which I received on 19 May. It read: 'I am directed to let you know that your letter (dated 8 May, '73) was unnecessary as the fact is that I told you to meet the Bishop after spending the night, saying

Mass in the morning and taking breakfast. But you did not care to do so'. On the 19th itself I reached the Bishop's house with this letter to confront Fr Chollambel with the lie his letter contained. Fr Chollambel with a meaningful wink apologized in advance for having had to sign such a letter which he would not have done but for the order of the Bishop. A priest is ordered to serve his Bishop by signing a letter of falsehood under order! I was reminded of the ritual prayer, part of the Mass: 'Ecce agnus Dei, ecce qui tolit peccata mundi'. (Behold the Lamb of God/the Bishop; behold he who takes away the sins of the world/the Bishop!)

# 15

# The Direct Payment – Fixation of 'Voluntary' Contribution: Rocks the Diocese

The Bishop in his letter dated 26 January 1973 addressed to Fr Joseph Puthenpura, with direction to communicate the contents to me, ordered: 'Re. his contribution to the Education Fund, he has to say YES or NO for what he likes to do. If he is convinced of his moral obligation let him do what his Bishop asks. If not, let him have his salary in full and continue as lecturer rather than as priest-lecturer' I could only understand it as the Bishop's demand that I surrender my priesthood if I declined to surrender my salary to him. In reply I reminded him of my early offer to contribute as other priests would to the Diocesan Education Fund after my repayment of the education loan taken for my university studies.

Meanwhile, all the priest-teachers assembled in Uzhavoor Presbytery discussed in detail the contradiction in the Bishop's fixing the priest-teachers' voluntary contribution and the various possible retaliatory measures on the part of the Bishop consequent to our refusal to accept his fixing our 'voluntary' contribution. We decided to stand unanimous and go to any legal step if the Bishop would dare for any drastic retaliatory measure. In the meantime the Bishop ordered Frs. S. Uralil, lecturer in B.C.M. College, and Joseph Manapallil, H.S.A. in Kaduthuruthy High School, to go on a long leave and to accept pastoral duties in two parishes. Seeing that the issue was getting more and more complex, about 85 priests of the diocese submitted a memorandum suggesting a conciliatory stand that the Bishop's fixation of the voluntary contribution of the priest-teachers be accepted for three months and after that the decision could be revised in consultation with the priest-teachers concerned. But this conciliatory mediation was on condition that the Bishop would relent on his stand towards Fr S. Uralil and Fr Joseph Manapallil. But the conciliatory attempt collapsed when they met the Bishop the following day (3 June 1973) on the advice of the Coadjutor Bishop Kunnacherry, as the Bishop insisted on the two Fathers going on leave and taking other pastoral assignments. Purpose once formed, death or victory! He had also instructed the H.M. of Kaduthuruthy High School, Fr Theranthanam, and the B.C.M. College Principal Sr. Savio not to allow the two to sign the attendance register on the 4th June, the day of re-opening after the mid-summer vacation. However, the H.M. Fr Theranthanam admitted Fr J. Manapallil to sign the attendance register on the day of the re-opening. But Sr. Savio, hesitating to take any bolder stand, for which she was indeed competent, refused to allow Fr S Uralil to mark his attendance. Fr Uralil reported his presence for duty in writing to the Principal and to the Manager – Bishop- with copies to the Vice Chancellor and to the Director of Collegiate Education. The stage was now set for legal confrontation with the Bishop.

On 7 June I met Fr Uralil in B.C.M. College and was told that the Bishop had called him and, having lost all temperamental control, burst out shouting: 'Don't step in to the college, you, you petty fellow....If you are not ready to obey the Bishop, throw away your cassock and get lost....'

In Kaduthuruthy the development took a different twist. The Bishop appointed a local young lady to Fr Manapallil's 'leave' vacancy and asked her to reach the High School with her father and join duty. The lady, with her father, approached Fr Mathew Cherucherril, the local manager of the school with the Bishop's appointment order. The manager congratulated her on her appointment and told her: 'But the post is on the top of the coconut tree. If you can reach it, take it' and sent her to the headmaster. The latter told the poor girl and her father that Fr Manapallil was teaching and consequently there was no vacancy. However this sordid scheming of the Bishop to get the local people united and roused up against Fr Manapallil and against the clergy in general piqued the priest-community. They no more felt any qualm of conscience in sending to the higher authorities a carefully and legally worded petition against the management even in the background of the recent tense fight between the government and the private managements over the college problem which had become a serious political issue – the government determined to take over the private colleges if the strike continued and the management determined to defend and protect the college through organizing college protection squads.

The next day, (8 June) morning the Bishop reached Kaduthuruthy, ordered the headmaster to write off Fr Manapallil 'to leave for one year' and summoned the lady, who reluctantly obliged the Bishop by engaging class for one hour. After the Bishop's departure, Fr Theranthanam noted down the Bishop's arbitrary and illegal procedures in the log-book and got it signed by two teacher-witnesses.

On the 10th morning the Bishops called Fr S. Uralil's father and threatened him with dire consequences to his son as priest unless he got him to obey the Bishops. In the evening, about 30 priests of the Diocese met at Kaduthuruthy Shanthi Bhavan and after serious study of the problem from all perspectives, took a unanimous decision to tell the Bishop to desist from proceeding any further with actions on the priest teachers and to revoke his orders to Frs. Uralil and Manapallil to go on leave. They were ready to threaten him with en bloc withdrawal from all pastoral ministry in the diocese if the Bishop refused to relent. Four copies of this unanimous decision were rushed to all other priests of the diocese through messengers and almost all of them agreed to stand with the Shanthi Bhavan decision. By now almost 85 priests of the diocese were in the fray and their memorandum signed by 85 priests in active priestly ministry was sent to the Bishop by registered post on 14 June 1973. On the 19th there was a joint meeting of the priests at Kaduthuruthy. They decided to form a priests-association and approved an adhoc committee for further actions. During the deliberations Fr Mathew Cherucheril made a casual remark referring to the comment of the German doctor Rhode, former medical officer of Caritas Hospital: 'Many priests of the diocese suffer from nervous breakdown. I advise the priests of the diocese in general to keep away from any contact with the Bishop'. I was reminded once again of Fr Vishakhanthara's advice given to me in 1954 or so: 'Before you join the seminary, you are natural. In the seminary you feel supernatural. Once you come in touch with the Bishop, you begin to feel unnatural'.

Without further ado let me come to the denouement of this sordid melodrama. The Bishops finally had to relent and to revoke the orders given to Frs. Uralil and Manapallil to go on leave, re-instated them and agreed that the priest-teachers have the moral right to fix their voluntary contributions to any cause whatsoever. However, the Coadjutor Excellency, Bishop Kunnacherry, expressed in one of the priest-meetings, convened in relation to the same 'Direct Payment Issue' his preference to have only S.S.L.C. holders and no P.G. degree holders as candidates to priesthood. Naturally enough a slightly mischievous thought came to my mind: 'Why S.S.L.C. holders? They are literate. They may indulge in reading, and get ideas and consequently begin to question arbitrary authority, creating inconvenience or perhaps even embarrassment to those in authority. So illiterate but hefty block-headed ones may be preferred to be vested in cassocks and laid Episcopal hands upon to condition them and use them for priestly rituals, much to the comfort and convenience of the dogmatic, infallible, divino jure hierarchy escalator to heaven after death'.

### The Smothering Grip Gets Tougher

Following my request to divide the burden of hostel duties and to lesson my burden, the Bishop issued order No. 63B/73, dated 1-6-73, relieving me of my duties in the hostel and directing me to shift my residence to St. Rock's Church Presbytery at Areekara, although I could easily stay in the hostel with the new young priest wardens or in the Uzhavoor Church presbytery.

On an on-the-spot personal inspection and enquiry I found very serious inconveniences for my stay at the Areekara Parish presbytery. Fr John Kadavil, the vicar and my one-time colleague in the petit seminary, informed me that there was only one room now free for the use of M.L. Members, for guests and for me to stay in. Further, there was not even a chair to sit on, a table to write on, a cot to sleep on or a cupboard to lock my little belongings in. I had to provide all these things at a heavy expense from where? Besides, I had to leave my motor bike on the public road day and night, as there was no cartable path to the church compound. The rain and the heat of the sun that I would have to endure for daily journey to Uzhavoor and back were in addition to the above. However, all these inconveniences and hurdles could with greater satisfaction be endured if my presence and service was in any way needed there.

I explained to the Bishop all those difficulties in detail. But the adamant and inconsiderate insistence of the Bishop on my immediate shift of residence to Areekara pushed me to the brink of severing all my connections with him as my Bishop and to seek my own residence. So I consulted Mr P.P. Jose who immediately agreed to share with me his bachelor residence of one or two rooms at Uzhavoor. 'Father', he told, 'If you intend to take a strong decision, have absolutely no worry about a residence. You are welcome to stay in my cottage with me'. The Rev. Mother of the local convent consented to supply my meals provided I employed a boy to fetch my meals from the convent. So in my reply dated 3 June to the Bishop's order mentioned above, I thanked him for taking so much care to arrange for my residence at Areekara presbytery, and added: 'The serious inconveniences for my stay in Areekara can be overcome by my finding a befitting residence at Uzhavoor, without at the same time giving you any unnecessary worry over the problem of a convenient residence for me.

'Regarding the rumours about my 'moral debility' and your paternal advice on my dealings with female folk, which you find fit to give place in your Curia letter, I hasten to assure you that in exercising and enjoying what I believe are my God-given rights regarding my private personal life and in the conscientious discharge of my duties, civic, professional and social, I have been very sincerely trying to be guided by the Christian principles of Justice, Truthfulness and Love, trying my very best never to violate any one's rights or to create inconveniences to another person. As to rumours, there are plenty of them about every one of us. I give to rumours only that importance which they deserve. Besides, they are the fruits of the culture and sense of moral values created by centuries of what are traditionally believed to be 'Catholic Christian traditions and preaching, but which now boomerang on us'.

The Bishop in return served on me an ultimatum dated 8 June 1973, ordering to submit explanation for the 'breach of contract' (refusal to surrender my aquittance roll salary to the Education Fund as my voluntary contribution) and to shift to Areekara, all 'on or before 11th inst'.

My reply to this ultimatum dated 12-6-'73 refrained from anything pertaining to the 'breach of contract', if any at all, on the moral principle learned in the Seminary 'contractus turpis non obligat': a dishonest contract does not bind'. Besides, the matter was being seriously handled by the priest-community of the Diocese.

With regard to the shift of residence, I reminded him of all the grave and absolutely unnecessary inconvenience involved in the shift of residence. 'All these serious inconveniences', I pointed out, 'take added intensity when we think of the easy accommodation facilities available in the hostel. I am willing to pay for my boarding and lodging in the hostel, and Fr Warden is willing to accommodate me subject to his conditions for my stay', and that too in the company of the priest-wardens. So I submitted: 'I pray you, my Lord, not to insist on my shifting my residence to Areekara but to spare me the intolerable and unnecessary inconveniences this shift involves'.

Pat came the reply dated 14-6-73 from the chancellor, Fr P. Poochakkattil, under order from His Excellency to inform me that 'the order dated 8th June 1973 stands firm and admitted no consideration' reminding me of the words of Pilate in John, 19, 22: 'Quod scripsi, scripsi: What I have written stands written'. Next day I wrote back to Poochakkattil: 'You have simply brushed aside all the serious and concrete difficulties and inconveniences connected with the shift of my residence to Areekara with one easy stroke stating that they are not satisfactory. I believe that a Bishop who assumes the authority to decide where a priest should reside, has also the duty to look to the necessary convenience of the residence....It was to avoid these serious inconveniences and to tide over the difficulties that I planned to reside in the hostel under the care and in the company of two priest-wardens. You say that the hostel is meant for the students. But more than 15 rooms are vacant in the hostel and teachers too have been and are even now residing in the hostel....If, however, I am not to stay in the hostel, I beg to be permitted to reside at St. Stephen's presbytery, Uzhavoor. Or if I am to stay only at Areekara, I expect to be instructed as to how to overcome these serious inconveniences'.

The Chancellor's reply dated 18-6-73, again 'under direction from H. Exc.' came by the return post: '...the reasons already stated and repeated.... are not at all satisfactory. Hence, you are again ordered to shift at once your residence to Areekara'.

I felt my way cleared to shift my residence to Mr P.P. Jose's bachelor quarters. But then came counsel from different sources to postpone it. On 21 June the Principal, Dr Simon Kottoor advised me to postpone the shift 'at least till the joint meeting of the Priest Senate and the Pastoral Council, convened to settle the college problem, so that this your decision may not adversely affect the cause of the Priest-teachers'. Later some laymen, especially my friend and President of the College Protection Samithy, Mr Kuriako Vattukulam, approached me with the same counsel. Above all, on 22nd morning the copy of Fr Kandarappallil's 'Open letter to the Bishop' dated 20 June 1973 reached me. In this letter he had added that all the priest-teachers followed the Bishop's direction in the matter of transfer including 'those who lived in the Uzhavoor College Hostel also vacated and went to Areekara'. I immediately shifted my residence to Areekara as otherwise, I thought, the Bishop would take unfair advantage and ruin the weight of influence of priests like Fr Kandarappallil propagating that Fr Kandarappallil was spreading falsehood and citing my case in support of this.

On 25 June I wrote to the Bishop again explaining and repeating the grave but unnecessary difficulties involved in my shift of residence, unnecessary 'since neither my presence nor my service is needed here and since very convenient places are available at Uzhavoor presbytery, hostel etc.

'I therefore request you to kindly allow me to stay at St. Stephen's presbytery or at the men's hostel. If, however, you find it inconvenient to permit me to stay in either of these two places, I hereby inform you that I shall have to look for a convenient and suitable residence at Uzhavoor.

'If I do not receive any reply till next Saturday 30th of this month, I shall have to presume' accordingly.

### Time to Cut the Umbilical Cord

I waited till Saturday, 30th June but received no reply. I thought it was high time I cut my umbilical cord with my mother diocese. And I did it through my 'Open Letter to Bishop Tharayil' dated 30 June 1973.

### My Open Letter of Resignation

Uzhavoor
30–6–1973.

To His Excellency,
Dr Thomas Tharayil
Bishop of Kottayam

Your Excellency,

It is about ten years since I began my priestly ministry under you. When as priest I voluntarily placed my ministry under your authority and guidance, I expected that this would help to develop and foster to the best possible my God-given talents, humble though they indeed are, and to use my priestly life to the fullest extent for the glory of God and the service for the people of God. But, unfortunately, not only the bud of my expectation did not bloom, but I now feel stifled and my priestly life a splendid waste.

### You Need Slaves in Cassock

You neither need priests who think freely and value their own personality nor their personal abilities. But what you need are living machines who are just fit to carry out your own ideas and decisions. You have been trying to scientifically destroy, under cover of authority and tradition, those who are able and dare to think creatively, to take on new ideas and to criticize with sincerity and a sense of responsibility as befitting Christian priestly conscience those tradition and observances which appear meaningless in the light of new ideas. You not only refuse to respect personality and personal conscience, you are not ready even to tolerate them. Instead, you try to train and condition just a few slaves in cassock who are just 'obedient to the Bishop', instructed in rubrics to perform 'priestly ministries' which are mere rituals and who are 'faithful' to preserve intact the present structure, traditions and rituals which are means of livelihood to their custodians.

### Human Trade Under Cover of Religion

You have been trying to train a bunch of priest and nun slaves in the solitary virtue of 'obedience' giving them priesthood and religious habit and to tame them with the bridles of the three vows of poverty, chastity and obedience in the name of God, religion and salvation of souls and then to make use of them to amass money. This human trade has been a crude shock to my priestly conscience. Besides, many of them are being continuously immolated for the sake of the cruel satisfaction of your insatiable greed for power. My life of obedience under your authority has been terribly pained to see several human and religious values and human emotions and feelings of fundamental importance being sacrificed before the altar of your lust for power and money. As you know, my own personal experiences are sufficient proofs for these my statements. The file of my correspondence with you since 1953 which I have carefully preserved as a very valuable treasure will potently testify to these facts. Let me quote but just two or three incidents of my life to substantiate my statements.

## A Few Incidents Just for Example's Sake

While canons are still in force forbidding, under the penalty of 'ipso facto' excommunication, any one to force another either to join religious orders or convent life or to accept priesthood, you wanted me to join and to make perpetual profession in the diocesan 'religious' congregation directly under your authority. But as my conscience forbad me to make profession in the said congregation, I could not obey your order, for which you suspended me from saying Mass. What justification do you have?

I think it was in 1964 that I wrote and published some articles on the Rite-Restoration programme which was indeed rocking the whole Syrian Catholic Church of Kerala at that time. And you found them good enough at first to heartily congratulate me on my 'thought-provoking articles', as you yourself described them. But suddenly, at the instigation of I don't know who, you became displeased with those articles. Subsequently you convened the Diocesan Liturgical Committee to charge-sheet me for these articles. In that meeting I volunteered to unconditionally withdraw them and publicly apologize for them although prior to their publication they were censured and approved for publication by the then Vicar General and the then Chancellor (now Coadjutor). Still you ordered me to write as many articles contrary to my earlier ones, supporting those very views and ideas which were repugnant to my conscience and conviction. Was it becoming of your Episcopal authority?

You unilaterally fixed what I should 'voluntarily' contribute to the Diocesan Education Fund and issued orders to that effect. But I could not accept either the amount of my contribution you fixed or the principle which you wanted to vindicate, i.e., that yours was the right to fix what your priests should 'voluntarily' contribute and to impose your decision upon them. Your vindictiveness then took the shape of transferring my residence from Uahavoor, where I am teaching, to Areekra presbytery. As neither my presence nor my priestly service was in any way needed at Areekara, I repeatedly requested you to allow me to stay at Uzhavoor presbytery, or at the college hostel managed by two priests and thereby to spare me the many grave and unnecessary inconveniences involved in my transfer to Areekara. I made these requests when several rooms were available at the Uzhavoor presbytery and almost half of the hostel rooms were vacant, as is the case even now. But you chose to ignore my requests and tried to clinch your orders of transfer threatening me with dire consequences if I refused to comply with your vindictive orders. Was it for the greater glory of God, or for the good of the people of God or for the good of me who am your subject that you thus wielded your Episcopal authority, which, we are to believe, was given to you from God for taking care of those under your authority? Or was it for the cruel satisfaction of your insatiable vindictiveness or your lust for authoritarianism? My conscience finds it difficult to get reconciled to many of your ideas and policies. I shall expatiate them before long.

Under the circumstance I cannot render priestly ministry under you. My last ten years of priestly service under your authority have given me no sense of fulfillment nor any satisfaction except perhaps chronic peacelessness and a sense of unprofitable waste of time and health. I am unable to carry on this state of affairs any longer. Therefore, while I still profess my duty to dedicate my priestly life for the benefit of the people of God, I withdraw my priestly service from your authority and guidance. I desire and am trying to serve as a priest under any other Bishop who is ready to recognize and require my priestly ministry. It is my earnest desire to do something in peace for the rest of my life that induces me to this dangerous 'solitary life adventure'. I call my proposed course of action a 'dangerous solitary life adventure' because I am aware that the same kinds of power-centres exist as those which could turn against Jesus and clamour for his blood: those very same innocent but gullible crowd who but only on the previous (Palm) Sunday shouted 'Hosannas' to him. The same traditions still exist even now which once trained the crowd to blindly trust these power-centres. But entrusting to the kind Providence my priestly life which God Himself has been taming, training and protecting along the path of suffering, hardships and obstacles, I take this decision. I further purpose to serve and to discharge as best as I can my duties as priest and teacher to God, to the Nation, to the Society, to the Institution where I work and to my students'.

Sd/-
Fr. Abraham Vellamthadathil.

**Shift of Residence to Monippally**

Before releasing the printed open Letter I wrote to the Bishop on 4 July 1973 intimating him of my withdrawal of myself from active priestly ministry in the diocese assigned by the Bishop. 'As I am looking for a convenient resident for me where I can prepare myself better for the discharge of my duties as a lecturer and do some urgent personal work, I don't press Your Excellency for a convenient residence'.

I may be wrong to think that the Bishop had a premonition of the contents of my 'Open Letter', or it might have been a mere coincidence. Whatever it be, on the very 4 July the Bishop issued order No. 66B/73 transferring me to S.H. Presbytery, Monippally with charge as assistant Vicar without its remuneration.

Those were days of intense agony on account of uncertainty and indecision as to the steps of breaking off from the Bishop. Threat of excommunication? Possibility of instigated physical violence from gullible crowds or even hired musclemen? Recently my dear Therese had offered to console me by going to any level of nearness even up to marriage. Will she be able to withstand the pressure from all around or will she give up the promise? If so, should I think of marrying anymore? At any rate

I must carry on my priestly ideals whether I get married or not. A small residence of my own to live in? It was in those days of uncertainty and agony that Annamma Cheduthy, Mudiyoorkunnel, with an extra ordinary degree of humaneness and courage came to offer me her newly built single-roomed 'thekkany' (an additional structure to an existing building) for me to stay in 'until you conveniently make arrangements for your own residence'. She was supposed to be a widow of ill-repute among the pious ones who were regular faithful church-goers for prescribed ritualistic observances. While the 'approved ones' of the society around me would not think of accommodating a priest or even regard him as a man if he is an object of his Bishop's displeasure, the 'ill-reputed' Annamma Cheduthy reminded me 'the sinners and the publicans' of Jesus' time who loved and welcomed Him. On the day I received the Bishop's order transferring me to Monippally, my worried father fixed the purchase of a small house and plot close by the college campus. However in deference to the joint request of the Priests Forum that met at Fr Manalel's house, Poozhikol on 11 July 1973, I once again obeyed the order and on 14 July I shifted to Monippally with the minimum necessary personal things and clothing articles. On the 23rd the property purchase deed was registered at Ramapuram. In this effort Fr M. Karukakuttil helped me with a loan. On 31 July Fr P. Karappallil, Vicar, Monippally reported to me that Fr Karukakuttil was taken to task for helping me and the latter went back to his parish at Punnathura after threatening to offer his resignation from active priestly ministry.

The joint meeting of the Cenacle Executive and the priest-teachers, held at Kottayam T.B. on 11 August to discuss the Bishop's latest circular No. 230 dated 31 July 1973, announcing his intention to divert the priest-teachers' contribution to P.P.F. and to give education scholarship to poor deserving students of the community from other (diocesan sources). The joint meeting felt the circular had an unholy, clandestine agenda on the part of the Bishop to alienate the sympathy of the laity from the priests and to turn them in his favour in his tug with the priest-teachers under cover of steps and decisions apparently innocent and well meant

## Bidding Farewell to Monippally Presbytery

By 15 October I completed my three months stay at Monippally as 'Assistant Parish Priest' to help the vicar Fr Karappallil. During this period only once I was given the opportunity to say the Sunday Mass and preach. I took up the matter with Fr Karappallil on Sunday 14 October. And he openly told me that being hefty and healthy enough to run a parish like Monippally all alone, he did not need any assistance from me. Fr Karappallil, I have always found, was a smiling figure. But more often than not it was not he who drank brandy or arrack, but it is brandy/arrack that drank him. And then he was capable of indulging in such actions as opening my private room with false keys and inspecting my records and documents. In fact I served on him a notice dated 28-12-'73 calling for his explanation, with copies to the Bishop and to the convener of Priest Cenacle, Fr Thevarmannil. Fr Karapallil pleaded that it was with the knowledge and consent of the Bishop that he violated the privacy of my locked room.

Severely stung by the vicar's insulting remarks I wrote to the Bishop on 18 October 1973 resigning my 'charge' as assistant vicar at Monippally. I concluded it thus: 'Even though temporarily I accepted your appointment order in spite of the grave inconveniences, consumption of time, energy and money involved in my daily journey to Uzhavoor and back, that too without any remuneration, only because I thought your appointment order was based on a real and not a non-existent need. I therefore regret and not without protest that such orders are issued to priests assigning them to tasks which do not in fact exist'. This letter was followed by the Bishop's Secretary, Fr Stephen Muthukattil, dated 20 October '73, written under Bishop's order directing me to 'continue your stay at Monippally presbytery till you are allowed to leave station'. I continued my stay there till 22 November without any further information. So, on 22 November 1973, I shifted my residence with my father to my newly bought house, renamed 'Therese Ville' just a football ground away from the college and the men's hostel. I continued to say Mass in the Hostel chapel together with the two priest wardens and help the other priest-fraternity in priestly service within the diocese.

### Investigations from 'Holy Sources'

On 8 December 1973, Feast of O.L. of Immaculate Conception, the second biggest church festival at Uzhavoor, the Coadjutor Excellency Bishop Kunnacherry in his message delivered at the market-chapel found it proper to denounce 'false prophets' who preach the gospel of love and called upon the people of Uzhavoor 'steeped in their forefathers' tradition' to deal with these false prophets as they deserve! Many priests and a few laymen standing with me in front of the preacher told me that the preacher obviously had me in mind.

Soon the warden, Fr Meledom, one of my own students, was ordered not to permit me to say Mass in the hostel chapel. I wrote to the Bishop on 12 December begging 'to be intimated of the reasons, if any, why I should not be allowed to offer holy Mass in the hostel chapel where a considerable number of the local faithful gather to attend the Mass of all days, especially on Sundays'. Till 28 December I received no reply. All the while I continued to walk down the hill and up the hill to the Church to say Mass and back home. I wrote to the Bishop again on 28 December reminding him of my request to be permitted to say Mass in the hostel chapel.

### My Prayer Room Changed into Altar

As days were getting more and more eventful and that too at ever greater momentum, I felt the dawn of January 1974 as the dawn of a year expected to be a 'Turning Point' in my life. I began to think of a family, as a source of security next to God against the hostile atmosphere. I expected Therese to keep her promise and come into my life as help to be more deeply and exemplarily dedicated to God's service as a priest. But subsequently, unable to withstand the social pressure, as I feared, she turned back from her stand.

Having received no reply to my letter to the Bishop dated 12 December I visited Fr S. Uralil at Mallossery on 18 January. Frs. Karottukunnel and Alex Chettiath too were present. I discussed my plan to turn my prayer room into an altar and say Mass there. 'Why not?' they said although Fr Karottukunnel had some scruples about its propriety. Soon I was supplied with all the utensils and vestments necessary – all lent to me by other priests of the diocese. And on 1 February 1974 I started saying Mass in my residence. A few of my very old neighbours used to attend the Mass, said at my private residence. I felt absolutely no conscientious objection in doing so. In fact, I remembered the two years of post graduate studies at Dharwar during which I had said Mass in my living room in the University hostel. However on Sundays and on other days when priestly ministry was needed, I said Mass at Uzhavoor or in other churches as invited by priests there for help.

On the evening of 11 February 1974, Fr Joseph Puthenpura, came to my residence, reportedly under direction from the Bishop, and threatened my father, my grand mother and my niece staying with me with 'suspensio a sacris' (denial of Sacraments) unless they compelled me to go back to my residence at Monippally presbytery. I had a little argument with him over the logic of punishing my aged parents and little niece for my disobedience. He told me that his was not to look into the logic of, but obey, the Bishop's order. However we parted friends after his sharing a bottle of beer with my father.

## Media Publicity Focused on Me

By now I had published in *Vaidika Miṭram* [The Friend of the Priest], a popular clergy Monthly, (issues of July, September 1973, February 1974) some articles such as 'Is God Jealous, Religion Sadistic?', 'Time For Christianity to Look Forward', 'Priestly Ministry In Modern Times', 'Obedience and All That' etc. These articles reflected a critical approach to the traditional 'Other-worldly Spirituality' and asceticism. The last one was meant to highlight the route taken by the Priests-Bishops tug over the college issue of Direct Payment to its destination. These articles naturally triggered off sharp controversy. All my messages delivered practically in all the churches in the diocese and even outside as guest preacher reflected a rational critical outlook on the traditional faith-spiritual practices and fetched me a lot of comments from the clergy and the laymen, mostly laudatory. V.M. issues brought out critics praising and criticizing me for my 'advanced' [to some] and 'unorthodox' [to others] views about religion and morality. Even Fr John Ancot, my former Rector at the Papal Seminary and later spiritual Father wrote in one of the issues of V.M. 'Our friend Fr Abraham seems to have forgotten the theology he learned in the Papal Athenaeum'. To this I very humbly and respectfully replied: 'Not because I forgot, but because I studied Philosophy and Theology at the Papal Athenaeum'. But the widest and the severest controversy about and focus of attention on me was triggered off by my press conference held in Kottayam on 11 February 1974 on 'The Church should Re-consider Its Position on Birth Control'. I argued for the change on the basis of the change of the dogmatically taught and traditionally held end of marriage brought about by the Vat. II document. According to the traditional teaching, procreation of the children was the primary end of marriage and the 'mutuum adjutorium' [the mutual help of man and woman for their human fulfillment of the Natural/God-given need for each other] was only secondary. According to the Vat. II document, the primary-secondary difference was eliminated and the two were regarded as two ends and therefore of co-ordinate status. The press conference was given wide publicity by practically all the media on the following day highlighting details.

### Instigating Laymen against Me

I expected that my press conference and the written article on the same would pique my Bishops and provoke their fury. I expected them to meet ideas with ideas. But later I realized that they were interested to meet ideas with rods and clubs, if necessary, even with hired muscle power. I suspected, they would side-track from the doctrinal issue into a Church-disciplinary issue. Fr J. Puthenpura gave me a hint at this possible side-tracking when he came to my residence on 21 February with instruction from the Bishop that I go back to Monippally presbytery and stop saying Mass in private prayer room. I requested him to give the instruction in writing. But he refused to oblige me. So as a strategic move I decided to abide by the arbitrary order of the Bishop to go back to Monippally.

On 24 February 1974, it being a Sunday, I reached Uzhavoor church to say Mass. At the vestry Fr Puthenpura, accompanied by about half a dozen men, said he could not permit me to say Mass unless I stopped saying Mass in my residence and went back to Monippally. I readily agreed to abide by the order, although he never expected this sudden change of attitude in me. He wanted me to give it in writing and I agreed to that too. He then turned to those around us and asked them whether he should allow me to say Mass in the church. They burst into words of sheer abuse and threatened me with violence. The Bishop had not taken any disciplinary action against me so far. But Fr Puthenpura thought it in order to ask his 'yes' men's permission for me to say Mass!

On the following day, 25 February 1974 I said Mass at St. Mary's Church, Muttom and gave a message during the nuptial ceremony of my nephew. There was no objection from any corner. Three days after on 1 March I said Mass in the college for the teachers and the students. There was no objection from anywhere either. It was indeed a challenge to the local parish priest who resorted to hire muscle power to obstruct my saying Mass in the church.

In the evening Mr Kuriachen Edattukunnel, Chackochen Chirakkara [both active members of the Parish Pious Associations], Kuriako Mudakkodil and Thommachen Velooparampil came to my residence as critics to express their protest and opposition to my out-of-the-way actions as a priest. I received them into my little study room, opened to them the file of my documents and records and discussed the whole story up to that moment. After about four hours of intimate exchange they left me as friends convinced that those in ecclesiastical authority should have met ideas with ideas and not with rods and clubs.

They were followed by the visit of Sri Cyriac Puthiakunnel, brother of lecturer Fr Luke Puthiakunnel and President K.C.(M) Party Mandalam Committee, on 12 March. He is still a friend of mine. With him I had elaborate discussion on the theological and moral aspects of the issue of Birth Control. He came to report to me of the Bishop's attempt to resort to political force to counter me. He told me of Fr Peter Uralil's visit to him seeking his initiative and political influence to 'get people united so as to seat Fr Vellamthadathil where he should'. The meeting was dramatic, as Mr Cyriac described it. Mr Cyriac asked him: 'Why should people get united to seat the mere one-man force Fr Abraham on his seat? Just one man hefty and strong enough with muscle power could do that job of seating him?' 'Cyriac', argued Fr Uralil, 'Only the people getting united could strengthen the Bishop's hand'. 'What!' Mr Cyriac responded, 'has the Bishop's hand got paralyzed due to rheumatism? Listen, Fr Peter. All that Fr Abraham has done is that he conducted a press conference and wrote an article on it, arraying his theological and rational arguments. Eminent priests like you are there in the diocese. Why don't you or they point out when, where and how Fr Abraham has gone wrong and show why his views are wrong. Once he is proved wrong and unorthodox, the Bishop could proceed with disciplinary action against him. Instead what need or justification is there to organise laymen like me to meet ideas? Why should you get baby-monkeys to grab at hot rice?' Rather embarrassed Fr Peter returned to where he came from.

## Instigations from 'Holy Pulpits' again

Once again the Coadjutor Excellency Bishop Kunnacherry during his Uzhavoor Market chapel sermon on 26 December 1974, let out a tirade, probably goaded by my presence among the audience just in front of him. He delivered thus: 'There are some who turn against when they are in a position to stand on their own legs. One may have education, degrees, job, money, property, house, health and beauty. But without obedience all these are in vain'. I felt very complacent at the implicit admission that the obedient ones are those who have no education, no degrees, no job, no money, no property, no house, no health and no beauty. Only they can be kept in the fold under the 'pastoral' care. This fully confirmed what the venerable Bishop Sebastian Mankuzhikkary honestly and openly admitted on 1 September 1973 when I met him by prior appointment to discuss with him my ideas on 'Priestly Ministry in Modern Times' and on Birth Control. The Bishop probably thought it unnecessary to go into those points. During our interaction I suggested that many priests are unhappy in life. The Bishop sharply disagreed with my view saying: 'They are not in chains, but free to give it up and go if they are unhappy'. 'Go where?' I argued. 'What security of life do they have outside the performance of rituals upon which they live? Do many of them have any qualification to be employed even as clerks except the training to perform rituals?' 'No, Fr Abraham', the Bishop countered me 'I don't agree with you'. With a gentle note of challenge I suggested: 'Make, then, a declaration to the effect that those priests unhappy with their priestly service can leave the service. They will all the same be given the same financial security from the church. After all by the declaration, you have nothing to lose but only to gain credibility, as admittedly none will go and your claim will stand eminently vindicated'. The Bishop thought for a moment and said: 'There lies the crux of the problem, Father'. And I came away. Nearly one year later I found an anonymous [understandable] statement of a 'Diocesan Priest' published in *New Leader* (Madras, Sunday 9 May 1974) which clinched my argument with the Bishop. Let me quote: 'If there is anyone who needs to be liberated so badly in the Church, he is the diocesan priest.... Few realize the misery he is in, and he himself is unable or afraid or reluctant to complain about the sad plight....Even if the proper person is chosen [to episcopacy], it often happens that through the force of the system and through the influence of the sycophants, who as a rule surround persons in power, he is slowly led to the illusion that he is no ordinary man but one born to rule and to subjugate others and endowed with extraordinary powers of intelligence and competent for any work.

Canon Law provides the Bishops with all sorts of props to keep an absolute sway over the priests under him. There is no independent judiciary in the church....Sometimes the accused himself is the judge or the judge stands committed to defend the accused.

'Consequently, priests are in effect slaves of the Bishops, subjected to their whims....A priest cannot develop his personality and talents, unless he curries favour with his bishop, through foul or fair means. Once a Bishop remarked: 'I don't care for talents among my priests. What I want is humility and obedience'. How can human dignity and freedom be preserved in such a system?'

### Complaints against Instigated Violence

I complained to the Bishop on 26 February 1974 against the treatment meted out to me at the hands of the vicar's hired men in the church vestry: 'I don't remember to have ever been summoned, questioned, warned or punished by you for any reason except your 'suspensio a sacris' in 1966 for not agreeing to make the religious profession in the diocesan congregation of the O.S.H.' What redressal was to be expected when the accused himself was the judge! I complained to the Apostolic Internuncio New Delhi on 1 March 1974 and my complaint met with the same fate. In my letter to Fr Thevarmannil, convener of the 'Priest Cenacle' dated 3 March '74 I added: 'For me my relationship with my Bishop has reached its climax with his move to deal with me with the hired musclemen. He goes to men in the street to deal with me. All I have done is to have come out with some ideas.... I think it is a sordid game played on me by instigating the 'faithful sheep' [or rams shall I say] against me....Am I a wild fowl to be chased with sticks and stones....I have a right to be treated as an educated man, if not 'an obedient priest'....I have only a few ideas for my defense. If those ideas are wrong, let the Bishop and my priest-fraternity declare my ideas wrong on ground of reason. I should like to know if the Cenacle or the priest-fraternity has anything to tell me about my present position'.

**Priest Senate Convened, but Dispersed**

On 15 March 1974 I sent a similar complaint to Fr Karottukunnel, convener of the Diocesan Priest Senate. I am not sure whether this complaint had any role but the Bishop directed a subsequent Priest Senate meeting to be convened to think of suitable disciplinary action on me on my 'Open Letter to Bishop Tharayil' dated 30 June 1973. As per the report of the proceedings I received later, the Priest Senate considered that issuing this type of Open Letter was unprecedented. 'Ha', the Bishop said, 'That's why I have convened all of you for your counsel as to what action should be taken against Fr Abraham'. One of the Senate members, I was told later, said: 'Before proceeding to consider the nature and degree of punishment, we would like to know whether the Bishop denies or admits the truth of the events related in the Open Letter under the paragraph 'Some life Experiences''. In an angry outburst the Bishop folded the Open Letter and dumped it into his long pocket and dispersed the meeting. No further Senate Meeting was ever held since then till the Coadjutor Excellency took over the reign of the Diocese from the senior Bishop through a circular on grounds of superannuation according the criteria laid down by Vat, II regarding the retirement of the Bishops. The takeover was a slightly different type of a coup d'etat.

In a letter dated 29 March 1974, sent to me through the Principal Rev. Dr Simon Kottoor by the Chancellor, of course under the order of His Excellency, the Principal was sharply accused of 'conniving with Fr Abraham Vellamthadathil', and 'allowing him to say Mass in the college for the staff and students'. His reply to these charges dated 30 April was one that the authorities really deserved. The first allegation he described as irresponsible and baseless. To the second he replied thus: 'There is no question of my 'allowing' Fr Vellamthadathil to say Mass since he has permission [as a priest]from the Bishop to say Mass in the Diocese, and, pray, let me know if that permission has ever been withdrawn by the Bishop through any notification according to any procedure. If not, there is absolutely no point in your allegation'. He further stated in his reply that he expected the Diocesan Curia to maintain certain standard in its procedure and to withdraw the allegations 'as any honest gentleman should do'.

## Umbilical Cord Finally Clipped

The Coadjutor Excellency by now having taken over the reins of the diocese from the senior one, Fr (now Mgr.) Joseph Kandarappallil was appointed as the new Vicar General. On 23 July I met Mgr. Kandarappallil during the meeting of the Cenacle of Kottayam Priests at Poozhikol. He then suggested that I go over to the Bishop's House 'to talk matters over' with him. I agreed to go over any day on condition that the authorities first redress my complaint against the local parish priest who mustered and instigated musclemen to abuse and insult me. Through another phone message sent via the Principal he made his suggestion a second time. To this I replied on 3 August: 'Isn't it absurd that when I am invited by the priests of the diocese to help them through various priestly services, Fr Puthenpura and two or three of his hirelings think it proper to threaten me with violence against my saying Mass in the Uzhavoor church? Until the authorities concerned looked into the matter, I may not be able to think of any 'talking the matter over''.

Yet, out of my deep respect for dear Mgr. Kandarappallil, I met him at the Bishop's House on 22 August. After a long exchange between us, I agreed to his first suggestion to be willing to render priestly service in the Diocese provided it was needed and respected in the diocese. To his second, that I let the new Bishop have a new start by 'closing the old chapter and opening a new', I submitted that an unnatural death calls for an inquest. I wanted to have a thorough investigation into and assessment of my 'wrong' doings, and ideas, as there was no need to fear of anything 'wrong' on the part of the 'jure divino infallible church authority'. Mgr. Kandarappallil sternly insisted on my agreeing to close the old chapter and open a new because 'as priests we have great responsibilities and duties to forgive and forget and to protect the good names of many persons concerned. You should obey me and cooperate with me to work for the good of the diocese'. I came away after requesting him to allow me a day or two to pray and ponder over what he suggested.

On 4 September I met the Senior Bishop at the Bishop's house, as wanted by him through the Uzhavoor vicar. I met him with a hope that he would be ready at least for a friendly and open talk. But instead he had a monologue consisting of the usual clichés of the stuff like 'save your soul', spirituality and insistence on 'Faith' and 'child-like obedience'. He only added insult to injury suggesting 'You are wrong in having owned a new house and property, because you come from a small family after all'.

On 7 September I sent word to Mgr. Kandarappally through the Principal Rev. Dr Simon Kottoor agreeing to the suggestion 'to close the old chapter and open a new', ready to inter all the sordid experience I had to endure up to now. On 13 September I reminded Mgr. Kandarappallil of his earlier assurance to discuss the matter with the Bishop and do what he could. 'Though after a long struggle and wriggle with myself, I accepted your suggestion because of my deep respect for and faith in you. You will also understand the long suspense and indecisiveness I have been wading through. Therefore I expect to be informed without any considerable delay if Kottayam diocese needs my service as a priest. If it doesn't, then I have decisions to take for myself'. Meanwhile I had developed an acute pain on my leg which my friend and doctor of the local government dispensary diagnosed as psycho-somatic – the effect of the prolonged intense mental tension I had been facing all this while.

After nearly two months, I met Mgr. Kandarappallil on 7 November 1974. Much to my utter surprise and moral indignation he told me: 'I am sorry I am helpless in the matter.

The Bishop is not disposed to consider my suggestion favourably. He wants you to go back to Monippally, and give him a letter of apology asking forgiveness for the many offenses of yours and requesting him to consider your case sympathetically'. I replied to it: 'Monsignor, you are person number two in the Diocese, older, educated and therefore more experienced than the Bishop. If your suggestion, made in consideration of the good of the Diocese, did not carry two-pence value with the Bishop, what human dignity and consideration are we poor ordinary mortal priests to expect at the hands of such a Bishop. Above all, if he thinks I have committed many wrongs and offenses, being my Bishop he has the power and the duty to summon me, frame a chargesheet against me and to proceed with the disciplinary action. That being the case, should I volunteer and take the initiative to equip him with the deadly weapon of an advance letter of apology for what crime I am yet unaware of'. 'I am sorry, Father', Mgr. Kandarappallil added: 'I am helpless in the matter anymore'. And I replied: 'Thank you sincerely for all the troubles and worries you took upon on account of my wellbeing. Please don't worry any more over me. I am taking my own decision, relying on Providential arrangements for my future life'. With that I clipped my umbilical cord with my 'Holy Mother the Catholic Church'. I felt the 'dazzling dawn' not far off.

## A Farewell Request to Bishop Kunnacherry

Uzhavoor,
21- 11-1974.

To Bishop Kuriakose Kunnacherry
Your Lordship,

Rev. Sr. Florencia F.M.M. wrote to me on 5-11-1974 quoting the following from your letter which you had sent her concerning me: 'Even though he has deserted the priestly ministry given to him, and draws the full salary from the college, and says without permission Mass at his residence, *we have not taken any action against him.* How can a Bishop be more tolerant than this? I will be only happy to rehabilitate him if he feels sorry for his actions and is ready to live according to the laws of the church'.

Strange indeed that I had to learn it from Sr. Florencia's letter that you Bishops had been very kind, merciful and tolerant towards me, and if it is so, you have my thanks. But then, my uncle and my cousin, Sr. Christine R.J.M. informed me that when they called on you at Puthuvely on Sunday the tenth of this month you told them that you have kept me in 'punishment' for my 'offences'! If my uncle and my cousin did not tell me a lie, I fail to understand how you could make such contradictory statements without violence to conscience, if you have that thing. I regret to have to say that persons of your position should make statements according to the convenience of the moment without respecting the demands of Truthfulness. You further seem to have told them that in one of my letters, supposed to be written years ago, I have acknowledged my 'serious offenses' and tendered my 'apology' for the same [Yes, a letter of apology from me, requesting pardon for my many offenses and crimes was an object of your long standing dream, as I heard it from Mgr. Kandarappallil on 7 November 1974]. I remember to have come across the same story in the curia letter from the Chancellor dated 29-3-1974 to which I have answered denying the truthfulness of the story. You might have known that both the curia letter and my reply to it were published in the May issue of Vaidika Mitram (1974). I am surprised to note that you have ventured to repeat the story to credulous pious souls without any one responsible ever having thought of accepting my demand to prove it by producing the letter which is supposed to contain my acknowledgment of 'offenses' and apologies for the same.

Taking into consideration your position and authority, and the uncritical obedience to and blind faith of the faithful in their Bishops, I should think that your irreconcilable statements can only create confusion and mental disturbance to the simple credulous people.

I pray you, cease from such contradictory statements which

only serve to mislead and misinform the simple faithful and my innocent relatives who have been taught only to believe and obey their bishop'.

Sd/-
Fr A. Vellamthadathil.

**Anxiety of the Priest Fraternity Allayed**

Many of the priests, particularly the senior priest-fraternity expressed their anxiety over what they thought I was going to discard my priestly status. I tried to allay their anxious concern. In my reply dated 30 January1975 to Fr M. Cherucherril's letter dated 18 January I recalled how on very many occasions I stood by and obeyed the counsels and guidance of the priest-fraternity of the Kottayam Diocese, given individually and jointly on many critical moments when I was on the verge of taking decisive decisions of far reaching consequences, including even the last attempt of good Mgr. Kandarappallil to save my priestly ministry in the Diocese which ended a fiasco. Then I added: 'If the personality of one of the V.G.'s rank merits no recognition in the Catholic structure, you can understand what would be the fate of persons like poor me. I cannot understand the use of any priestly ministry in a structure where personal values....have no recognition. Hence after the failure of Mgr. Kandarapallil's effort to make use of my priestly life and ministry, I took a definitive decision not to waste my life and ministry under a monolithic administrative machinery that tries to roll over and crush every personal value within its vaults.

'Whether you believe it or not, I sincerely own that I have not regretted the Christian priestly grace that God has deigned to grant me and I hope I shall never have to regret for it. And once a priest, I cannot but be a priest forever. I have decided to get married with the hope and earnest prayer that after God, a family would be my next protection in this my unequal struggle with the mighty machinery and power of the Church authority....'

# 16

# 1968–1975: A Period of Ideological Fermentation

The period between 1968 and 1975 was one of hot bubbling fermentation of ideas for me. During this period, the ideas of religion and morality that I was brought up and drilled in from my infancy by din of daily by-hearted prayers, ritual practices and Sunday catechism classes underwent a drastic transformation. My exposure to the influence of my professors and to the secular University courses I took to and to the student community of young men and ladies largely worked as the fermenting agent or catalyst. The traditional spirituality in which I was drilled and conditioned through my upbringing and the seminary formation was the other-worldly spirituality of renunciation of 'the world, the devil and the body' as the three-tier enemy in the path of 'saving one's soul for life in the next world'. The one spiritual weapon against this three-faced enemy as prescribed by the 'divine-right' infallible magisterium of the 'Holy Roman Catholic Church' was the faithful observance of the church prescribed rituals and asceticism or the life of mortification of desires. This infernal thrust on the practice of asceticism to curb desires and defeat the 'enemies of the soul' used to generate in me a mischievous but prima facie reasonable doubt: if mortification of desires is virtue and the path of salvation of the soul, the greatest virtue and sure path to heaven is suicide because it is the voluntary mortification of the greatest desire of all: the desire to live. Where there is no desire, there is no life because life is nothing but desire.

However the Holy Roman Catholic Church infallibly teaches that asceticism and mortification of desires is the path to salvation or victory over the triple enemy of the soul. The Christian tradition is full of stories of monasteries and nunneries with weird ascetical practices, sprouting up like mushrooms. They vied one with the other in the practice of severe mortification of natural human desires by privations of life's basic needs and comforts and even inflicting severe bodily tortures on self to suppress the instincts of life's desires, particularly the bodily desires for food and sex, the most condemned of these desires being the sexual desire.

It was only later that I came to realize that it was a distorted or perverted adaptation of the Indian concept of the 'Absolute Renunciation of the Individual' as the path to the realization of Moksha or to the realization of the real self as identified with the Universal Disinterested Witness that ultimately man is. But the Catholic Churchian path of asceticism aimed at the transportation of individual souls into the heaven above there somewhere. The self-arrogated 'infallible Magisterium' took upon itself the service of the only one and exclusive heavenward escalator. From my life-experience of nearly thirty five years of making confessions and nearly twelve years of hearing confessions, I came to learn that centuries of church-prescribed religious practices could only develop a two-dimensional sense of sin consisting of failures in the church-prescribed rituals and indulgence in sexual urges even if it be in any minute form. Recall the traditional catholic principles of moral theology defining the three essential constituents of any mortal sin, namely, gravity of matter, full awareness and freedom. But in matters regarding sex, there is no gravity of matter: 'in rebus de sexto, nulla datur parvitas materiae'. [Highlighted in Chapter II above]. I have heard of Spiritual Fathers counseling their spiritual children to go to the bath with two towels lest they may commit the sin of even looking at or seeing their own corporal areas of sex! I have heard penitents confessing sins of failures in the observance of ritual practices and of the 'impure sins' of 'boys looking at girls and girls looking at boys'. But I have hardly heard any penitent confessing failures in his/her civic and social responsibilities or violation of Natural Justice.

The Christian life came to be described as a perpetual struggle or striving through the narrow thorny paths at the end of which one reaps the fruits of the victory over this struggle against the triple enemy of the soul in a life of bliss in heaven after death. The basic content of the message of the traditional Christian spiritual life seemed to consist in renouncing the mortal life here on earth to gain the immortal life there in heaven after death.

Once on invitation from the Uzhavoor parish priest I joined the catechism teachers' picnic to Kurishu Mala on 24 April 1972. The impression I got from the ashram life there only confirmed what I had thought of ascetic monastic life and goaded me to write the article: 'Is God to be sought in forests and dens?', published in Vaidika Mitram, June 1972. It was this article that had provoked my former Rector and later Spiritual Father, Fr Ancot to gently scold me of my 'forgetfulness of theology learned in Papal Athenaeum'.

I felt theirs was an apostolate among the cows, these being the only creatures well-cared for. I was shocked by the unhealthy sight of meals taken in buckets to the labourers. I thought what the buckets contained was food for pigs. It was a God-forsaken hilly place, 'unpolluted' by the 'worldly' influences or conveniences of man's scientific and cultural advancements, as if the God of the Christian monks seemed to be pleased only with primitivism in dress, food etc. But for the din of a few ploughing machines and lawn-mowers the atmosphere was gloomy as though with the dooms day silence. The inmates apparently absorbed in 'holy contemplation of God', had hardly any social life: no talk, no jokes, no peels of laughter, nor warmth of human friendship and touch. Not a trace of any sprightly cheerfulness could be seen reflected on their faces. The only graceful objects I could see were some beautiful calves trotting about, a few flowers and the few young girls, students of Alphonsa College Pala who had come on a similar picnic....In the place of healthy and sprightly human communications, the inmates appeared to be in communion with 'an awe-inspiring God, confined in the recesses of the weird buildings, in a tabernacle within a granite wall, black with smoke and sticky with oil oozing out from holes on the wall used as pits to burn oil lamps. There is not the poetic sound of children playing about, no giggling girls, no women nursing their babes or serving meals to or chatting with their husbands, parents and relatives, no din of boisterous laughter of young boys playing on the ground, no men around tables playing at cards, no modern, 'profane' worldly melodies or duets except the tinkling of the metal disks ornamented with the images of cherubs and seraphs with innumerable small bells dangling from the edges of the discs. The inmates shake the discs while chanting the ceaseless hymn of the angelic choir 'Holy, Holy, Holy Lord, God of hosts ....' May be due to my own 'perverted view' this holy, silent, monastic loneliness reminded me of a song in the movie 'Thommante Makkal' describing a family where the brothers, once brotherly, friendly and sprightly, were now not even talking to each other: 'The haunted home. The house without laughter, the nest without chirping of the chicks, the house haunted by Satan'

There was no smell of any flowers tickling and exciting sensations of sweetness. Instead there was mortifying smell of cow-dung coming from the cow shed. There was a chapel or shrine built on the top of a steep, rocky hill challenging the adventurousness of many pilgrim souls in our picnic party. It was about 11.30 a.m. and the sun was getting from warm to hot, 'The shrine is an ideal spot of loneliness for priests to make retreat and find God. Nobody to disturb. Only a few monkeys are there,' one of the inmates explained. The mischief-mongering perversion in me remarked: 'In the company of the monkeys they can praise the Lord' and there was a suppressed laughter. Some pious nuns and teachers invited me to venture to the hill-top to visit the shrine and adore the God living in that loneliness, forsaken and neglected by humans who are busy with the 'worldly' affairs. 'What, if by the time we reach there God decides to go to another higher hill-top?, I said rather mischievously. 'I would rather eat my lunch here and thank God rather than venture the trek up the hill there'!

I began to examine the church-prescribed life of suffering and renunciation or the other-worldly spirituality and treading the narrow thorny path to heaven in the light of Jesus' words: 'I have come that you may have life and have it more abundantly'. Again; 'I came to preach the Kingdom of God here on Earth'. I began to suspect that the traditional other worldly ascetic spirituality of self renunciation is a deviation from the path to the Kingdom of God and life in its abundance here on earth as preached by Jesus. Again Jesus severely criticized the Pharisees saying: 'John the Baptist led a life of ascetic renunciation and you accuse him of having been possessed by the devil. The Son of man came as friends of sinners and the publicans, eating and drinking with them and you call him a glutton and drunkard'.[Mathew, 11, 18 & 19] Besides, I also suspected a kind of utter hypocrisy in the preachers of this life of universal renunciation and asceticism teaching the faithful to look up to heaven for eternal bliss after death, thereby depriving them of the abundance of God-given life here on earth, while those who show them this path of renunciation live an abundantly luxurious life of bliss rolling on wealth and looking right down on very concrete, pleasure-giving earthly realities. I could not reconcile myself with a God who is proclaimed as Goodness and Mercy and Love, yet tantalizing His poor ordinary human creatures with intense desire of life in this abundantly rich and beautiful world which He has created for man and takes a kind of sadistic pleasure by punishing with eternal hell these poor creatures who try to satisfy their God-given hunger by taking in the God-given tasty food, to fulfill their sense of beauty by enjoying the beauty God has lavishly provided all around them, to sweeten the faculty of hearing by enjoying the heavenly music which fills the whole Nature.

Above all is the supremely divine design of the fulfillment of man in woman and of woman in man by mutually sharing the love and liking for each other through sex. The human fulfillment through sex when it is a sharing of mutual love and liking becomes the supreme divine gift to man whom 'He created male and female'. Any desire can become selfish greed and thereby sinful. The movie, 'The Ten Commandments' depicted a scene in which the young Pharaoh of Egypt gets infatuated with the young lady who is in love with Moses. The mighty Pharaoh, who thinks whatever he lusts after is his, tells the young lady: 'I love you'. The lady replies: 'I don't love you'. Back comes the King's insistent demand: 'I like you'. And the lady replies: 'I don't like you'! Pat comes the over-powering view of the mighty King: 'Whether you like it or not I like it'! This is not the mutual sharing of mutual love and liking as God intended it, but lust and violation of the border line of Justice and therefore sinful.

On the other hand, ordinary people of genuine original innocence, not distorted by any conditioning and drilling in the other-worldly spirituality of regarding the body on par with the devil, do fall in love with genuine love. The one and important theme of almost all immortal works of Art and Literature, from Homer's *Iliad* up to modern pieces of art is Love. And the characters who stand in the way of and obstruct the flow of genuine love to its natural fulfillment, for example, characters like Iago have always been looked upon as 'villains'.

Life is the sum total of all the desires. It is fulfilled when all the God-given desires are fulfilled as God has ruled it through Natural Laws. [Ethics or Moral Philosophy teaches: 'Nature is the Norm of Morality'] The fulfilled man, both male and female, then turns to his Creator and says: 'Thank You, Lord, for this my happy life'. Is not this the best form of prayer, and praise and offering to God that pleases Him? Is it not the best act of thanksgiving, the best act of adoration: namely, the realization that creation was the act of the Infinite Bliss to share this bliss with other beings? This realization is summarily described within the Philosophical principle: '*Bonum est diffusivum sui ipsius*: Goodness is self-diffusive'. Is not 'the abundance of life' that Jesus came to preach this fulfillment of life through the fulfillment of all the desires, as life itself is the sum total of all desires? Yet the 'Churchianity' teaches that life is a struggle against all desires. It is mortification of desires here on Earth for fulfillment and bliss high up there in heaven after death!

I remember what my young cousin, a teacher in a Catholic management school, once told me what she had heard of her 'holy' parish priest, holy because 'he leads a very ascetic life of mortification and privation. He spends most of his time for prayer more often than not with extended hands and kneeling on rough ground. He fasts quite often and takes his scanty rest on a thin mat spread on the floor, though he has a beautiful soft bed with soft pillows and cozy, feather- soft sheets'! I told her in reply: 'Do you want to say that your God in heaven takes a sadistic pleasure in seeing the poor emaciated priest going on fast, torturing his body with self-inflicted pain and sleeping on the hard floor and feels complacent to reward him with a seat in heaven? Or am I to believe in a God who, seeing his priest eating well, getting a sound sleep in his cozy, soft, comfortable bed, gets jealous of him and threatens him with the denial of a heaven after death because he eats well and sleeps comfortably? No wonder we have ever so many angry atheists who refuse to believe in such a sadistic and jealous God. On the other hand, what would be the level of your parish priest's holiness, if after a satisfactory meal and night of sound sleep with pleasant dreams wakes up in the morning to sit on his bed, stretching himself to quicken his blood circulation and then with a bowed head and folded hands he prays: 'Thank You, Lord, for the last night's cozy, comfortable sleep and for the light of this dawn. Help me to spend your gift of this new day according to your holy will'?

The only limit for this fulfillment of man's life and therefore the forbidden border of the hell of sin is the limit imposed by the consideration of man's social nature and the consequent obligation that follow the fact that each man is a member of the human community having equal rights of fulfillment. Hence the sense of justice is the rock-foundation of the structure of Christian spirituality, the foundation of the Kingdom of God, upon which love builds its structure up and up to God the Infinite Love. Violation of this boundary of justice leads to the world of selfishness which is the hell of sin and suffering. The ideal of Jesus' message of life demands the shunning of the 'I-attitude' and the taking up of the all-inclusive 'we-attitude'.

Christian life has therefore two dimensions of love to maintain: the vertical dimension of the love of God, Who is Truth, Justice, Love, Grace, Mercy and Goodness. The other is the horizontal dimension of the love of one's neighbour as oneself. The denial of the I-attitude and taking up these two dimensions of love which completes the cross define the symbol of Jesus' discipleship, namely, 'Deny yourself, take up the cross and follow me'. This cross of the two relationships of love is different from the cross of suffering which the selfish Chief Priests and Pharisees and we the selfish ones imposed on the Son of man and impose on the human community. The cross of the symbol of Jesus' discipleship is the means of redemption from and panacea for all the sufferings of man. It is the sum total of the whole core of Jesus' message: 'Love God your Lord [Truth, Justice, Love] with all your heart and with all your soul. This is the first and the greatest of all commandments. The second is as important as the first: Love your neighbour as yourself. In these two commandments are included all the Laws and Prophets'.(Mt. 22, 37-40) But unfortunately our society has everything else except these two and consequently is drained of moral and ethical values, though the society and the 'Faithful' are drowned in and smothered with Laws and Prophets, rituals, Canon Laws, commandments of the church etc.

Dr S.K. Desai, one of my professors in the Karnatak University, once said: 'We people of India distinguishing ourselves as orientals, take pride in the spirituality of asceticism and faithful observance of religious rituals, and condemn the westerners as materialistic atheists. But if one wants to meet gentlemen, one must go to the West'. This reminded me of Henry Cardinal Newman's illustrious definition of a 'Gentleman': 'A gentleman is one who never offends another man'. Saintliness is gentlemanliness and vice versa. I have closely watched ever so many icons or statues of 'saints', all of them in a mood and facial expression of deep contemplation, gloomy asceticism, prayerfulness with hands extended or looking upward to heaven up above there somewhere. But I have never seen a 'saint' with a smiling face, expressing contentment with the happy and abundant life here on earth thanking God for this life.

My suspicion got clinched that the Churchianity we profess is deviant from the message of Jesus' 'abundant life in the kingdom of God here on Earth'. It began to rule and guide my intellectual life and my daily practical life till finally I found a thorough confirmation of my suspicion when I came across the words of the great German theologian Holger Kersten years later in my mid-sixties: 'Jesus' message has been distorted beyond recognition'.

These reflections of mine goaded me to write articles like 'Is God Jealous, Religion Sadistic?', 'Is God to be Sought in Forests and Dens?', 'Time for Christianity to look Forward' (not upward to empty space, not downward to the earth below one's feet, but forward to the horizon which is symbolic of the meeting of heaven and earth, of the spiritual and the worldly), 'Priestly Ministry in Modern Times', 'The Need of Reconsidering the Church's stand on Birth Control', all of which were published through the pages of *Vaidika Mitram* (The friend of Priests) run by Fr Christie Daniel. The messages I was invited to give in churches on their titular and other important festivals all over the diocese were studded with these ideas and were looked upon by most audiences as most welcome modern ideas, by some with suspicion as unorthodox. Almost all the youthful active priests welcomed them with euphoria. My sermon at Paingulam Cherukara Church, for example, delivered on 21 November 1970 was spirited enough to provoke a lively discussion among the priests like Fr S. Uralil, Cyriac Kooplikat, Thomas Valloppally who were invited for the festival. Fr Kooplikat observed: 'The theme of your sermon was the same as in your article: 'Is God jealous, Religion sadistic?' We shared the following conviction: 'So far we have been preaching too ascetic a morality that seems to be an injustice towards the faithful in this that it deprives them of the God-given opportunities of happiness already here on earth....We must be extremely careful and cautious and think many times over before we impose a law on them as God's will. Individual life experiences should be regarded as of primary importance and their happiness even here on earth as the will of God should be the chief concern of religion'.

## A Re-consideration of Sex as God's Gift

The traditional morality on sex, considered as a curse and unavoidable evil, had served to impose on my conscience an intolerable burden of guilt, as every minute indulgence in the area of sex, even a touch or a look was considered as mortal 'impure' sins. (It would seem to give the impression that cheating or cutting the throat of another would be a 'pure' sin.) The presence and any contact with girls, especially the beautiful ones, were supposed to be considered highly dangerous zones and therefore to be shunned as dangerous pests. But the dawn of my perception of God's creation of man as 'male' half and 'female' better half and of God's divinely designed plan of human fulfillment of man in woman and of woman in man through the union of these two halves, through the mutual sharing of love and liking through sex as the supreme divine gift to human happiness, brought down the unnecessarily and intolerably borne burden of the sense of guilt considerably. I felt relieved and free in considering the basic facts regarding sex. The company of and contacts with girls, even very beautiful ones, were no more looked upon as a source of curse and guilt burden, but as an opportunity to heartily thank God for endowing me with such a sense of beauty and for creating such exquisite beauty to fulfill this sense of beauty. Among my friends and visitors were also young beautiful nuns and young and exquisitely beautiful girls. They were welcome to visit me without any fear or inhibition. I remember the visits of Alice, leaning on the right arm of my armchair with her left hand holding the left arm of the chair and singing sweetly like a skylark. The fond angelic little Celine trotted in to talk about her world of innocence and trotted out like a dear pet lamb and I prayed: 'Lord, I thank you for the rich love and affection she bears me'. Alice once wrote to me that she would come with her beloved B., hoping for an opportunity to enjoy the affectionate company of each other without any fear of watchful eyes and without inhibition. 'Oh, yes, why not?' was my reply. God unites them because they were in fond love towards each other. And a few days later she came. She was all affectionate to me as I was to her. She felt confident that I understood her and was interested in her real peace and happiness. Soon enough B. also arrived. I tried to make him aware of the sanctity and sublimity of love as God has designed it. I then left them to their own convenience and went to engage my class, making it possible for them to have some time to share their intimacy and affection. I assured them that God will smile over them and bless them if only they understood passionate intimate love as He has designed it for the humans.

Sr. Sy. wanted to leave convent life for good and to go to Madras on 8 June 1971. Her mind was an ocean of anxiety, indecision and what not. She wanted to leave without informing her Superiors for fear of being harassed to any extent. I did not want to disturb her plans, but advised her to give information through a letter as soon after her leaving as possible. I assured her: 'Dear my sister, I'll be at the railway station to wave you off to Madras. Be assured of my brotherly and affectionate heart that will weep with you weeping and laugh with you laughing. Share with me through letters your joys and sorrows the future may have in store for you. The dear Lord protect you'. We both wept together mixing our tears in an affectionate hug. Thank God, she was able to leave as planned, in spite of the huge hurdle and terrible storm stirred by her superiors and the Bishop as she had expected.

On 13 May 1971 I attended the vestition ceremony of some aspirants to sisterhood at S.H. Mount Generalate. The sight of the professing sisters prostrate on the ground, covered with a black sheet with the tinkling of the bells tolling the knell and the officiating Bishop pronouncing to them: 'You are dead to the world and to you in order to live to God' made me much disturbed and morally indignant. With a heavy heart I reflected whether this kind of self-immolation was necessary or even useful to live for God. Was it not but a rotten vestige of an obsolete, medieval, desert–oriented other-worldly spirituality, a kind of subtle but perhaps bona fide spiritual injustice done to these beautiful young daughters of God, created to be happy even here on earth.

On 14 July1971 during the catechism seminar for priests held at S.H. Mount, one layman speaker, Mr N.J. Thomas, expected 'good example of Christian life from the priests'. 'Well,' I responded, 'all that the priest is expected to do is to keep away from any contact with women, to say Mass, administer sacraments and sacramentals and preach. Which of these can be an example of Christian life to the laymen....Priests must be ordained from all walks of life and show good example of Christian life as businessmen, politicians, doctors, lawyers, parents, teachers etc. Priesthood should not be a means of livelihood. It should be the additional divine grace added to human life in all its spheres....'

The Coadjutor Excellency did not seem very pleased at my remarks, especially after other priests such as Fr Thomas Valloppally and Cyriac Kooplikat elaborated on the point, much to the consternation of the Bishop. On 15 May 1972 I attended the nuptial ceremony of my colleague Mr T.M. James with Leelamma. In my message delivered on the occasion I said: 'When we take into consideration the importance of marriage and family in the present context of the unchristian and disturbed social and political life, marriage and family life is perhaps the greatest form of missionary activity'. The Coadjutor Excellency thought it his canonical duty to make furtive and unfavourable comment on my statement.

On the morning of August 2, 1971, I had a visit from Leelamma, a very affectionate girl capable of sincere love. The same day, I received a letter from Sr. A.si and another from my dear MAJ, both overflowing with tender affection and intimacy. Once again I thanked God for such overflowing tenderness and affection that added bliss to my life. Again, before long, a visit from MAJ and CMN on 11 September proved them capable of being more affectionate in their deeds than in their letter announcing their visit. I thanked Almighty God for such sweet ones sharing affection and love. I felt convinced that sharing of love, frank communion and uninhibited intimacy could give a direct experience of divine grace in life.

On September 30, 1971 during the diocesan clergy retreat at Vadavathoor Seminary, the preacher Bishop Joseph Rajappa almost broke down sobbing while referring to the critics of the church. 'The church deserved to be loved and not criticized' he said. Chiefly the preacher had in mind the critics of the Church's 'mandatory celibacy, the greatest and delicate gift of God, which we carry in weak earthen pots. Lest we should lose this gift, we should keep away from ladies who are a threat to our chastity'. Ladies created as a threat to men? Blasphemy, I mused. The Bishop further went on to say that celibate clergy was a glory of the Church because 'even the enemies admire this glory of the Church'. Once again, I mused, is it not a tragedy indeed that these probably bona fide people see nothing in the church to love and admire except the mandatory celibacy, the so called 'gift of celibacy', which they are presumed to admire, but they would not love, much less accept as an ideal for imitation. Later I heard a small group of 'orthodox' priests justifying celibacy because, 'Sex is an immensely great urge and the sacrifice of this urge is a worthy sacrifice to please God'.

I interacted with them: 'Our urge to live is much stronger than sex urge and logically therefore an act of voluntary suicide would be the greatest sacrifice we can offer to please God. And every voluntary, self-imposed mortification, by its verbal meaning, belongs to the same species of suicide, as life is the sum total of all desires. Is God placated by our suicide? The presentation of a God who is pleased according to the measure and level of the voluntary mortification is the surest short-cut to irreligion and the destruction of faith in God, a loving father'. I saw the pious orthodox group winking and blinking and mumbling: 'Do you mean to say, Father, that our theology and moral codes should be written out afresh and our venerable traditions given up?' 'Why not, if reason demands it?' I said.

It was in October 1972. My cousin and niece, both named Annamma, wanted me to give them tuition in English. The only convenient place available was a room in the Girls' Hostel, Shanti Bhavan, as they felt embarrassed to come to the boys' hostel. Within a few days news came that the sisters including Sr. Goretti, head of the Department of English, felt terrified at the thought of my giving tuition to two girls in a private room and advised me in Fr Principal's presence not to do so, because

'What will be the reaction of the people around us, Father?' And as if by way of reflex Fr Principal responded: 'No tuition as the scheme of direct payment has come into force'! I controlled myself from blasting out at them. 'What reasoned-out valid argument do you have against my giving tuition to them or are you ruled and guided by the gossip of the rabble? If I am denied the most ordinary family relationship and the most natural and human relations under the myth and idol of celibacy, I will not hesitate to cast it away and decide to have a family,' I said.

Later I told the Warden of the Girls' hostel, Sr, James: 'I suppose you will have no objection of the two girls going for tuition to Mr Sunny Thomas, a lecturer having a wife, while the society cannot trust a priest with his own close relatives, probably because unmarried men in cassock are regarded as brutes and not men'. Sr. James felt the poke and apologetically said: 'Personally I have no reason to object to your giving tuition to those girls'.

On 1 January1973 on my way back from Kottayam, I paid a visit to some of the aspirants to Caritas Secular Institute, getting ready for 'religious' profession. From my interaction with them on the course offered to them during the Novitiate I felt they were being drilled in routine course of sheer formalities as canonical legalities to get them bonded by 'vows' to run the Caritas Hospital at practically no expense but the grub of these 'vow-bound' brides of the Lord in heaven! None of them was being given a personal message or programme of life suitable to their temperamental dispositions whereby they could probably have a genuine sense of fulfillment and achievement. My sadness at this was intensified when one of them remarked, half jocularly and half ironically: 'All these are ultimately on account of the six inch stomach we have, Father. We came here because we had no other go'. The bitter irony of the discontentment of these supposed dedicated spouses of the Lord 'specially called by God for His service' came out in all nakedness. The girls were all very young, healthy, beautiful and bursting and bubbling with energy, life. And the little conversation left me clinched in my critical attitude towards the way in which precious human and God-given opportunities are marketed and utilized in the name of 'religious life'.

### An Unexpected Precious Visit

I had a very surprising but unforgettable visit from Mercy on 11 March 1973. I felt much flattered by the absolute trust and overwhelming affection she showed in boldly visiting me all alone – a sweet graceful beauty. I found her rather disturbed and tense. To my natural and usual greeting enquiry: 'Are you happy, Mercy?' she burst into sobbing, leaning on my chest saying: 'Father, you are the first to ask me about my happiness. There are many to scold and goad me on'. In fact she came to unburden her exhausted mind. During the long talk that followed she revealed to me the terrible ordeal of mental agony and tension taking her almost on the verge of a breakdown, all on account of some home troubles. I remembered how mental pressure similar to hers took me to an actual breakdown and insomnia while in the seminary. My heart began to beat with hers in harmony. My emotions began to flow with hers. I explained to her my own terrible ordeal of similar nervous crisis due to reason analogous to hers: due to lack of cordial love and cooperation among my near and dear ones. Besides, being exquisitely beautiful and highly intelligent, Mercy had a delicately sensitive soul. She immediately recognized a similar delicately sensitive soul in me. It pained me acutely to know that such a dear sensitive soul had to undergo crushing tortures of even physical violence from her own very dear and near ones who should have been a source of solace and comfort to her. I tried to understand her with the sympathy and understanding that my own experiences made it possible for me to have. I longed to comfort her and wipe her tears trickling down her rosy cheeks from her pretty eyes. I thought that perhaps no other two hearts could understand each other more intimately and with greater sympathy than ours. And I suggested it to her boldly that I would be only glad and go to any degree of heroic daring to give her affection and every sense of security and protection that my poor human heart and soul and life is capable of. I assured her that she could with complete freedom and confidence and intimacy ask of me anything if that can in any way add to her sense of security, peace and happiness. I thanked the dear God to see Mercy leave me for home after a warm tight hug with a greater peace and better nerves than those she had when she came.

As wanted by Mercy, I met her at her residence on 30 March. We had a very long and intimate talk during which we opened our hearts to each other more closely. Before I left she promised to meet me at Uzhavoor. And she made her second visit to me on 8 April. After long hours of chat and exchange of affection in an absolute mutual trust and confidence, she left at 2.30 without taking lunch, because 'I have promised my mother that I will dine today only after coming back home'. Since Mercy did not take lunch, I too refused to go for my lunch, leaving her in my room hungry.

On 11 April, I received a long letter from my beloved Mercy, giving me an indication that she was ready to share with me her life with all its joys and sorrows in answer to my earlier assurance that I would go to any degree of heroic daring if her peace and happiness would require it. The letter led me to the chapel where I prayed over it for a long time. I felt sure that it was the all holy divine Providence that had been bringing us closer for a definite purpose.

Mercy visited me a third time on 16 April. We talked for hours. That day she took lunch with me. In the evening before she left she leaned on my chest and told me she had chosen to share with me her life with all its sorrows and joys. I hugged her close to my heart with all the warmth and affection my heart was capable of. Tears of joy that rolled down from my eyes got mixed with those from her eyes and flowed down her sweet soft cheeks. Then we consecrated our mutual affection at the feet of Jesus crucified, kissed the crucifix together calling Jesus to witness that we loved each other and asked to bless our love. I then saw Mercy leaving for home with a smiling face, and, as she assured me, with a peaceful heart. Later, on 6 May I came to know directly from Mercy's brother that he was displeased with her for her visits to me and with me for admitting her without his permission. His main grievance was that he was afraid of the social set up and the gossip of the rabble. I told him back that by principle I would be absolutely and contemptuously indifferent to the often worthless and always adverse reactions of the rabble when I have to care for the good of individuals like Mercy. I tried to allay his anxiety by assuring him that bye and bye he would be convinced that he had nothing to be anxious about Mercy's visits to me.

The persistent and long silence on the part of Mercy that followed worried me much. And I visited her at home once again on 29 May in order to relieve me of the heavy suspense as to the reasons of her silence. Much to my surprise and sorrow Mercy hesitatingly gave me to understand that she may not continue to have contact with me 'If my brother J. does not like it'. On further discussion I was given to understand that she was discouraged by one I knew very malicious. It took a few silent minutes for me to regain my peace of mind. Then I told her that just as I had offered 'to go to any degree of heroic daring' if that could give her happiness, peace, security and affection, so also her decision to stop contact with me would find myself equally contented as long as that would give her the same peace and sense of security as I had desired for her. Before I left her, she promised she would write to me once more in a week's time. And she kept her promise. She sent her letter through her confidant, one Mr Abraham, with whom I had a long open and intimate exchange. When he left I returned through him all the letters Mercy had sent to me, as she had requested in her latest letter. Years later I came to know with a heavier heart that fate was rather very cruel on her and the future ahead of her had a very hard and miserable experience in store for her in which she continues even now, unless I am happily mistaken in this my last observation.

# 17

# Decision to Get Married

After cutting the umbilical cord with my 'mother Catholic Church' of Kottayam diocese, my next concern was to look for a visible source of protection next to God. I knew that the hostility of a powerful Christian community and a Catholic college management could resort to any means to get rid of me from the service of the college too. During the period of disturbance consequent upon the dispute over the direct payment and the fixation of voluntary contribution, some of the senior priests of the diocese had forewarned us the junior teaching priests against possible maligning and traps through bribed and indoctrinated young ladies, sent to our residences to get us entangled in allegations for disciplinary proceedings particularly in a community of gullible, blind followers of religious leadership. The four-page long charge sheet dated 23 September 1974 and supplemented by an addenda charge sheet of even date was a clear indication foreboding lightning strokes of vindictiveness from this catholic churchian college management. Besides, those were days when the University Appellate Tribunal was not operative, having been struck down by the Apex Court on plea of the minority communities that it stood in the way of their arbitrary demands. One of the senior practicing lawyers of the High Court, decorated with knighthood and the title of Chevalier, was reported to have advised the Bishop-Manager: 'The proper opportunity has arrived. The management has only to frame a chargesheet on any persona ingrata, conduct a domestic enquiry, get a report from the paid enquiry Officer sustaining the charges and dismiss him. The decision will be final in the absence of any Appellate Tribunal'. I think I obliged the Management with the explanation that the charge sheet deserved. But I expected the wounded viper to miss no chance to dig its venomous fangs into the very heart of its victim. So I decided upon having a family as my visible source of protection next to God.

I could think of one reliable and competent person with whom I could discuss and weigh the pros and cons of my decision to get married – Fr Christie Daniel of Quilon Latin diocese, Manager and Editor of *Vaidika Mitram.* He has known me from close quarters through my articles published in the columns of V.M. I rushed to Quilon and revealed to him my decision to get married. 'Get married and waste the God-given opportunity to fight for ideals?' Fr Christie shouted at me. 'If you throw out the priestly title you wear, who will care for your ideas and read your energy-packed articles?' I had expected this very reaction to my decision from him. 'Yes, Father Christie, I intend to get married, and I am more strongly determined to continue as priest and never to give it up'. 'What? You intend to get married and continue to say Mass and function as priest?' Fr Christie was stunned and completely surprised. 'Are you kidding, man?' 'No, Father', I said, 'I am quite serious'. Fr Christie got up from his chair, took my hand in a violent shake and hugged me and said: 'Then I'm with you'. Very soon we came to the business and its details. 'We will seek out a girl through matrimonial advertisement,' he said and drafted the advertisement himself: 'Wanted: an educated Bible-loving Bride for a college lecturer'. I rushed back, gave the advertisement to Manorama office, Kottayam, and which other papers, I don't remember.

Within a week's time I received a large number of responses. I rushed to Quilon with them. Of these Fr Christie chose eight responses for preliminary enquiries, giving first priority to the response of Rev. K.C. Samuel, vicar, C.S.I Church, Kunnamkulam. He being a priest would understand us better, we thought. Soon enough we in our catholic priestly cassock rushed to Kunnamkulam and met Rev. K.C. Samuel. He had responded to the matrimonial for his daughter Annammal, pet-named Ammal, with master's degree in Economics, and then teaching in a temporary vacancy in Vimala College, Trichur.

After the usual preliminaries and a little more of details, Rev. Samuel said with considerable hesitation: 'It may be embarrassing but, to be honest, how can I proceed further without seeing the person concerned and having a little exchange with him?' 'Oh,' said Fr Christie. 'You don't have to take much trouble to see the person. He sits just in front of you'. Rev. Samuel, startled and surprised, took a thorough look at me in my cassock. Fr Christie soon eased the situation saying: 'It is for him that we have come for the marriage negotiations. And I know him from rather close quarters.' And then he explained the whole story of my adventurous background without any mitigation. Rev. Samuel himself seemed to have an element of adventurous daring in his blood. All his worries over uncertainties were allayed by the assurance that Fr Christie vouched on my behalf. When we found him rather inclined to look upon the proposal with favour and a spirit of adventurous challenge, we made bold to suggest to him to let us have an opportunity to see Ammal. 'Oh yes,' he said, 'but my family is in Trichur. Let us proceed.' Then he turned to me and said: 'You better change your cassock and put on a shirt instead, so that we may spare my family specially Ammal, a crude surprise, and leave it to me to acquaint my home members with your background story.' We were fully prepared for this suggestion and soon the three of us reached 117 Nehru Nagar, Trichur. We had a short interview with his family members present, including the protagonist Ammal. We then came off after giving a hint to Rev. Samuel that if Ammal and other members respond favouably, he could proceed with the matter further and we both were fully satisfied with the interview and the negotiations done so far.

I divulged the news to some of my colleagues and friends in the college and in Uzhavoor, It spread like wildfire. Many of them heartily congratulated me and promised full cooperation while some others, I felt, changed the shape of their faces when they passed me by.

Very soon Rev. K.C. Samuel sent his green signal with a photo of my would-be wife as I had requested. It was followed by a short visit from Rev. and Mrs K.C. Samuel to have a closer survey and inspection of my cottage. Again another visit from Ammal's, brother, George S. Paul, Lecturer in Physics, Christ College, Iringalakuda and his friend Sri Chandran confirmed the green signal. Soon enough a small get-together was hosted in my residence for further details and the wedding was fixed to be held in the All Saints' CSI Church Trichur on Thursday, 6 February 1975, along with the wedding of Mr George S. Paul.

**Another Unexpected Visit**

Soon I had an unexpected visit from Sri Abraham Vettimattam, one of the lay leaders of the Knanaya Catholic community and a distant relative of mine on the maternal side. 'Are you going to get married, Father?' he enquired rather anxiously. 'Yes, I am' was my rather cool reply. 'Oh, we feel having been deceived by you'. 'How is it that you feel deceived over my marriage? Why, I shall take care of my wife and you can rest assured of no worry on that account'. 'I don't mean that way, Father', he explained: 'We feel let down because you are getting married outside the community'. 'Outside the community? No, I assure you, Sir. I'll marry only within the human community'. I thought he felt the pungent irony of my words. 'But, Father', he continued after a pause of uncertainty: 'If you can give up the idea of getting married, I shall obtain from our Bishop Kunnacherry within two days his order of pastoral appointment for you to a church convenient with your work of teaching in the college'. 'Mr Abraham', I responded to him with as much self-restraint as I could muster. 'If you think the level of my self-respect is so low as to give up my word of the settled marriage negotiation with a family of honour and respect, because of your offer of Bishop Kunnacherry's pastoral appointment order, I'm sorry, you're absolutely wrong. Didn't you know earlier that I have been staying in this my cottage for the last two years saying Mass in my private prayer room, contrary to all our sacred canons and customs? Did you ever feel bothered about it and go into the causes of such a situation and take me to task for my mistakes if you detected any?' After a short pause again he continued: 'Yes, Father, I agree that it is all too late that I thought of getting involved in this affair'. After a little more friendly exchange over a cup of tea each, Mr Abraham left me.

## Membership in the Church of South India

Yes, I had cut the umbilical cord with Knanaya Catholic Church. But I still had the same Faith I was drilled in from my infancy, unaware of the possible practical complications regarding the legal formalities connected with my marriage. However, having been engaged and experienced in active pastoral ministry and therefore wise and practical minded, Rev. Samuel began to think of the completion of legal formalities of the marriage, especially of the N.O.C.: who would issue a valid and legal N.O.C. to my getting married? So he rushed to Uzhavoor with the suggestion that I should take membership in the CSI Church. 'Taking membership in the CSI Church, casting away the faith I was brought up in without knowing anything about the Faith of the C.S.I.?' I asked in utter surprise and confusion. 'If that is a condition for the marriage, I would rather give up the marriage proposal itself'. The practical minded Rev. Samuel told me: 'It's not a matter of Faith which is a matter for each one's conscience....As a member of the CSI Church you can get the required N.O.C..' I found it a counsel that deserved due consideration and promising him that I would duly consider the matter, I sent him back on assurance that I would meet him the following day. The next day I reached Kunnamkulam with Fr Christie and submitted my application for membership in the CSI Church and we returned after confirming the place and time of the wedding as fixed.

## The Wedding

February 6, 1975. With more friends and well-wishers including some of my colleagues and a couple or more students representing the rest than my immediate relatives, Fr Christie and I left for All Saints' Church, Trichur in a convoy of cars. I was closely following the text of the Order of Service during the ceremony and felt it very beautiful and meaningful. The following Sunday 9 February, I attended the CSI Communion service. It led me to a delightfully surprising realization that the order and the structure of the CSI Communion Service is almost totally identical with the Latin Catholic Communion Service that I had most comfortably followed for eight years in the Papal Seminary, Poona. With that I was totally relieved of my faith conflict I had experienced when Pappachy (that's how we his children used to address Rev. K.C Samuel) came to me with the suggestion of taking CSI membership.

On return from the church after the Sunday service, I was confronted with a pointedly sharp and logical question posed by Ammachy (that was how we her children used to address Mrs. Thankamma Samuel). 'As a Catholic priest,' she confronted me, 'you had taken the vow of celibacy and now you broke that vow by getting married. What guarantee is there for us to rest comforted that you will not break your marital vow pledged to Ammal?' 'There is no parity between the two vows, Ammachy,' I told her without any hesitation. 'The first one concerned an ideal and the second concerns a person. It is a duty to break the first one on realization that the 'ideal' is irrelevant and contrary to God's law as revealed in Nature, whereas it is a sin to break the second vow made to a person involving deep responsibilities, and Ammachy, you continue to pray God that I never commit that sin'.

In the afternoon Ammal and I accompanied by Pappachy and Ammachy came off with my relatives who had arrived to fetch us home. After a day's rest Pappachy and Ammachy left for Trichur. 'Separated from the affectionate and protective care of her parents, brothers and sister, my beloved Ammal felt a short outburst of emotion. But very soon she took to her new circumstances in all care and with full heart, much to my happiness and relief of unnecessary worry about it' [Diary Entry].

# 18

# Vindictive Spirit Unleashed

I had only waded through the narrow strait of vindictive lava. I knew that the sea was just ahead for me yet to swim across. The goodwill and friendliness shown to me by ever so many persons of understanding and my faith in the invincibility of Truth, Justice and Love helped me to muster all my courage and to plunge into the sea of turbulence ahead.

The storm started with Bishop Kunnacherry's circular No. 7 dated 11 February 1975 declaring me as excommunicated and directing the priest-fraternity and the faithful including all the nuns under his care to ostracize me from human fellowship. After reading the circular from the pulpit of Uzhavoor Church on Sunday 16 February, Fr Joseph Kalapurackal, assistant vicar of Uzhavoor, came straight to pay me and wife a visit at our residence. 'Hi, Fr Abraham,' he greeted me, 'I am coming after announcing your excommunication to the people during the service. How is your wife called?' 'Ammal', I answered. 'Hi, Ammal and Abraham,' he continued, 'My hearty congratulations and good wishes to both of you for a very happy and God-prospered family life. As for the excommunication, you need not worry about it. It is, after all, Bishop Kunnacherry's excommunication. We need not worry as long as God does not excommunicate us'. We thanked him cordially. And he left after sharing with us a cup of coffee and a piece of cake.

Another visitor was Mr Kuriako Vattukalathil, President of the College Protection Samithy formed in 1972 in the wake of the government's threat to take over all the private colleges that were unwilling to implement the Salary Direct Payment Scheme. As I was convener of the Samithy we had come in close cooperation and intimate friendship. 'Will you excuse, Father, my failure to attend your marriage ceremony at Trichur?' he started apologetically. 'I felt between the devil and the sea when on the eve of your marriage I got a message from the Bishop, sent through a special messenger, asking me to keep off from any cooperation with you and not to attend the ceremony in Trichur'. 'I fully understand you, Kuriakochettan,' I responded, 'Have no worry over it. Your absence that day of my marriage is never going to disrupt or even touch the intimacy we have built up'.

## Office Staff Nuns Out to Erase the Priesthood in me

According to Catholic dogmatic theology, as taught even from the infancy through catechism and pulpit sermons, of the seven 'sacraments', Baptism, Confirmation and Ordination, once administered, impress 'an indelible mark upon the soul of the person baptized, confirmed and ordained'. However the college office superintendent, Sr. Tarsisia, seemed to have vowed to wash my soul clean of this 'indelible mark of ordination' by scraping off the 'Rev. Fr.' from my name in the Attendance Register and replacing it with 'Mr.' I guess that she must have undertaken this Herculean task of erasing the 'indelible' mark as a service to someone above the Principal of the college, because the Principal had several times warned her against it and struck off the 'Mr.' and corrected it into 'Rev. Fr.' On 5-6-75. I found it repeated in my salary Aquittance Roll. I refused to sign it until it was corrected. My diary has the following entry for that day: 'Puny little stupidity coming from a puffed up head of a 'pure pious catholic nun' who wants to be more catholic than the Pope'. On Friday 3 October 1975, the September Salary day, I found my name in the Aquittance Roll as 'Mr Fr Abraham'. I could only impute it to the stark ignorance or hellish meanness of some of the office staff nuns, the 'holy consecrated earthly brides of the Lord, their heavenly bridegroom'! I found this 'holy meanness' stooping to a stinking level, when I noticed that the envelope containing my salary bore the words 'Abraham Vattanthadam'. At first I thought it sufficient to look down at it with the level of contempt the writer deserved. But many of my colleagues, including Sr. Goretti, head of the department of H.O.D. of English and the Vice Principal, advised me to complain against it. The issue later on taught me that I should not believe all those who smile at me as there can be 'smiling and yet smiling villains'. Even Fr Principal took an attitude of indifference on the issue more out of cowardice, I believe, than want of concern. At any rate, I showed my protest against his indifference through a letter dated 27 October: 'Now you seem to have chosen to disown me, probably because you have come to the knowledge, at least at this late hour, that I am but a small fry, a sure target of the mighty angry human organization. You have only to gain and nothing to lose by disowning a profitless friendship with me....I have not put my ultimate trust in any human power but in the divine Providence, and if God will not fail those who trust Him, I shall not be disheartened. I have fought with mighty men, all the while keeping up certain standard of nobility and respect....But some of the Rev. nuns of your office seem to be out to drag me to their stinking level of mean personal fight of no standard. You know, I cannot afford to stoop to that level'.

Without further delay I sent a complaint to the Director of Collegiate Education explaining the unequal struggle I was forced to be engaged in. I think it was just by divine providence that I met Prof Dr Ayyapa Panicker of the University Institute of English on 1 November 1975 with a copy of my complaint. Prof Panicker gave me a close friendly understanding hearing to the whole background of the college management's hostility towards me and its possible after-effects upon my family security. He advised me and very effectively helped me to make the whole Collegiate Education Department aware of this unequal struggle. He used all his immense popularity among and influence on all the top officials of the Higher Education Department. His advice and help were highly commendable and necessary as later experiences showed me.

On 7 June 1975 my wife and I paid a casual friendly visit to the new Uzhavoor church vicar, Fr Mathew Naduvileparampil. Before we left he expressed his regret for his inability to visit us at home, though he was much inclined to it because 'Bishop Kunnacherry has forbidden me to visit you and family'.

On Monday 14 July 1975 I reached the college on invitation from Mr Sunny Thomas to help the choir by playing the harmonium to sing some hymns during the Mass. Fr Principal instructed Mr Sunny Thomas not to have any choir at all if I am to be included in it. Then Fr Principal told me: 'Fr Abraham, I can safely call an atheist, a Hindu, a Protestant or a Jacobite to join the college choir. But I am afraid to enlist your cooperation because that might invite the Bishop's displeasure on me.' Pathetic catholic priestly life, I thought. What a life of slavery and fear!

On Saturday 11 October while in the CSI Central Kerala Diocesan Council, Rev. Kokan, Secretary of the Trichur Christian Eccumenical Committee, informed me of the Trichur Catholic Bishop Kundukulam's complaint in the Committee against the C.S.I. cooperation and part played in my marriage ceremony 'a dissident priest of our denomination without our consent'. Rev. Kokan reported to have replied to Bishop Kundukulam saying: 'Spirit of ecumenism does not mean that when one denomination proceeds to victimize and sack a person it judges outlawed, all the others should join hands with it'.

## Attempt to Wedge My Family Relationship into a Crack

On 20 November, 1975 my brother Joseph visited me to discuss the proposal of his daughter Annamma's marriage with Philip. Annamma had been staying with me since my marriage and even before. During our conversation he told me that his parish priest Fr Mathew Koratty took my simple-minded father to severe task for my breaking off with the Catholic escalator to heaven! I also heard from another source that the same Fr Koratty had exhorted some of his pious sheep to pray that I might fall out with my wife and our family life might be broken up and ruined. Though I felt a little indignant at it, my next impulse was to feel pity for the miserable 'faith' and crudeness of the fellow. Eventually the betrothal of Annamma and Philip took place, officiated by Fr Koratty, the vicar. I attended the function. But, once again by providence I had a foreboding that Fr Koratty would use the occasion of Annamma's marriage to wedge my relationship with my family into a crack.

In the first week of January 1976, Fr Koratty told my brother that he would refuse to solemnize Annamma's marriage if I was invited and if I came to attend the function. 'Tell your brother not to come for the function,' he told my brother. Stunned at this crude and cruel suggestion, my brother felt a moment of agony. 'How can I tell my brother not to attend the marriage of my daughter, whom he as her guardian brought up? I would request you to just drop a line asking him not to come and he will understand,' my brother whimpered amidst sobs. 'I tell him?' Fr Koratty shouted back. 'That's none of my business. I've much better things to do'. My brother left him with mind full of darkness and uncertainty. The news leaked out and reached me. I rushed to my brother. 'Have no worry, Chettan. My wife and I will be with you for all the celebrations of the wedding except for the function in the church. The attempt to wedge our family tie into a crack we will defeat'.

My words seemed to allay his agony. However, the news reached the groom's relatives. Simple, but sufficiently enlightened and God-fearing as they are, the groom's father came to me: 'We insist on your presence even during the ceremony in the church', he said. 'Why! Persons of all religions, even atheists attend catholic marriage ceremony. Why not a well-recognized priest of a Christian denomination like you?' I thank God for such simple, but reasonable and broad-minded attitude. 'Since you insist on my presence, I'll come for the ceremony,' I said. 'But I'll come with alternative arrangement to conduct the ceremony, if Fr Koratty refused to conduct it'. 'Any arrangement you like,' Philip's father said: 'We'll stand by you.'

I was in Trichy as an accredited visitor attending the CSI Synod held from 13 to 15 January 1976. On the last day, Bishop T.S. Joseph in consultation with the CSI Moderator Bishop Ananda Rao Samuel and Bishop M.M. John and Bishop T.B. Benjamin gave me authorization to solemnize Annamma's marriage at the Bride's house according to the Syro Malabar Catholic Rite in case Fr Koratty refused to solemnize it in my presence. Equipped with this unusually granted privilege I returned home.

On Sunday 18 January, Ammal and I reached my brother's residence, with all the necessary ritual vestments and requirements needed to conduct the ceremony and celebrate the nuptial Mass, all lent to me by my understanding priest-friends of Kottayam Knanaya Catholic diocese. 'Son,' my father held me close to him and said: 'Fr Koratty has announced during the service this morning that all the parishioners loyal to the church should be present in the church by 9 a.m. tomorrow for a 'joint work' [the church building was then under some major repair works]. I am afraid his secret agenda is to unleash violence on us and chase us away. Why should we take that risk? Why not we avoid going to the church at all and conduct the ceremony at home in our pavilion erected for the reception?' 'No, Achachen,' I tried to explain, 'That would give him an easy opportunity to achieve his sordid scheme and wash himself clean of the dirt saying: 'they did there at their home something I do not know what'. The hellish depth of his sordid scheme will reach the public only if we go to church and suffer the humiliation of being sent back rejected'.

Soon I went around and met almost all our relatives and friends and explained the situation to them and instructed them never to get provoked at whatever I may have to hear or suffer physically. 'Only see to it that Ammal is protected against any assault'. She was then seven months pregnant. 'We will see to it that she comes out unhurt,' they guaranteed me. I arranged with a small group of understanding members of the parish to interact with the vicar as authentic witnesses over his objections if any against the ceremony.

After making all the arrangements for the ceremony to be conducted at home if it became necessary, we reached the church for the ceremony, scheduled to commence at 10. a.m. We found hardly any one come for the 'joint work' as called for at Mass the previous morning. As the vicar did not turn up for the ceremony even 15 minutes after the scheduled time, the small group of my enlightened and understanding friends arranged by me approached Fr Koratty. 'As long as the excommunicated priest is within the Church or church compound, I refuse to officiate the ceremony,' he categorically said. 'But Father', one of my chosen friends pleaded: 'You conducted the betrothal ceremony in this church attended by the excommunicated Fr Abraham, and you had no objection'. 'So was it then, thus is it now,' was the vicar's reply. 'But', the group pleaded again, 'Fr Abraham was present in the cathedral church for the burial of Bishop Tharayil on 27 July 1975. Why was he not chucked out of the cathedral and the cathedral compound before the burial service?' 'Who are you to question?' was Fr Koratty's reply. Again they requested: 'Please give your objection in writing that we may appeal to the Bishop for his permission, as all arrangements for the marriage have been made ready and the invitees are come for the marriage celebrations and reception'. 'My will is not inclined to oblige you with anything in writing'.

As I saw the people around getting impatient and morally indignant, I intervened and told them: 'You heard Fr Koratty saying that my presence and that of my wife is the only objection raised against conducting the marriage ceremony in the church. So we are leaving the church compound.' After a short silent prayer my wife and I drove off in a car and reached my brother's residence. The bride and the groom along with all the relatives and friends got out of the church and followed us. I conducted the wedding ceremony after duly completing the necessary legal formalities and celebrated the nuptial Mass, all in the same Syro Malabar Catholic Rite. In my short message I added: 'If 'church' means an imposing edifice of bricks and mortar, the Thodupuzha Lakshmi Theater should be considered a church! On the other hand, if church means the assembly of God-believing people, there is a living church here under this modest pavilion'.

I wish I were wrong in thinking that the unholy, or shall I say, inhuman agenda to wedge my family relationship boomeranged on all those who masterminded it. Enraged at this fiasco, Fr Koratty during his Sunday sermon on 22 February referred to 'The modern Luther', 'who is out to ruin our church. I admonish the loyal ones to beware of him'. At about 7.30 a.m. that day I was at my brother's, attending a tea-party held in honour of the newly wedded. We got information that a few musclemen equipped with rods were found loitering on my way to bus stand in a manner that evoked suspicion. Probably they were expecting me on my way to catch the last bus to Uzhavoor. But we stuck to our fixed schedule to return the next day. Any way some of our friends warned me that unless I was cautious, my life might be in danger because of the ghost of vengeance of the infuriated and rebuffed catholic authorities concerned. At sharp contrast with the treatment of Fr Koratty was that of his successor, Fr Abraham Nedungat who on 7 November 1978 welcomed me to the sanctuary to attend and even to participate in the official functions related to the wedding of Ousu Joseph Pathirikara.

## Diverse Reactions to Me Married

Mrs Gene Gadbury (R 13 BOX 157, Muncie, Indiana 47302, U.S.A.) and family were my benefactors helping me through my studies and even after in all my needs. I was rather worried as to what their reaction would be when I informed them of the circumstances leading me to leave the Catholic Church and get married. In their reply dated 22 November 1976 the Gadburys wrote: '....It is really a shame that the Bishop has given you so much trouble. We believe that you have done what you have to do. These are very confusing times for the catholic people. My ideas have changed a lot just in the last year. I feel that how you really feel in your heart is how God will see us. Some of our church laws are way out of place for these times. I think many catholics are just going by their own conscience. Most of the ones I know do practice birth control without feeling any guilt. I can see how it would be even more urgent in India....We hope you are very happy and am sure you will continue to do God's work and live a good Christian life. You know in your heart that you are doing the right thing, so I am sure God will continue to bless and guide you....'

Again on 11 January 1977, Mrs Gadbury wrote to me: '....I thank you for the pictures of your wife and beautiful son....Your father looks in good health. Your wife is a beautiful lady. You must be very happy. I have always admired priests and the work they do, but felt it must be lonely without some one to share all your hopes, longings and joy....From the tone of your letter it sounds as if the Catholic Church there considers themselves a little above the rest of the people. If this is true they must have lost the meaning of what a true Christian really is. To me it really doesn't make all that much difference what church you belong to if you do what is right, mainly kindness and love for your fellow men regardless of the colour of their skin. I really feel that when all is said and done, these are the things the Almighty is going to judge us on'.

Contrasted with the above attitude of the Gadburys was the attitude taken by a senior priest of Kottayam Diocese, then parish priest of Memury Church where I was the parish priest in 1967. He had been holding a top level office in the diocese. On 21-12-1976 I reached Memury church to redeem and hand over to the Vicar the fixed deposit that had been pledged in favour of Memury church as security to Electricity Department in 1967. Seeing me there after nearly ten years, the sexton boy Jose came to join us. During our conversation the senior priest vicar commented: 'Your wife is a black lady isn't it?' 'I am to take care of my wife whether black or white. It is no one else's business', I replied. 'But what made you infer that my wife is black?' 'Why, she is a member of the C.S.I. church'. Immediately our sexton boy Jose intervened. He asked his parish priest: 'Do you know our present Kottayam M.P., Father?' 'Why, of course, Mr Varkey George', the vicar replied. 'What is his colour?' Jose continued. 'Of course, very fair coloured, as white as an American sahib'. 'Do you know that he is a member of the C.S.I.?' Jose confronted his much embarrassed parish priest. 'Well, Jose,' I remarked with a wink, 'It is an irony of the mischievous Fate that Fr J.M. is your parish priest and you his sexton. It should have been the other way about'.

### Attempt to Trap me

On 18 February 1978 I left for Bangalore with Ammal and my

baby son Jeslie to begin the first semester of my doctoral residential studies in the United Theological College (U.T.C.) on study leave up to 30 March 1978 and then to renew my leave sanction from the beginning of the next school year in June. Accordingly, leaving my family back at U.T.C. student quarters, I reached Uzhavoor on 27 March. On 31 March morning I reached the college and marked my attendance and submitted my application for leave from the re-opening in June and left for Bangalore to join the second semester of my studies. Ammal and I were expecting our second baby by the fourth week of May. On 29 May, Ammal got admitted in the Baptist Hospital Hebbal, Bangalore, to undergo caesarian operation the following day. On 13 June I got an urgent message to reach my brother's home on an urgent issue. Meanwhile my father, all anxious to see his two grandchildren came to Bangalore. Again on 24th I received urgent call from my nephew. Leaving my two little kids including the 21 days old daughter and Ammal all weeping and sobbing I left Bangalore for my brother's to handle the urgent issue.

The 27th June was the college reopening date. I thought of paying a visit to the college to say 'hello' to all the staff and then to return to Bangalore. By the time the Principal, Rev. Dr Simon Kottoor, had retired and Rev. Sr. Goretti had been appointed Principal, leaving the office of H.O.D. of English to the next senior most staff, Sunny Thomas (later national coach for Olympics Shooting Competition). Mr. Sunny Thomas told me that on the 26th afternoon Sr Goretti had instructed him to set the time table assigning duty to me too from the re-opening day onwards as the Manager had decided not to grant me leave for study! The new Principal, being a nun in the diocesan congregation for women, was more pliable for Bishop Kunnacherry than the former Principal and was ready to render any dedicated service to her Bishop who was the earthly representative of Jesus, her heavenly 'bridegroom'. I told Mr Sunny that probably I might prove myself too large a creature to be caught in a mouse trap.

On the re-opening day, 27 June, I met Principal Goretti in the morning. She told me that the management has rejected my application for leave for studies and a Memo had been dispatched to my Bangalore address under certificate of posting [for evidence I suppose] on Saturday 24 June calculated to reach me on 26 or 27 June in Bangalore! The situation was almost overcharged with intense tension. However, mustering all the poise of my mind and self-control I was capable of, I told her: 'I expected a minimum level of the human at least in you that should have persuaded you to send me a wire at least on Friday 23 June when the Memo reached you. But quite unexpectedly, Providence brought me here in time to sign my attendance on the re-opening date'. I then signed the attendance register.

Next I met my friend, a doctor, Mr Bhaskaran then on government service at Kadaplamattam, got a medical certificate, applied for medical leave in the presence of Prof C.K. Abraham as a witness and left for Bangalore. Back at U.T.C. quarters, Ammal handed over to me the Memo forwarded by the Principal. The post mark on the envelop showed the date and time the memo reached the Bangalore post office: 27-6-1978, at 10:00 hours, dramatically enough simultaneous with the time I should have been, and by kind divine Providence I was present at the college to report for duty!

## They Stick Together the Lot of Them

On 30 June 1978 I reached the Catholic Archbishop's House, Bangalore, with a hope to get an understanding hearing from Archbishop Packiam Arokyaswamy to the tale of my woes. I was met by a good old retired catholic priest residing on the campus with whom I shared the experiences of my woes I had to endure at the hands of my former catholic bishops. He then warned me against further disappointments by going to the Archbishop for sympathy and understanding. 'One rogue needs other rogues for mutual safety', the good old Father told me. 'They stick together, the lot of them. And so one Bishop will never give away another'. After my interview with the Archbishop I heartly thanked the good old Father whose assessment of the prospects of my visit to the Archbishop was flawless. The interview magnificently confirmed what he had warned me against. After listening to me for some time the Archbishop said: 'The story of your experience with your two former Catholic bishops is incredible and bizarre, and would destroy the credibility of the Catholic hierarchy, if it were true'. I appealed to him to take some time and trouble for God's sake to verify the truth of my story. And the great Archbishop pronounced his final verdict: 'It is difficult to ascertain the truth of these facts'. I came away confirmed in what the good old retired Father had told me about the Catholic Bishops.

## Ecumenical Movement: Pursuing Ideals or Mutual Back-Scratching?

On 18 July 1978 I met Rev. M.A. Thomas, Director of Ecumenical Christian Centre, Whitefield, Bangalore. We spoke of the earlier correspondence between us about the marriage of Annamma with Philip and about the past events which led to this pass. In his reply dated 25 April 1977 he was kind enough to point out my 'foolishness' in leaving 'the great Roman Catholic Church'. To this I gratefully replied, on 15 July 1977: 'If by greatness you mean power, money and influential institutions, then I am not at all sorry for it. If you mean that there are very holy men in the Catholic Church also (in spite of its being the Catholic Church) let me be the first to agree with you. But I think they are holy not because they are Catholics, but because they are Christians. In fact I can say, perhaps more authoritatively than you can in this case, that the Catholic structure as such can be very unchristian and inhuman because having claimed to be infallible and therefore unquestionable, it can effectively protect and perpetuate gross injustice'.

However during our personal interactions he felt sorry for not having shown in his correspondence that understanding which the matter had deserved. At any rate, he explained, he never suspected any such ugly situations. And he added: 'Do not expect any sympathy, or interference from other churches which are associated with the ecumenical movement. If the events had taken place fifteen years ago,' he continued: 'half a dozen churches would have come to Marika and taken up the case to exploit the situation in their favour. But the present mutual understanding and policy of non-interference in the internal matters of other churches, promoted by the modern Ecumenical Movement, would make any other church reluctant to intervene.'

'But,' Fr. Thomas kindly advised me: 'if you quit the churches associated with the ecumenical movement and approach the Evangelical Churches of Thiruvalla side,....you will certainly get very quick and favourable response. But the course of action you suggest may be next to impossible'. 'But Fr Thomas,' I said: 'I cannot dissociate myself from the ecumenical movement....I cherish great hopes of Ecumenical Movement in the pursuit of Christian values and ideals and justice in the churches'. 'What you say is indeed the ideal,' said Fr Thomas, 'but the ecumenical movement is run by men, not by ideals.' 'That,' I responded, 'fills me with a sense of cynicism to hear these things of the Ecumenical Movement....It is sad indeed to hear that the much hoped for Ecumenical Movement is degrading itself to the level of Managers' Association, trying to maintain the status quo of each church, safeguarding the interests of the lucky ones at the leadership and protecting the frontiers of each one and close the door to the victims of ecclesiastical despotism seeking refuge, instead of pursuing, in a united effort, the Christian Mission of Justice and Love, serving the common cause of the Christian message, while recognizing and respecting legitimate and unavoidable denominational differences. I expect Ecumenical Movement to be an effort to rise above, and in spite of denominational limitations'.

Fr Thomas then confidentially told me of several non-catholic Bishops – Bishops who are scared of the power and influence of the Roman Catholic church which is wealthy enough to literally purchase the faithful of their churches for money and empty these churches. 'I feel the fear is mutual,' I supplemented his statement, 'The Roman Catholic Church which is more aware than any other church of the internal weakness it has come to suffer, particularly after the second Vatican Council, is more frightened of its own survival and is scared of the united moves of other churches. This is the only way I can explain the haste, tolerance and rather belated good-will shown by the Catholic Church to take active participation in the Ecumenical Movement. But if the driving force of the movement is mutual scare and mistrust resulting in the restless anxiety to maintain the status quo, the Movement itself would turn out to be another human device to protect the frontiers of each other to safely continue the practices of deluding, exploitation and oppression within each other's habitat safely. Even groups of bandits or robbers enter such mutual understanding and cooperation for plundering and call it ecumenical movement for easy mutual back-scratching'!

At the same time I must acknowledge with deep gratitude to God and flawless honesty the love, honour and care and concern with which my then CSI Bishop the Rt. Rev. T.S. Joseph of Madhya Kerala and the two retired Bishops M.M. John and T.B. Benjamin dealt with me and my issue with the Catholic management. Of course Bishop Joseph belonged to the community dumped by the white-skinned ones as 'Backward class', the only one from this community to be elevated to this position till 2011. I have thought of him as a man of deep Faith in God and great humility of heart, emptied of the ego of the incumbents from the 'forward communities' like his successor, and therefore there was room left in his heart for the Holy Spirit to live in and operate through this humble holy Bishop.

## An Ominous Darkness Looming Large

The Management's drama of attempt to deny me study leave, played through the new Principal, Sr Goretti, gave me a premonition of a foreboding prospect. Sr Goretti, being a member of the diocesan congregation for women, was of course a pliable and docile character to play the chief role in the vindictive drama now moving to the climax. The letter from Prof. K.M. Mathew, Secretary A.K.P.C.T.A. Uzhavoor Unit, and a man of strong Knanaya Communal solidarity and incumbent of the post of Principal after Sr Goretti, gave me a feeling that I cannot rely upon all those colleagues who smiled at me, especially those of the Knanaya Communal fellowship. In this letter he informed that the A.K.P.C.T.A. unit decided not to act on my complaint because it was addressed to the Staff secretary!

I returned from Bangalore and joined duty in the college on 28 August 1978. I felt an ominous darkness looming large over the future of my teaching career, particularly in the wake of the University Appellate Tribunal having been struck down in favour of the minority communities. On 25 October I met Dr Paulose Mar Gregorios, guide for my doctoral studies on 'Freedom and Authority'. During our discussion I related to him certain facts of my relationship with Bishop Kunnacherry indicating the possible threat to my college teaching career under his vindictive spirit. 'I am not surprised at all,' His Grace remarked. 'Being myself a Bishop it is not proper that I pass remarks on other Bishops. But regarding Bishop Kunnacherry, I must say, I am sorry for the diocese of Kottayam for Kunnacherry's being raised as its Bishop. Much good could have been done by the Christian Bishops, if not for Bishop Kunnacherry. He is basically immature and insecure'.

The fear of the management's gangs aching to spill the venom and the consequent uncertainty and insecurity of my wife and two kids loomed large above me often disturbing my sleep. But my experiences of the Divine Providence raising the right persons or events at the right time to save me from dangers helped me to boldly and cheerfully push on. On a casual visit to Prof Narayanan Nair Poovathinkal, Uzhavoor, on 28 October, he enlightened me on many points in matters of procedure and formalities regarding service as a lecturer. Pursuing the tips he gave me, I had a personal talk with Sr. Goretti on 30 October about the possibilities of my keeping away from the Bishop-Manager: the possibility of my working elsewhere while keeping my lien in the college until I got a permanent employment else where or my retirement. This was only to protect the benefit of my pension for my family. I promised to seek all possibilities of getting my lien transferred to another management under the same University of Kerala.

The very next day I heard her Master's voice through her mouth: 'The manager's policy, followed so far, is to sanction extraordinary leave only for one year. The Management would be happy at your keeping away from it.'

The Principal continued a kind of step-motherly attitude towards me. On 24 September 1979 she tried to take me to task. That day I reached college at 1.50 p.m. for invigilation to begin at 2 p.m. The exam had started at 1.30 p.m., instead of the usual time. This had been notified – but on the 20th when I was on leave. She then took up the charge of my leaving after first hour though I had applied for leave only for the afternoon that day. I had left only after completing my forenoon duty. However when I pointed instances of other teachers taking half day leave without even ever stepping into the college that whole day, she raised her voice in anger not knowing what exactly to answer. I ignored it and came off. I felt that these were only symptoms of the deeper malady of vengeance.

Meanwhile I got a letter from the U.T. College Principal, Dr Chandran, dated 3 September 1979, informing me of the success of my assessment examination assessed by the supervisory committee consisting of Dr Chandran, Dr Paulose Mar Gregorios and Dr Mundaden. They found my assessment examination satisfactory enough to recommend me to the Serampore Senate for the next stage of my research. 'On the whole we felt that you have sufficient awareness of the main problem you want to probe into', Dr Chandran reported, 'and that you have good scope for a meaningful research'.

Eventually I got admission at the Princeton Theological Seminary, U.S.A., and sanction of scholarship to continue my research. But I needed leave from the college Management for two years. On my request for mediation, Bishop Paulose Mar Gregorios and the retired CSI Bishop, M.M. John, wrote to Bishop Kunnacherry in the second week of March 1980 recommending me to be sanctioned two years study leave.

## Shift of Residence to Vadavathoor

It was time for us to think of putting my baby son Jeslie into a suitable kindergarten. Ammal and I could not think of sending him to schools in Uzhavoor run by nuns under catholic management. On 23 December 1978, I had come to the CSI Church Vadavathoor to give a 'Christmas Message'. Ever since then we had been thinking of shifting our residence to Vadavathoor, a suburb of Kottayam. Among the several considerations which led us to this inclination were the Vadavathoor CSI Church fellowship, the prestigious Catholic Institution of St. Thomas Apostolic Seminary with its immense library and above all the several first rate schools and higher educational facilities within a conveniently reachable distance. Several members of the CSI Church like Dr Mathew Thazhathu Bethel (affectionately called Dr Appachen) including the then Church worker and later pastor Rev. Joyce Daniel put in strenuous effort looking out for a convenient residence for us in Vadavathoor. Providence helped our dream come true.

On 9 May 1980, Bishops T.S. Joseph, T.B. Benjamin and M.M. John came to bless my new residence at Vadavathoor to grace with their presence and blessings the commencement of our new chapter of life. On 14 May, Ammal was interviewed by the manager of Girideepam School Vadavathoor. The next day on arrival at Girideepam to buy books for Jeslie to his U.K.G. class we were told that Ammal could join the School staff without further delay.

# 19

# The Catholic Vindictive Grip Tightened

On 1 July 1980 I told the Principal that I would be applying for study leave of two years. As was usual with her, the next day she told me in her Master's voice that leave might not be granted unless for higher studies in the subject I was teaching. Once again I pointed out the precedent of a lecturer, Mr Regimon, who had gone on leave to study Theology in Poona. 'That is at the Manager's discretion,' she replied, as usual, raising her pitch. 'Your quoting the precedent of Regimon will only worsen the situation.' I met Bishop M.M. John and explained to him the possible refusal of leave. He sent me to Dr George Jacob, former Vice-Chancellor of Kerala University. The latter put me in touch with the then Registrar for the latest statute regarding leave taking. On 11 July, I met the registrar. He advised me to tap political sources to influence the management. 'Law is helpless in getting the leave sanctioned,' he said.

I had applied for a loan from my provident fund in June 1980. On 14 July I applied for leave without pay for two years. But the college office refused to complete the required formalities connected with my applications. On 18 July I met Dr George Jacob again. He gave me the idea to apply for leave to pursue a programme of Ph. D. in literature. 'I am ready to be your guide. Once you get leave, you can pursue your course of studies and it concerns no one what you study and what thesis you present and what degree you get and so on,' Jacob said. The college office was bent on mixing up the PF loan application and the leave-without-pay application to complicate matters.

On the 21st I met Fr Philip Kamicherry, the senior-most priest, then resting in Vianey Home for aged priests, to plead with Bishop Kunnacherry for the favour of the leave sanction. He felt helpless and said: 'He is bitter with you and will certainly deny you any favour if he can legally do so. Do you then think it worth my incurring his displeasure in my old age?' I came away with my profound respect for him intact. Seeing that the college office was complicating the issue, I approached the Principal with a letter withdrawing my leave application. She then told me that I was to communicate with her only in writing. My loan application was returned for want of certain details from the office. I felt harassed to a degree beyond my endurance. I felt myself on the verge of a nervous breakdown. I approached some of my sympathetic colleagues for advice. But they were unwilling to help me: 'Why should I burn my finger and incur the displeasure of the office and the management?' was the common refrain.

My written request to speed up the process of my P.F. loan was met with the answer: 'The office will carry out its function according to its convenience'. I felt psychologically oppressed. On 22 July, on enquiry at the D.D. Office in Tripunithura about the fate of my loan application the section clerk told me: 'The other day Sr. Tarsisia came here and when I told her that the college office could have prevented the return of the loan application, she told me: 'I knew it would be sent back, and that was what ought to have been done''! On the insistence of Dr George Jacob, I reached the Bishop's House for a sympathetic hearing of my problems with the college office. But I was denied audience with the manager-bishop. According to his secretary, Dr John Padinjarekut: 'You have seriously offended the Bishop by your decision to join the C.S.I. and to carry on your priestly ministry there,' he told me. 'You should have remained a layman in the Catholic Church.' I replied: 'I am prepared to make any amendment for any personal offenses on my part. As for my decision to quit the Catholic Church and to join the C.S.I., it was a matter concerning my own religious conviction and peace of my conscience. If somebody gets offended on that account, well, I am helpless in the matter'.

My repeated requests for an audience with the Bishop were summarily rejected. Rev. Padinjarekut enquired of me about the 'rumour' from 'a very reliable source' that I was regretting the religious decision I took. And I replied: 'In this matter I am more reliable and I assure you that by divine grace I have absolutely no regret till now about the decision'.

September was a period of acute harassment from the Principal and the college office. The prolonged harassment on every minute routine affairs related to my college duties and formalities and my response to it had already given me sufficient mental tension to feel physically exhausted, so much so that I had trouble lasting the full hour of each class without breathing trouble. On 19 and 21 August, I had to end my classes before time on account of breathing trouble. On 22 August all the other teachers were given the month's salary in advance as was usual with the Onam festival. But I was not given my salary nor was I told the reason for this. I was on the brink of a breakdown and decided to keep away from this vindictive atmosphere on consideration of my health. I took medical leave for a few days. On the second day of my leave I went to Kottayam vegetable market. There I saw a poor lady in the midst of vegetable waste-dump searching for pieces of thrown out vegetable market waste. The sight of this poor old unhealthy lady's struggle for mere survival piqued my pride. 'If this poor lady could withstand these hardships in her effort for survival,' I asked myself, 'why, am I not a coward if, with more than average education, with a lecturer's job and salary, I am unable to ignore the puny little petty taunts of a small group of 'holy nuns – consecrated brides of their heavenly Bridegroom?'

I mustered all my mental courage and strength, decided to face the situation with manly courage, cancelled my medical leave and joined duty in the college. The Principal questioned me on joining duty after taking medical leave. 'Well, Madam,' I said, 'here is my health-fitness certified. Some of my students of final year literature degree class had enquired about my health and persuaded me to discontinue classes. In answer to their enquiries I explained it away saying that certain amount of tension due to certain pressures was responsible for the exhaustion.

**Memo Served and Domestic Enquiry Ordered**

On the advice of many friends, I decided to send a petition to the Vice-Chancellor against the harassment meted out to me by the college office with the connivance of the Manager. I prepared a petition in triplicate. On 3 September, in the presence of the head of the department of English, Mr Sunny Thomas, as a tacit but willing witness, I submitted my petition in duplicate to be forwarded 'through the proper channel' and produced the third copy for the Principal's attested acknowledgement. 'If you are unwilling to attest acknowledgement, I expect all the three copies to be returned,' I told her. In that case, she knew, I would send them to her by registered post with acknowledgement due. 'I have to verify the third copy to make sure it is a true copy. You may collect it later,' was her reply. I went to engage classes. After two consecutive periods once again I felt exhausted and short of breath. I had to stop class a little before the end of the period, as the students also requested me to do. I went to the Principal for permission to leave the college a little earlier in order to consult a doctor. She then returned the third copy of the petition without attesting acknowledgement and refused to give back the other two copies. 'This is illegal', I said. Pat came her 'lady-like' response: 'You have cause for another petition now. Proceed with it'. As my feverishness was getting worse, I left.

The next day I demanded the return of the copies of my petition, but was summarily denied. 'I'll sit here in your office till you either acknowledge receipt of or return the petition in triplicate,' I answered. 'You may sit there,' she said and left the room. After about two hours I went out to the toilet and returned to find the Principal's room locked. I continued standing outside the locked room exhausted, worried and almost broken down. To the queries of some of my students who saw me standing there in that condition I explained the reason. 'Father,' they told me 'you need not wait here today.

Tomorrow you will get either the acknowledgement or the originals back'. And so I left.

On the way back, I met Bishop T.S. Joseph and Rev. Sam Mathew [who became the second successor to Bishop Joseph] and explained the new development. 'We are outside the matter of your college discipline and so helpless. However, pray God and proceed prudently,' they advised me.

The next day, at noon, the students gheraoed the Principal and her office staff for nearly four hours at the end of which she consented to hold a joint meeting of all concerned including the student representative the following day to discuss the problem in detail. That evening I met Metropolitan Paulose Mar Gregoios and explained the turn of events. 'Knowing Bishop Kunnacherry as he is,' the Metropolitan said, 'a man without any element of Christianity or humanity, I think this might turn out to be a State-level issue, if not a national one [perhaps he had in mind the absence of a University Appellate Tribunal]. Perhaps Bishop Kunnacherry might chicken out from this, awaiting a better opportunity'.

On 6 September the Principal convened the meeting. She gave her own explanations, indicating that disciplinary action would be taken against me 'for instigating the students to gherao the Principal's office room' and dispersed the meeting saying that it was only an explanatory meeting. On hearing the new developments, the Metropolitan said: 'Now that things have reached the present stage, we need not be very anxious for a cheap talk. Let us now wait for the full development of the course of action'.

As expected, on 15 October, the Principal served on me a 'memo of charges' of 'three grave misconducts' including 'inciting the students to gherao the Principal. The service of memo was officially witnessed by Prof K.M. Mathew, [who was to succeed as the next Principal] with acknowledgement of the same got signed by me. On 20 October I submitted my explanation prepared under legal guidance of Advocate Sri. Sankunni Menon. The explanation was signed and witnessed by a couple of my colleagues. Mr Sunny Thomas, who had a prior talk with her, told me to meet her alone. I did not want to meet her alone. But, as Mr Sunny told me, she began to dodge accepting my explanation. She was running like a rat to escape confronting us by leaving her official seat. Once I hastened after her and met her near the Hostel and asked her when she would be available in the office to attest acceptance of my explanations. She refused to give me a definite answer. I gave a written statement about the Principal's dodging the acceptance to the staff secretary Mr Kurian Lukose. Seeing me hastening after her several times like this, the students naturally asked me what the matter was and I had to explain to them the situation. They offered to be witnesses to my submission of memo–reply. On Tuesday 21 October, at 1.20 p.m. I saw her coming from the hostel. But seeing me waiting at her office she went straight to engage a class. I saw her hastening to her office at 3 p.m. Immediately, I requested some of my colleagues Mr B.J. Antony, Mr E.A. Thomas and Mr V.J. Joseph to come with me to witness my submitting the memo-explanation. I got another shock when they refused. A few of my III D.C. students ran to my help and in their presence I submitted my explanation though she still refused to sign acknowledgement of acceptance. The refusal of my colleagues to even witness my submission of memo-reply was indeed very painful to me.

On Tuesday 26 October, I reached college as usual at 8.15 a.m. and went to the office along with Mr V.J. Joseph to mark my attendance when I saw 'Late' marked on my attendance column and over my signature in the previous day's column. On enquiry the Principal answered that when required she would say she mistook the column for that of someone else, the column that bore my signature!

### Absence of Appellate Authority Causes Mental Turbulence

On 4 November, I received Bp. Kunnacherry's 'memo of charge' sent by registered post. Next day I met Bishop T.S. Joseph and explained the developments up to date. He gave me five letters addressed to some Bishops of the Jacobite, Orthodox and Mar Thoma Churches seeking help in the matter, particularly in the wake of the absence of an Appellate Authority over the private management's disciplinary authority, now endowed with an absolute character. Two days later I met a University Syndicate member, Mr C.Z. Scariah who assured me all possible but limited help under the legal situation. My mind was turbulent, full of agony and the darkness of insecurity. I met many people who had influence somewhere or the other, and all of them felt deeply concerned over my helplessness at the hands of the private management's disciplinary authority. I decided to fight till the end and then to work as a porter in Kottayam vegetable market wearing my priestly cassock if dismissed from my college service.

### The CSI Bishops Intervene

On Bishop Benjamin's advice I discussed the problem with barrister P.K. Kurian, Partner of Menon and Pai, Ernakulam. After a close study and assessment of my plight of legal insecurity against the Management's absolute authority in the absence of an Appellate authority, Mr Kurian gave a report to Bishop T.S. Joseph dated 16 November 1980. He told me that I have no legal protection against the Management's vindictive harassment. He concluded his report thus: 'On the basis of the law as it stands today, the right of the management to take disciplinary action against a teacher is absolute and the same cannot be set aside ordering re-instatement. If a person is wrongfully dismissed, then like in any private employment such a person is entitled to approach a civil court for relief. If the civil court finds that the dismissal is wrongful, then that court can only award damages. However the point to be noted is that re-instatement is a remedy which a civil court in the circumstances cannot grant....I personally feel that any final decision of the court will take five to ten years. While an Institution can afford the luxury of litigation on for such a long period, whether the individual can suffer it is different matter altogether....What I have in mind...is the privations involved in having to face such a situation for a long period, with the chances of taking employment elsewhere during the period being restricted'.

I engaged Mr Sankunni Menon and Mr P.K. Chitra Bhanu as my advocates to attend to the affairs consequent on the serving of memo on me. On 12 November 1980, Metropolitan Mar Gregorios assessed the college situation as sufficiently serious. 'Will your Church take up the case and fight it out in the court?' he asked. In fact the C.S.I. Bishops T.S. Joseph, T.B. Benjamin and M.M. John spared no effort in their attempts to save me and family in this moment of agony and uncertainty. Their attitude brought much comfort and courage to my aged and agonized father and Ammal. On 25 July, Ammal and I had visited Bishop T.S. Joseph to share our woes and worries with him. I had given him a signed blank letter head of mine as a guarantee to the effect that in case he felt the need of making enquiries about my grievances and found me wrong any where he could take any drastic step against me. 'If you find me to have acted in any way unbecoming of a priest-cum-lecturer, you can adequately punish me', I assured him. 'If you think I am unjustly persecuted, I request you to intervene on my behalf to bring a sense of security to me and family'. He promised he would and he did, as I shall explain further below.

On 17 November, after classes, Mr K.C. Joseph, my colleague, told me: 'Bishop Kunnacherry told us, the leave committee, that he would not grant leave on loss of pay until Fr Vellamthadathil is ousted from the college. He will not extend any help or concession to you'. This only confirmed what Bishop Tharayil's driver told me the previous day. According to the driver, another colleague, Mr T.M. James, had said: 'We know the Bishop is murdering conscience. But what can we do? He has promised the teachers to grant all favours they request if only they would cooperate in ousting Fr Vellamthadathil'.

On the basis of the suggestions of several Bishops, Bishop Joseph met Bishop Kunnacherry, but to no result. Out of his honesty and concern for me he suggested to me that I pamper Bishop Kunnacherry with a 'general apology' to avoid losing my job and the regular income it gave me. But I realized that any such 'apology' would have been a fatal weapon in Bishop Kunnacherry's hands - he would not even have to hold the farce of a formal domestic enquiry. Domestic enquiry under the situation would in effect mean nothing but the persecutor sitting in absolute judgement over the persecuted.

On 1 December 1980, Mr Joseph, my colleague, told me to plead with Bishop Kunnacherryonce more. I replied that Bishop Kunnachery was relying on the advantage given to him by our distorted legal system made by our politicians in unholy alliance with the religious leaders on the basis of vote banks, an unjust legal system conferring absolute authority to the accuser over the accused. 'Please ask Bishop Kunnacherry,' I told my colleague, 'whether he can agree to the judgment of an impartial enquiry, as I have already suggested to some others, done by a committee appointed by any competent authority, most preferably by the Christian Bishops. On my part I may be dismissed if the impartial enquiry finds me guilty. If I am cleared of the charges, I am willing to leave the service of this college. At any rate, don't plead for my maintenance or that of my family; plead for the course of justice in my case'.

In yet another attempt to wrench me out of the octopus grip, Bishop Joseph, through an appeal dated 1 December 1980 and jointly signed by Bishop M.M. John and Bishop T.B. Benjamin, pleaded with Bishop Kunnacherry for an alternative solution. Let me reproduce the appeal in toto so that it may speak for itself:

Dear Thirumeni,

We understand that Rev. Abraham Vellamthadathil is under disciplinary proceedings initiated by you as Manager of St. Stephen's College, Uzhavoor. He had been telling us of severe harassment from the college office stating that his complaints to you remain unheeded even to date. He is convinced that the disciplinary proceedings have been initiated without bona fides, and he appeals to us on principles of natural justice for a chance to have the charges gone into by an impartial commission and suggests that the charges against him be gone into by a commission of the Christian Bishops of Kerala, though it is the statutory right of the Manager to institute his own enquiry commission. Rev. Abraham looks upon the disciplinary proceedings as a serious threat to his person and career as a lecturer with eleven years of service and according to the present state of University Statute, he has no appeal and so no legal remedy against the proceedings which according to him is motivated by hostility.

'Under the circumstances, we suggest, as a practical measure to solve this problem, Rev. Abraham be granted leave from Uzhavoor college for two or three years on loss of pay, with the understanding that as soon as an opportunity presents itself, he will be absorbed into one of the colleges under the CSI management. We hope that this suggestion would be agreeable to you since Rev. Abraham thus comes away from the college under your management. This will help him too by safeguarding his career as a college lecturer with eleven years of service and with a fair reputation of being a good and efficient teacher, as you yourself acknowledged to Bishop T.S. Joseph. *The suggestion will also save us from the embarrassing inconvenience of pressures from groups and people under our care to make some kind of public statement of facts involved in this problem.* [emphasis added]. We wish to go to any extent to avoid the need of such a step which, we fear, will unfavourably reflect upon the good relations that now exist between our churches.

Looking forward to your more soft and sympathetic stand on the matter, we remain,

Yours with fraternal greetings.'

The CSI Bishops knew Bishop Kunnacherry too well to expect any positive response, though they were sure the letter would create a rumble in him regarding the possible damage on his public image that could result from a total neglect of such a reasonably and maturely worded appeal from three Christian Bishops. Hence they jointly signed an appeal to the Archbishop, Dr Antony Padiyara, dated 15 December 1980 with copies to Joseph Cardinal Parekkatil, to Mar Thoma Mathews I Catholicos of the Orthodox Church, to Alexander Mar Thoma, Metropolitan of the Mar Thoma Church, to Dr Joseph Kelanthara, Archbishop of Verapoly and to Bishop

Kunnacherry, certainly, requesting him to wield his influence, if any, on Bishop Kunnacherry as the latter's archbishop, although the CSI Bishops were well aware that the Archbishops have no jurisdictional power over the local suffragon bishops.

Once again I reproduce the joint appeal in toto:

'Your Grace,

Please find enclosed herewith a copy of a statement of facts published by Rev. Abraham Vellamthadathil, describing some of his experiences as a lecturer from the management of St. Stephen's College, Uzhavoor. We are constrained to believe that the statement is substantially true and feel concerned about him.

Rev. Abraham is now being proceeded against by Bishop the Rt. Rev. Dr Kuriakose Kunnacherry on the basis of a charge-sheet containing charges punishable even with dismissal from the college. Your Grace will certainly understand Rev. Abraham's mental agony and feelings of pain and legal helplessness, under the shadow of the disciplinary proceedings now initiated against him by the college management, which seems to be wanting bona fides. He looks upon the management's action as a serious threat to his character and career as a lecturer with eleven years of service, against which he has no legal remedy under the present state of the University Statutes. Rev. Abraham approaches us with an appeal on the principle of natural justice for a chance to have the charges against him examined by an impartial commission and suggests that the charges be examined by a commission of the Christian Bishops of Kerala. Of course it is the statutory right of the manager to institute his own commission to enquire into the charges leveled by the manager himself.

We tried to solve the problem with a sincere spirit of understanding and cooperation in accordance with the spirit of the present ecumenical relationships existing among us as Christian Bishops. Accordingly, Bishop T.S. Joseph approached Bishop Kunnacherry offering to take Rev. Abraham with him for a personal talk of reconciliation, hoping to ease the tension existing between the two. The same measure was adopted a few months ago by Bishop M.M. John too. But Bishop Kunnacherry refuses to meet Rev. Abraham or to have any reconciliatory talk with him. As a practical measure to solve the problem, we already suggested to Bishop Kunnachery to grant Rev. Abraham leave from the college for two or three years on loss of pay on the understanding that as soon as an opportunity presents itself, Rev. Abraham will be absorbed into one of the colleges under the C.S.I. management. This, we thought, would be agreeable to Bishop Kunnacherry, who, understandably enough, wishes Rev. Abraham to leave the college under his management. We also thought this would help Rev. Abraham to safeguard his career as a college lecturer with 11 years of service and with a fair reputation of being a good and efficient teacher, as acknowledged even by Bishop Kunnacherry himself to Bishop T.S. Joseph. But we regret to say that Bishop Kunnacherry is unwilling to take an understanding and helpful attitude in the matter suggested by us. This seems to confirm our suspicion that Rev. Abraham is being victimized for having left the Catholic Church and joined the C.S.I. Church where he continues as a priest.

We hope that your good influence will prevail upon Bishop Kunnacherry to take a more soft and sympathetic stand in the matter. This will also save us from the embarrassing inconvenience of pressures from groups and people under our care to make some kind of public statement of facts involved in this problem. We wish to go to any extent to avoid the need of such a step which, we fear, will unfavourably reflect upon the good ecumenical relationships which we Christian Bishops in Kerala have been at pains to create and to maintain.

Looking forward to your good will to mediate in the matter under consideration, we remain,

Yours with fraternal greetings'.

The modest but unmistakable indication of a public statement of facts by these Bishops seemed to have given Bishop Kunnacherry some jitters about his public image which he was desperately trying to project in gorgeous colours. I felt the momentum of the domestic enquiry was brought down to some extent.

On 26 December, Prof Zachariah Chakkalayil (my neighbour, who had retired as a professor at a college in Bombay) after listening to the saga of my persecution, remarked: 'I wonder how you can go on smiling like this. If I were in your position, I would have gone mad'. 'But I didn't,' I replied, 'because my trust is in God who is Truth, Justice and Love'.

Rev. Theo de Sales S.J., a former colleague, and then Rector of the Papal Seminary Poona, wrote to me on 3 January 1981. In my reply dated 27 January I wrote: '... It was indeed very kind of you to have thought of me and family, it was indeed a comfort and relief to have been reminded of your fellowship and brotherly concern at a time when I felt cruelly persecuted by my former catholic Bishop Kuriakose Kunnacherry. He thinks it chivalry to drag me to war with him.

'Bishop Ambrose Abosolo of Vijayapuram diocese told me that one would not believe that a Bishop would do such things and that my complaints would be looked upon as attempts of a crack-brained one who is out to calumniate his Bishop'.

### The Lane the Enquiry Farce Traveled

The formal domestic enquiry procedures started on 14 January 1981 under a retired district judge, P.T. Mathew. For various reasons the enquiry process went on for nearly one year until I got the copy of the enquiry report, signed by the Bishop-manager Bishop Kunnacherry dated 10 December 1981. And the enquiry officer was loyal and faithful to his employer in reporting that he had found all the Bishop's charges leveled against me true. With that the drama of the case trial of the accused by the accuser sitting in absolute judgment came to its finale. But the drama was not without some comic relief.

At the very first meeting with the inquiry officer even before the enquiry began, the retired judge P.T. Mathew said: 'There is no reason to say that in your case Bishop Kunnacherry is victimizing you because leaving the Catholic church has become the usual thing among priests and nuns'. Thereby he struck at the very root of my defense plea at one easy stroke.

My advocate, Mr Chitra Bhanu, immediately countered it saying: 'The rejection by the management of the joint appeal of the CSI bishops was a proof valid and strong enough to suspect victimisation target behind the domestic enquiry initiated under the absurd legal system of allowing the accuser to sit in absolute judgment over the accused.'

On 7 February, the Principal, Sr. Goretti, was examined. In the cross examination she was asked whether she had given up addressing the accused as 'Father' and instead addressed him as 'Sir'. 'I always addressed him only as 'Father', she deposed under oath of truthfulness taken in the name of God. 'Here is a memo you served on him. How have you addressed him in the memo?' Back came her admission: 'Yes, I have addressed him as 'Sir' since his marriage'. The staff council resolution in the original recommending disciplinary proceedings against me and presented as Management side Ext. No. M6 dated 6-9-80 was taken up. The Principal confirmed it as original, signed by all the council members and by the Principal during the council meeting itself. 'How is it then,' Mr Chitra Bhanu asked, 'that its Photostat given to the accused and presented as D Ext. No D2 does not bear the Principal's signature?' A slight disfigurement of her beautiful face was her only answer.

One of the management witnesses was Prof M.C. Mathew, Pathupara. He represented the manager's case vigorously indeed. During the deposition he explained how he was an eyewitness to all the members of the staff council including the Principal signing the resolution Ext. No. M6 during the council meeting. He identified the resolution in the original. When in the cross examination he was shown its Photostat, No. D2 not signed by the Principal he stated: 'Ha! I did not expect they would make such a stupid blunder'!

On 2 March 1981 I had an intimate talk with Kerala University Registrar. On his advice I consulted the University Advocate at High Court, Mr Bhaskaran Nambiar. Mr Nambiar said: 'Unfortunately the Minority Rights Provision has been interpreted giving absolute power to the management. Once they try to victimize you, you better resign and quit instead of wasting your time and money and unnecessarily taxing your brain'. The same day I also met a senior advocate at Kerala High Court and father of Justice K.S. Radhakrishnan, Mr Siva Sankara Panicker. His view was: 'You have to face the domestic enquiry. Defend yourself there. If its verdict is unfavourable, appeal to the Vice Chancellor. If the V.C.'s verdict is also unfavourable, then we shall take it to the High Court'.

On 1 June 1981, the day the college re-opened after the summer vacation, I joined duty, much to the bitter disappointment of the nuns in particular who had thought that the disciplinary proceedings would be completed and I would be eliminated before the reopening. The Principal nun had hinted to Ammal on 4 May when she went to the college with my authorization to take my April Salary: 'The enquiry is being delayed on account of centralized valuation. But there is still one more month'. Mr Sunny Thomas, understandably enough turned down my request to appear as witness before the enquiry officer because 'I will have to say the truth,' he said, 'and the Management might take it ill and I would be courting the displeasure of the management for no benefit to any because at any rate they will eliminate you. I'm afraid of the management who might start victimizing me next.'

One of my students, M.C. Kuriakose, was examined as DW1 on 10 June when the office superintendent Tarsisia and other management representatives were not present, unlike in all previous sessions. On 16 June, during the examination of another student, P. Salim, the Management advocate, Mr P.C. Abraham, remarked to Tarsisia and others including the Pro-manager Fr, Jacob Kollaparampil: 'because you were absent last time, the case took a bad turn. The witness (M.C. Kuriakose) denied several of the allegations leveled by the management....' 'That is the usual method of the case, to assert what did not take place and to deny what actually did take place,' the superintendent nun commented unaware how her witty remark could boomerang on herself. And it did boomerang as the enquiry officer said with an unnatural and flattering smile: 'Am I to understand then that your statements also were in accordance with 'the usual method of case'? 'I then remarked:

'Not only the superintendent, but also the Principal and the Manager-Bishop, too, act in accordance with the 'usual method of the case'. That is why they could produce Photostats of documents avoiding the signature that is found in the original'. I thought my remark was telling enough for those concerned to feel stung.

The evidence taking was closed on 5 August and the arguments started on 19 September. My advocate seemed to relax the need of working upon the evidence as he felt I had bright prospects of being appointed in the newly-sanctioned Melukavu College under the new CSI Bishop, Mani. I intervened: 'The prospects are not that bright as you think because the new Bishop the Rt. Rev. M.C. Mani is admittedly a 'Bishop of peace' and rigorously ruled by the spirit of the modern ecumenical movement. At any rate I would like to know the findings'.

So he decided to argue the case seriously. At the very outset of the argument, Mr P.T. Mathew said: 'In the argument of the case there is only one point that needs argument as it is not clear: 'I mean the charge of the Gherao'. Later, I enquired from my advocate what the enquiry officer's remark meant. Whether all the other allegations have been proved or *not* proved? My advocate, who had been assessing all the depositions, assured me: 'The remark definitely means the second: namely no allegations have been proved'. I fear my advocate had for a moment forgotten that it was a domestic enquiry and my fear was confirmed later by the enquiry report which found all the allegations true! On 1 November the proceedings were concluded and the verdict was expected to arrive any day.

Those days were days of intense agony for my family and immediate relatives, thinking over the heavily dark, uncertain and insecure future looming large on me, my wife and my two little kids under the absolute authority which the politically woven legal fabric around the Minority Rights Provisions had endowed the management with. On 7 December 1981 I met Bishop Thomas Mar Athenasius of Mar Thoma Church at Manganam seeking his influence and help. 'There is no use my intervening in the matter,' he told me, 'Bishop

Kunnacherry's mind is set. You report the matter to the Vice Chancellor'. On 9 December I reached college and reported the latest position of the enquiry to the staff. They seemed to be interested in discussing the problem. But then they thought: 'It is better to dissociate ourselves from the issue' and advised me to pursue further legal steps. But which step? They had no answer. I left the future of my helpless family for the disposal of Divine Providence and waited.

# 20

# From Frying Pan to Fire

## The Rt. Rev. M.C. Mani: Successor to Bishop T.S. Joseph

I have already mentioned about the letter of Bishop T.S. Joseph dated 1 December 1980 and subscribed by the two other retired CSI Bishops, M.M. John and T.B. Benjamin, addressed to Bishop Kunnacherry requesting him to give me back to them alive. I regret my inability to adequately pay back my debt of gratitude for the letter. Coming from a backward class community, rather black-skinned but fairly white-souled, Bishop Joseph was ruled by the holy spirit of Truth, Justice and Love rather than by the mutually back-scratching spirit of the modern ecumenical movement, formed parallel to the political alliances of internecine and mutually repulsive political parties. Bishop Joseph retired and was given farewell on 18 January 1981. The Rev. M.C. Mani was consecrated as the Rt, Rev. M.C. Mani, Bishop-successor, on 8 February 1981, a very fair-skinned personality from the forward class Syrian community. From the very beginning he was very enthusiastic to foster and to be ruled by a strong, modern ecumenical spirit. The presence of Bishop Kunnacherry on the Rostrum of the C.M.S. College Great Hall during the gorgeous reception given to the new forward class community Bishop was a solid proof of this strong modern ecumenical spirit. I recollect what a beautiful, mid-aged respectable lady told me later, extolling the fair, attractive, agile personality of our Bishop: 'We must have Bishops like Bishop M.C. Mani. What an attractive personality! With Bishop Mani seated in the middle, wedding and family photos will look extra graceful'. It was quite instinctively that I responded: 'We can look for and find fairer and sprightlier personalities among film stars as candidates for Bishopric'.

However, my first meeting with Bishop Mani, on 25 February 1981, was a shock for me, provoking me to ask myself whether my leaving the Knanaya Catholic Church and entering the C.S.I. Community had been a leap from frying pan to fire! My unequal struggle against a mighty vindictive management, empowered with an absolute disciplinary authority with an absurd legal set up not permitting any appeal, had almost vanquished me and my family, mentally as well as physically. Naturally, I approached my new Bishop with a turbulent mind expecting a patient and understanding hearing, and a ray of hope, of help and protection under his new position and influence. Rev. M.C. Mani appeared very gentle, smiling, friendly and sympathetic towards me before the diocesan council convened to elect the Bishop panel. I too was a member of the Council and one of the qualified voters in the panel election. I requested him to follow up the protective hand extended by Bishop T.S. Joseph to fetch me a feeling of security. The response I got was highly disheartening and confirming a decision and policy to abide strictly by the spirit of modern ecumenical movement. These are the words that I heard falling from his recently consecrated mouth: 'No synod executive, not even the diocesan council executive, will take up your case. The priests of the diocese are not particularly happy over your change of denomination.[The ecumenical spirit of mutual understanding, I felt, to protect the frontiers of each member church, closing the door to the persecuted refugees from other denominations!]. They are rather indifferent. You are not even on the clergy roll of the Diocese, perhaps for no cause of yours [I wondered how then I could have the right to vote for the Bishop-panel in the just concluded diocesan council]. I (then as the diocesan clergy secretary) allowed you to vote for the Bishop-panel only because I was one of the candidates (!!). You must resign from the college. I am a Bishop of peace. The other three Bishop might sign a public statement. But not me.' As far as my experience goes, I have never come across any presbyter or church worker of the diocese showing in difference towards me. On the contrary they have called upon me several times to help them in the field of priestly ministry. I have rendered priestly ministry in almost all the parishes of the diocese and am doing the same even now. Above all I have with me the order issued by Bishop T.S. Joseph dated 2 October 1976 recognising me as one of the presbyters of the diocese. I have been assigned and have done pastoral (surplice) duties in several churches of the diocese. Ever since my shift of residence to Vadavathoor I have been and am an active member of the St. Paul's C.S.I. Church, Vadavathoor, conducting priestly services either jointly with the pastor or alone depending upon the need of the time, all these without asking for or receiving any salary or remuneration. Bishop Mani asked me to resign from the college. It was against all the instructions received from ever so many who are competent in the matter of service rules including the University registrar and the Vice Chancellor himself never to resign from the service of the college at Uzhavoor. And his words fell on my ear like a bolt from the blue. This was perhaps the shortest and the most effective means for him of rendering service to and establishing 'ecumenical peace' and sharing Episcopal-level shake hand on elevated public rostrums with Bishop Kunnacherry. Compared to the latter I am small fry for Bishop Mani. The suggestion to resign sounded like selling me into butchers' hands for the prize of ecumenical cooperation!

'Don't you think, Thirumeni,' I pleaded, 'that it is more heroic and manly to face dismissal, under the present absurd legal condition, after boycotting this one-sided enquiry?' 'Yes, you can boycott the enquiry and face dismissal. I am not going to give you recommendation for D.Th. scholarship'. He seemed to be bent on closing all the doors of refuge for the survival of me and family. I said: 'I thank you for the forthright frankness shown in your attitude. If I am not wanted or appreciated as a presbyter, I am prepared to leave the diocese and seek some missionary field.' 'No need to leave. You are welcome here. You resign from the college. When man closes one door, the Lord will open many others. I shall recommend you for D.Th. scholarship. That will take care of your family for two years. Afterwards you will have K.U.T. Seminary to teach or surely a pastorate in the diocese'! Once again the target is my resignation! That would clean Bishop Kunnacherry of the stigma and embarrassment consequent upon the domestic enquiry he has initiated to do away with me and save him from all inconvenience of any stain on his public image! What else is the purpose of the modern ecumenism if not the mutual back-scratching! For my resignation Bishop Mani would reward me with his recommendation for D.Th. scholarship and later with a pastorate in the diocese! But how all these if I am not in the clergy roll of the diocese? Rev. Dr Jacob Varghese of K.U.T. Seminary and Dr Ayyappa Panicker of the University Institute of English, both of whom I visited on 2 March 1981 and Dr Chandran of U.T. College, Bangalore, whom I visited on 20 June 1981, all advised me never to tender my resignation because it would cut my lien in the college and deprive me of the benefit of eleven and more years of continuity in the service.

However, pointing at the prospects of my being absorbed in the future vacancies that might arise in colleges under the diocesan management, especially in the expected new college sanctioned and soon to be started in Melukavu, also under the management of Bishop Mani, he demanded that I tender my resignation from Uzhavoor College. On 6 March I handed over to Bishop Mani my resignation containing certain hints of the process of victimization under cover of the private college management's absolute disciplinary authority. Bishop Mani wanted me to rewrite the letter of resignation indicating my voluntary resignation and removing all allusions to any victimization that might cast shadow or aspersion on the image of Bishop Kunnacherry. I obliged Bishop Mani, with full awareness that I was providing the two Bishops in strong ecumenical relationship with a fatal weapon they could use whenever they would wield it. That might also have been the reason why the momentum of disciplinary proceedings was brought down.

### Prospects of Appointment in Melukavu

Meanwhile the process of bifurcation of the Madhya Kerala diocese and the formation of the East Kerala Diocese was in full momentum. The area which would come under this new diocese is predominantly of scheduled tribe community, generally known as Mala Araya Community. Rev. Michael John, though coming from this community was a very white-souled, highly efficient priest who was on the Bishop panel with Rev. M.C. Mani and eventually he became the first Bishop of the new diocese. On 28 June 1981 I met Rev. Michael John. That time as convener of the college steering committee he was in the thick of work in preparation for the inauguration and commencement of the new college that was imminent. I met him with all the burden of my agonized heart, of which he was well aware. 'I have been thinking of you as the first Principal of the new college,' he told me. 'I was intending to see you tomorrow or so to know your mind'. The new college office was opened the following day.

Though allayed by the concern and affection shown and the prospects offered by Rev. Michael John, my mind was still turbulent and my nights restless. On 2 July, on the insistence of and accompanied by Dr T.J. Mathew (Dr Appachen) I met Bishop Mani to discuss the prospects of my being absorbed into the new college staff. Pat came the response from the glamorous-looking Bishop Mani: 'Melukavu College is still in the government's file. I haven't got any official information yet from the University and can do nothing about it until I get official communication. And then after advertisement for application, if your application is filed then it will be considered along with the other ones. I have just opened the college office and appointed Arby Varghese, Malayalam Lecturer, Bishop Moore College, Mavelikkara, as the Principal'.(Mr Arby later was ordered to go on compulsory leave and eventually dismissed from the service consequent upon grave mis-management of the college financial affairs detected by the department. And I was called upon to take over charge after Arby left. Details will follow.)

'Appointment of the Principal is already made?' Dr Mathew enquired utterly surprised. 'Yes', the Bishop replied, 'That chapter is closed as the manager appoints the person of his choice'. 'What do you advise me to do, Thirumeni?' I enquired.

'I have no advice for you.' 'But I am being consumed in the unending fire of uncertainty, insecurity and indecision. I came to seek your help to make a decision,' I said. 'You take the decision you want. I have no objection.' 'Oh my God,' I thought, 'with the fatal weapon of my plain and unconditional letter of resignation in hand, has Bishop Mani taken on from Bishop Kunnacherry the quotation to flatten me and my family for a lesson to intimidate other priests who might think of following my course for the reward of the glamorous Episcopal-level ecumenical shake hands on elevated public rostrums?'

'I have applied for junior lecturer post advertised for the Bishop Moore College in accordance with your advice,' I reminded him. 'If you get a selection there, well and good,' was the Bishop's cool, cold reply. 'Appointment of the Principal, done already, is much disheartening,' Dr Mathew said. 'We thought Achen's (that is my) problem could be solved with the sanction of Melukavu college'. 'If only I knew of it a couple of days ago,' the Bishop more soft and gentle with Dr Mathew, said, 'I could look into whether the case could be considered. Now, that the chapter is closed and the Bishop cannot go back over his decision….' 'On my return to Bangalore I had written to you. Did you not get my letter?' I put in. 'I'm too busy to read all the letters. Your letter must be on my table'. With this he entered his closet and shut the door.

It was hellish heat and darkness in my mind. At the gate of the Bishop's house compound I told Dr Appachen: 'I feel rather bad, Dr Appachen. I should like to spend a few minutes with Bishop Benjamin. I'll get a word of consolation from him that will ease my tension.' I was reminded of Bishop Mani's attitude to me shown in the diocesan office earlier. The new diocesan registrar, Prof K. Samuel, Principal of Peete Memorial Training College, Mavelikkara, asked me to discuss the problem with Bishop Mani. I waited for him till he was free from the diocesan executive committee meeting. As he came out of the office and saw me approaching him he took an attitude of indifference and went into the office again ignoring me. I waited. As he came out again, I approached him. Without even caring to look at me, he walked straight to his car to go to the Bishop's house.

I made bold to tell him: 'I have been waiting here to meet you. Could you spare a couple of minutes?' 'I don't know,' he answered. 'You must make enquiries at my office in the Bishop's House to see if I have any time to spare for you.'

Dr Mathew understood the tension of my mind. Leaving me at the gate he went back to the Bishop. After some time, Dr Appachen came out of the Bishop's room and beckoned me to the Bishop's room with him. Reluctantly I entered. And Dr Mathew started: 'Thirumeni, Achen expected at least a word of sympathy and consolation at this moment of acute mental tension….' At this I almost burst out and said: 'Thirumeni, I did not crave for my grub and job, but for justice which is being denied. I expected your help to get justice done to me. Now I feel being severely punished for leaving the Catholic church and joining the C.S.I. I have a saga of long-endured injustice to tell. But I have nobody to hear it. I have not begged for a bowl of porridge. I am prepared to face utter want and privation as I have faced poverty in my life before I became a lecturer. My grievance is that I have no legal protection and an impartial competent forum of authority to hear the story of my being victimised'. We came away after D. Mathew made the Bishop agree to consider my problem. As I parted with Dr Appachen at his clinic, he said: 'Go, Achen, without much heaviness and be at ease. The Bishop will consider and your problem will take a better turn'. I came off.

On 7 July, I shared my woes with Bishop Benjamin. 'He is a puppet in the hands of a few laymen,' Bishop Benjamin observed about Bishop Mani…. 'There is not even honesty in the diocesan affairs' and he continued to cite a few incidents to confirm, which I desist to quote from my diary notes of the date for obvious reasons. On 10 July 1981, Mar Gregorios admonished me: 'Reach a decision soon to come away from Uzhavoor. The deterioration of your spiritual and psychological strength warrants it….If Bishop Mani refuses to consider you at least as Vice Principal of Melukavu College…. Well, God will reward your decision. You start your full time study for D.Th.'

On 14 August 1981, I was interviewed for appointment in Bishop Moore College. The interview was held in the diocesan office. 'What do you prefer, Mavelikkara or Melukavu?' Bishop Mani asked me. 'I'm ready to work where my service is needed', I replied. 'Right then, it may be appreciated more in Melukavu,' he decided. On 4 September when I reached Melukavu Office and bought the application form, I heard rumours that my chances for getting appointed there were bleak as the scheduled tribe CSI community there had two candidates for the two vacancies available: one on the Open Merit quota and the other on the community quota. However I filed my application before the Principal appointed, Mr Arby Varghese, on 22 September. Then Mr Arby said: 'The steering committee which considered your case was of the opinion that the diocese must look after you in a way demanded by the occasion. Here I want only those to be appointed who have already come to the college and been working with me'. 'I apply as per instructions from the Bishop. That's all,' I replied and left.

I did not attend the interview at the C.M.S. College conducted on 17 October as the Principal, Mr P.T. Abraham, said that I was expected to join Melukavu College. 'Interview for Melukavu will be held later in Trivandrum or Kottayam, depending on the convenience of the government nominee and the University nominee to the Board of Interview'. But the interview was held in Peete Memorial College Mavelikkara on 27 November 1981. Bishop Mani's management selected P.T. Aleyamma, one of the S.T. Community on open merit quota, and Rev. K.J. George of the same community on the community quota. However, as I later came to know directly from the persons concerned, the government nominee, Dr Babu Paul, I.A.S., and the University Nominee Dr Andrews Valentine, ruled out the management board's decision and insisted: 'On the basis of the interview there is no question of appointing any one else to the open merit quota except Fr Abraham Vellamthadathil'. I humbly and earnestly thanked God for such honest and God-believing men at least in the laity. Dr Babu Paul and Dr Valentine, priests though not made by the imposition of Episcopal hands, but according to the order of Royal Priesthood, conferred by the touch of divine grace, put me in the path of justice. In the result Miss Aleyamma and I were selected for appointment on the community merit quota and on the open merit quota respectively.

### The Vice Chancellor Intervenes

I felt much relieved. I went on medical leave from Uzhavoor College to recuperate my already shattered psychological and physical health so as to join duty in Melukavu on time. However, formalities required for the change of management had to be completed. On 1 December I met University Syndicate member Prof C.Z. Skariah. He advised me to apply for relieving order from the Uzhavoor college management in advance. I was to join service under the new management only from the date of relieving. This was necessary to protect the benefits of my last 11 years of service and for the continuity of the same salary and pay scale as in Uzhavoor College. He must have foreseen the possibility of mischief on the part of the vindictive management denying me even the relieving order. Accordingly, on 2 December I submitted through the Principal my application for relieving order with effect from 3 December. Sr. Goretti forwarded my application to the manager, gave me a copy of her forwarding letter and instructed me to approach the manager in person. I immediately contacted Fr Jacob Kollaparampil, Pro-manager over the phone and received the curt reply: 'The manager's will is not inclined to grant you relieving order. If you want, resign and go.' On advice from Advocate Sankunni Menon, I met Bishop Kunnacherry, but got the same curt reply. Again with Advocate Menon's letter I rushed to Ernakulam and consulted Advocate Siva Sankara Panicker of Kerala High Court. 'The court can do nothing in the matter as it stands,' he advised me. 'Go to the Vice Chancellor.' I rushed to Trivandrum the same day and spent the night with Rev. Dr Jacob Varghese. The next day (4 December), I met the Vice Chancellor and submitted my petition. He wanted to consult the Registrar on the matter, but the Registrar was on leave. I spent that night too at Trivandrum and met the Vice Chancellor the following day. After consultation with the Registrar, the Vice Chancellor said: 'We are calling for the Management's reasons, if any, for denying you the relieving order. Meet me on 14 December. Meanwhile, go back and join duty in Uzhavoor'. I returned, filed my medical fitness certificate and joined duty.

## Denouement of the Sordid Tragi-Comedy

On Thursday 10 December at about 7.30 a.m. a messenger from the Bishop's House brought me a letter from the Pro-manager requiring me to meet the Bishop at his office between 8.30 and 10.00 a.m. Accordingly I reached the Pro-manager's office at 9 a.m. 'We are willing to give you relieving order along with the copy of the Enquiry Report and the manager's decision on the report,' the Pro-manager said. At about 10.15 a.m. His Lordship the Rt. Rev. Dr Kuriakose Kunnacherry alighted down the staircase. Handing over to me the papers duly signed he said: 'I am praying every day for you'. 'Thank you,' I said in reply. The Bishop continued: 'According to the findings of the enquiry, you are found guilty of all the charges leveled against you.' I felt like telling him to thank the faithfulness of the hired enquiry officer P.T. Mathew. And the Bishop continued: 'But I don't dismiss you from the service, but show you mercy'. 'Thank you' I repeated. I deliberately suppressed the words that came to the tip of my tongue: 'I too pray that God have mercy on you.' I left with the enquiry report and the relieving order, conveyed the information to Ammal, then in Girideepam School, over the phone and reached college. Neither the Principal nor the superintendent madam nor the Vice-Principal, nor the Professor in Charge, Mr K.M. Mathew, was present. I signed the attendance register for that day, that being the last day of my service in Uzhavoor College and returned home, after conveying the message to my friend the old, 'uneducated', but God-fearing Kuriakochetan Mudakodil. On reaching home my five and a half year old son Jeslie, said: 'Pa we have got over one big headache'. All were happy over the happy end of the sordid Uzhavoor drama.

The very next day, Friday 11 December, I joined duty in Melukavu at 9.30 a.m. After engaging three hours of class there I returned home by about 7 p.m.

The next day I met Mr Sankunni Menon and Mr Chitra Bhanu and showed them the enquiry report. Mr Menon commented: 'Let's rise above them. You write a series of articles on your experiences with the leaders of organized religions in your attempt to find the truth of religion. I shall certainly help you to get them serialized.' If this modest saga of my struggle 'From Dark Dungeons to Dazzling Dawn' is completed and gets published, one of the sources of inspiration behind the effort is these words of the late Mr Menon.

**Farewell to the Bishop-Manager**

I thought I should complement the transactions engaged in on 10 December 1981 between Bishop Kunnacherry and me with a letter of due acknowledgement of his largesse of 'mercy'. I abstained from giving it then and there orally for fear that my strong emotions might over-ride my self control and prompt me to make impulsive utterances before a great Bishop of the 'jure divino' hierarchy, unbecoming before a consecrated person, which might be a source of life-long regret for me. My strong emotions having subsided, I thought of complementing the Episcopal magnanimity with a due acknowledgement in the form of a New Year's day message and I wrote a letter and dispatched it by registered post with acknowledgement due. I reproduce below the letter in its entirety.

Vadavathoor P.O.
Kottayam-10.
Rev. Abraham Vellamthadathil

To
The Manager,
The Corporate Educational Agency,
Kottayam Diocese,

*Ref.*: Your Letter No. 3/MT/80 dated 10-12-1981, reg. your findings of the Enquiry

Dear Rt. Rev. Thirumeni,
Kindly refer to the letter cited above, intimating me of your

findings from the report made by the person you employed to enquire into the charges you levelled against me. Under the circumstances I am constrained to write this to you to plainly deny once again all the charges you had levelled against me, and to repudiate the supposed findings of the enquiry farce you had instituted. The proceedings had totally been devoid of any bona fides, but vitiated from its birth till death by your design, in connivance with the Principal and the Office Superintendent, both catholic nuns under obedience to you, of wreaking vengeance on me for my decision to leave the Catholic Church and to join the C.S.I. Of course you conceived and instituted the proceedings under the cover of our unhappy legal system of the 'domestic enquiry', shielded in this case by the shade of the Constitutional Provisions of the Minority Rights to the one-sided protection of the managements. But let me quote another Catholic Bishop, Bishop Isaac Yuhanon of Thiruvalla Diocese, from his Christmas message of 1980: 'Ours is an age whose characteristic is that law defeats justice'.[*Malayala Manorama,* Sunday 21-12-1980]. I repeat that you had no right to institute such mala fide proceedings against me under any of the provisions of the Kerala University First Statute 1979 or any other law, as no law can validly provide for mala fide disciplinary proceedings. The farce of the disciplinary proceedings ordered by you to victimize me and to satisfy your vindictive urge has been a violence against Natural Justice and elemental honesty, and the enquiry report a travesty of the sanctity of legal enquiry proceedings.

I admit that such domestic enquiries as in the case under reference have been and are possible in our society of persons with sufficient money to hire human beings even for assassination! Our society with its morality guided by the present religious leadership and educational agencies, has unfortunately come to such a pass as to be guided by the morality of money.

In the case at hand, you were the accuser and I the accused. And the order of Natural Justice is that both the accuser and the accused are heard and the case decided by an impartial judge. I suggest to you, my Lord, if you care for the sanctity of

Natural Justice and the courage born of bona fides to refer the case for enquiry by an impartial commission. I am fully prepared to face the consequences of such an enquiry.

Your letter cited above reads: '...as you have obtained an appointment in a newly sanctioned college at Melukavu, I do not consider it necessary to take any step now to impose on you the penalty of removal from the service of this college'. And you told me on 10-12-1981 in the morning that you were showing mercy on me in relieving me of my duties in the college. I should have appreciated your gesture, had you cared to show it when I applied on 1-12-1981 to be relieved. But you chose to turn down my application and I was thus left with no choice other than appealing to the good Vice Chancellor against your denial. Again, you could have shown me the same gesture when three revered C.S.I. Bishops appealed to you on 1-12–1980 suggesting to you to relieve me from your college for good by granting me leave till a vacancy occurred in one of their colleges where I would be absorbed into one of the colleges under the C.S.I. management. But you had chosen to ignore even that appeal and to proceed with the disciplinary actions you had initiated. Now when I appealed to the Vice Chancellor against your denial to relieve me, you suddenly decided to show mercy on me by relieving me. Dr Samuel Johnson had once said: 'Benefit delayed is benefit denied'. However, while I take the mercy you thus imparted to me in the same measure in which I deserve it, I too pray that God have mercy on you and those who cooperated with you in this enquiry affair including your witnesses and the author of the enquiry report.

Sd/-<br>
Rev. A. Vellamthadathil

Copy to:<br>
Vice Chancellor, Kerala University, Trivandrum<br>
The Dy. Director of Collegiate Education, Tripunithura.<br>
President, Kerala Christian Council.

# 21

# The Third Phase: Dungeon Darker and Narrower

With my farewell to my Catholic Bishop-Manager, and joining duty in Henry Baker College, Melukavu, on Friday 11 December 1981, I entered the third phase of my priestly and professional life-struggle. I thought fortune would favour me with peace and ease of mind. With my earlier experience, my faith in the 'ipso facto' sanctity of the 'jure divino' hierarchical escalator service to heaven, as arrogated by the Catholic Church, was almost flattened. Still I could sustain my optimism because of God-believing persons such as Bishops T.S. Joseph, Ambrose Abasolo of Vijayapuram Diocese, Mathew Kavukatt of Chenganacherry, Rev. Michael John, and several honest laymen. However with the third phase of my college career, in H.B. College, started under Bishop Mani's management, I lost all my faith in the 'jure divino' and 'ex opere operato' sanctity and holiness that theological studies in the Seminary had generated in me. I was fated to continue treading along dungeons far darker and even narrower. I remember having read Bertrand Russell's words somewhere: 'If dictatorship, let it be that under Aristocrats rather than that under rabbles'. This observation is very relevant and apt for a comparison between the first two phases under the Uzhavoor College management and the third one under Melukavu College management.

## Nineteen Months without Salary: All Thanks to Bishop Mani

My college salary was the main source of income for the maintenance of my family. Of course, I was rendering almost the same load of priestly service as many other priests in the CSI Central Kerala Diocese, though I was not a pastor in charge of any pastorate with remuneration. I had decided not to take any remuneration for priestly service, except perhaps actual T. A., if given. After joining H.B. College, I had to struggle with my household affairs for nineteen months without my college salary, all thanks to Bishop Mani's decision to appoint me as junior lecturer, instead of as lecturer in continuation of my eleven and a half years of service upon the same salary and salary scale I was drawing in St. Stephen's college, Uzhavoor. Even in Uzhavoor, I began my teaching career on 1 July 1970 as a lecturer on lecturer's salary scale. I wish I were wrong in thinking that the Uzhavoor College Catholic management appointed me straight as lecturer only because it was prior to the direct payment system enforced upon the Private College Agencies by the then Education Minister, Mr Joseph Mundassery, of the communist Government in 1972. Till then the private college teachers had to sign the Aquittance Roll for the amount of salary disbursed by the government through the manager and be satisfied with the pittance doled out by the managers.

The purpose of all the exercise behind the struggle for a relieving order instead of resignation from the service of Uzhavoor college was to protect the benefits of the previous unbroken service and for appointment in continuation of my past service and scale of pay and salary. Throwing all these benefits to the winds, Bishop Mani appointed me as junior lecturer upon the salary and scale of salary fixed for junior lecturer post. Once again I wish I were wrong in thinking that Bishop Mani was instigated to do so either by the craving for the 'modern ecumenical' bishop-level friendship with his immediately neighbouring Catholic Bishop Kunnacherry and for the warmth and glamour of public image accrued through hearty Episcopal shake hands on elevated public rostrums or to spill the venom of ire created by Dr Babu Paul, I.A.S. and Dr Andrews Valentine, government nominee and university nominee to the interview board respectively, who insisted upon selecting me for the appointment on the open merit quota against the management's decision to appoint their candidate. They had ruled out and defeated the management's agenda of appointing candidates of their choice. Whatever be the instigation, Bishop Mani appointed me as junior lecturer ignoring the benefits of my past continuous service including the imminent right of promotion as second grade professor. I explained to him how and why I was warned by competent authorities including top level university officials not to resign from the service under the previous management lest I should lose the benefits of my 11 years of previous service and how they intervened on my behalf to obtain relieving order from the adamantly unwilling Catholic management of Uzhavoor college, solely for the purpose of protecting my service and salary scale and pay of salary. But as he once earlier told me: 'A bishop must not go over his decision once taken,' much along the line of Bishop Tharayil's 'motto of life': 'Purpose once formed, death or victory'. On my complaint the University refused to ratify my appointment as junior lecturer and consequently the payment of my salary was held up. I was reeling under financial stringency.

On 25 October 1982, I shared my straining helplessness with the Vice-Chancellor. He discussed the problem with the syndicate member Mr C.Z. Scariah, and suggested to him to put in a word with Bishop Mani to appoint me as lecturer. Accordingly, I visited Prof Scariah at his residence in Chenganacherry on 28 October 1982. He sent me to Bishop Mani with a personal letter addressed to him, clearly stating that it was well in order to appoint me as lecturer in continuation of my previous service and benefits. On 30 October, on the occasion of the baptism of Dr T.J. Mathew's grandchild, officiated by Bishop Mani, I handed over to him Prof Scariah's letter. But to him it was only a 'personal' letter and not an 'official' one from the university obliging him to go over his decision once taken. 'Get me the Vice Chancellor's order to appoint you as lecturer,' was his response. I rushed to the University once again with the Bishop's demand and was told by the Registrar or the Vice Chancellor himself, I don't exactly remember: 'Tell your Bishop that the office of the Vice Chancellor is not to fly and scatter unnecessary papers as other [Bishop's] offices might do'.

On 1 February 1983 I met the diocesan lay secretary Sri M.M. Mani along with Prof K. Samuel, diocesan Registrar. The latter had a copy of the syndicate decision of 17 February 1982 approving similar appointments as in order. They agreed to discuss the matter with Bishop Mani that day itself. On 17 February, I urged the matter of my appointment as lecturer with Principal Arbey but 'The Registrar will object,' he told me. 'I'll face the Registrar's objection if any and find legal ways and means to get over it,' I replied. On 21 February he wrote to the Registrar a misleading letter the copy of which he showed me. Later, on 2 March, my colleague Mr M.K. Kurian told me not to expect much support from the staff as the Principal had started forming 'inner caucus and cabinets'. On 22 February I discussed the matter with Rev. K. Michael John, who was all in my favour. He suggested some strong measures along the Gandhian path to get my appointment as lecturer in order. In fact I told the Principal that I would rather end my life before I see my children starve.

On 3 March I met the University Registrar at Trivandrum. He said: "The Syndicate decision [ratifying similar appointments as well in order] is self-explanatory to those who can read and understand simple English, not necessarily to all managers and Principals who run colleges". The remark was telling and ironical enough.

Meanwhile my intense mental tension began to develop psycho-somatic symptoms. I met Dr Jacob Chandy and consulted him on my acute pain on my thigh. After analysis of the situation he remarked: 'Bishop Mani's pride will dig his own grave'. On 15 March 1983, during my meeting with Mr M.M. Mani and Prof K. Samuel, the former was fully convinced of the unfairness of my predicament and promised to take up the matter with the Bishop. But the latter seemed to stand on weak ground. 'I'll meet the Registrar tomorrow. Meet me on 19 March Saturday,' he said. But he would not have me accompany him to meet the Registrar. On Saturday 19 March after the ordination service held in the C.S.I. Cathedral, Prof Samuel wanted me to meet the Bishop and I did so. 'Not now,' he said in his usual curt style. 'When shall I come then?' I respectfully enquired.

'Some time later,' was his reply again. I decided to write to him on the matter, but before the diocesan office he asked me to meet him at the Bishop's House. On 23 March 1983, Principal Arbey showed me a letter from Bishop Mani demanding to meet him with the copy of the syndicate decision in favour of my appointment as lecturer. I got my last pay certificate from Uzhavoor College on 30 March and handed it over to Arbey. On 31 March, Bishop Mani signed the order of my appointment as lecturer. I consulted Prof Scariah on 5 April to make sure what all papers should accompany the appointment order to the University for approval. With all the papers, I reached the University on 12 April and got fully favourable response from all the top University officials including the assurance that the approval of the appointment and fixation of salary and scale would reach the college by the end of April. The University formalities for my salary protection having been completed, I rushed to the D.D. Office with arrear bills on 1 July 1983, the due date of my promotion as II grade Professor. After all the usual red-tapism at the D.D. Office for the passing of the bills and at the Treasury Office, Erattupettah, for the customary 'something', which they failed to get from me, I finally got Rs. 26,000 or so as arrears of my 19 months salary as lecturer and not as junior lecturer, on Friday 22 July 1983. I reached home with this 'hefty' sum of money with a baby doll for my little daughter, Maymol, as I had promised her.

## Excardination from the Central Kerala Diocese

After thanking Bishop Mani for signing the order appointing me as lecturer, I informed him of my willingness to render priestly services in the new East Kerala Diocese, recently formed on bifurcation of the Central Kerala Diocese, and short of priests, now that I was working in Melukavu where the new diocese would have its headquarters. The new diocese was expected to elect its panel of Bishop candidates very soon and the two most prospective candidates were Rev. P.D. John, who was the first choice of Bishop Mani, and Rev. K. Michael John whose love and care I have had from 1975 onwards. It was the latter, who, on the suggestion of the then Bishop of North Kerala Diocese,

Bishop T.B. Benjamin, visited me and Ammal at our residence at Uzhavoor soon after our marriage. He introduced me to Bishop T.S. Joseph and initiated me into priestly service in the CSI. Bishop Mani posted my request for consideration at a later time. The gesture was indeed an indirect but clear recognition of my place in the presbyter roll of the diocese. However, consider indeed he did as soon as the Bishop Panel election in the new diocese was completed and Rev. K. Michael John was installed as the New Bishop. By posting the consideration of my request to a 'later time', he succeeded in depriving Rev. Michael John of one vote in the panel election. And consider he did with a vengeance by deciding: 'You are removed from the Central Kerala Diocese. You are free to join any'!

I was on the Central Kerala Diocesan Clergy Roll, after all, as per the admission implied in the decision to remove me from the diocese. But to this date I remain a member of the Vadavathoor C.S.I. parish and therefore am on the clergy roll of the Central Kerala Diocese.

## Rev. K. Michael John Installed as Bishop

On 5 January 1984, Rev. K. Michael John was consecrated and installed as the first bishop of the new diocese of East Kerala. I prayerfully attended the solemn graceful function with intense joy and gratitude to God. Rev. K. Michael John got a thumping majority of the votes cast in the bishop-panel election, though I was manipulated out of his panel election by Bishop Mani. I felt a ray of light and gentle cool breeze stream into the dungeon, made darker and more uncertain after my farewell to Uzhavoor. I was sure of better understanding, care and trust from my new Bishop-Manager. Through his order dated 5 June 1984 he incorporated me into the presbyterian community of the diocese: 'You will have all the rights and privileges of a presbyter,' the order assured. Ever since then I have been assigned honourary priestly service in various churches in the Diocese.

The Mid February 1984 was a period of student indiscipline in the college, mainly due to party politics. The relationship between the Principal and the Staff was rather strained as the Principal over-ruled and called off certain minor punishments imposed on the students by members of the staff. This provoked the teachers and they decided to stand united and firm in matters of discipline in the classes and around. On 21 February, Bishop Michael John intervened and appointed a discipline committee with Mr M.K. Kurian as the convener.

## Involvement in Politico-Social Affairs

My acquaintance with advocates Sankunni Menon, P.K. Chitra Bhanu, V.B. Binu and others in connection with my legal fight with the Uzhavoor College Management had put me in touch with leaders of the Communist Party of India. Often I got invitations in large numbers to take part in party sponsored social and political issues which I honoured as far as possible. I was not aware that the 'caucus and inner cabinets' which were highly communal in nature were closely watching me in my politico-social involvements, with a view to make capital out of it when opportunity presented itself. Besides, one central figure of this caucus, a politician congressman, became the lay-secretary of the newly established East Kerala Diocese.

The diocesan council meeting of 13 October 1984 elected me to the Diocesan Executive Council with the highest majority of votes. The bishop-manager had already nominated me to the College Governing Board. The first anniversary of the Birth of East Kerala Diocese and the sixtieth birthday of Bishop Michael John were duly celebrated on 5 January 1985. The words of the chief guest of the day, Bishop Geevargese Mar Osthathios of the Syrian Orthodox Church: 'It is time for Christianity to give up minority rights and stand united for human rights,' were simply gripping and I felt justified in all the politico-social human programmes I got involved in.

## Professor-in-Charge of Principal

There was an emergency joint meeting of the Diocesan Executive Committee and the College Governing Board on 30 April 1985 to discuss the emergency situation in the college created by the report of the audit of the college office affairs by the Collegiate Education Department of 15 September 1984.

The report presented a rather sorry and sordid state of the college office affairs, particularly concerning the hefty amounts of educational grants and concessions disbursed by the government to the Scheduled Tribe and Scheduled Caste students who formed the majority of the student community. Let me quote from the introductory remarks in the report: 'It was found that the college is not having proper basic records such as Admission Register, Term Fee Register, Daily Fee Collection Register, P.D. Cash book etc.... The records and accounts are maintained most carelessly and irresponsibly. In the absence of proper record and registers, the audit was unable to scrutinize the accounts.... All records and registers have to be maintained afresh.... and produced for audit.' Quite expectedly, the Principal was ordered to go on compulsory leave and the Management was asked to initiate disciplinary proceedings against him.

In the vacancy created by the Principal's indefinite compulsory leave, the manager, Bishop Michael John, reposing his entire trust on me, which I reciprocated with the utmost possible loyalty, dutifulness and honesty, issued an order appointing me as Professor-in-charge with effect from 31 May 1985 and directing the Principal to hand over charge with records and registers duly signed and counter-signed. However the Principal did not even turn up to hand over charge and sign and counter-sign records. Under the circumstances I had no choice but to assume charge. Eventually Memo dated 10 August 1985 containing seven charges including grave misappropriations was served on the Principal, the first of which was his failure 'to hand over to Professor-in-charge [P.i.C.] Rev. Abraham Vellamthadathil, the books of accounts, registers etc. on your availing leave with effect from 1-6-1985'. Proceedings having been duly concluded he was eventually dismissed from service.

## A Blessing or a Curse?

I wonder whether my assuming charge was a blessing or a curse. I leave it to the readers to decide in the light of what followed. For me it was the dawn of a period of nearly ten long years of struggle against a simple but gullible community made hostile under the whip of a power-drunk, venomous ambitious caucus who wielded over this community a blind, almost dogmatic authority with no defense for me except legal battles. It was indeed a long period of test of fire at the end of which I emerged without even a scratch or a burn, all thanks to God Almighty in whom I put my trust when I took over charge. Somewhere in the middle of this struggle, even Bishop Michael John gave me up because he was forced to such a pass as to make a choice between me and the caucus-led community over which he was the bishop. And he made the choice in favour of the caucus-led community. To me therefore this long period of intense struggle was a great blessing in terrible disguise. If good Bishop Michael John ever thinks that I availed myself of his trust reposed on me as a defense in this again unequal combat, it was only for my self-defense and not for any financial gain as the denouement of this struggle will prove and he will forgive me with a smile.

## At the Helm of a Battered Ship

On 1 June 1985, I assumed charge of the college in the absence of the Principal Mr Arbey to hand over charge, records, registers accounts and balance if any and to sign and countersign. I felt myself like the captain of a battered ship about to sink. I invoked God's help and protection to keep it afloat and rescue it from sinking.

As a first step, I consulted Rev. K.C. Mathew, Principal of Moore College, Mavelikkara, and explained the situation and sought his wise and valuable guidance. And God acted on my behalf through him. He advised me to write to the Collegiate Education Department that in the case of Principal Arbey's failure to turn up to hand over charge I have assumed charge on a nil balance and that I would not be responsible for any failure or defects for the period prior to my assuming charge. I immediately carried out this piece of advice. I then instructed the various officials concerned to maintain recording every day-to-day office affairs in a temporary record each until permanent arrangements are made. I also visited Mr Sadanandan,

Superintendent, Deputy Director of Collegiate Education Office, Kottayam on 20 June and informed him of the situation. My next visit was to Mr K.M. Varghese, Principal of St. Mary's College, Manarcad for the help of a small team of efficient and expert office staff to work out a complete office work system in H.B. College and to initiate the H.B. College office staff into a flawless systematic and up to date maintenance of office records. He promised all possible help and cooperation and eventually generously implemented the promise. I continued daily personal check up of the temporary log book entries.

**The Shift of Girls' Hostel from Private-Owned Residence**

The classes were conducted in open rooms, partitioned by half constructed walls and movable screens under a temporary asbestos-sheeted roof. There was a small building on the college campus set apart and used by the former Principal as his living quarters. Now that I was given charge of the Caily Land Church along with the charge of the Principal I resided in the parsonage which is also close by the college. The building used as the Principal's quarters was now lying vacant. A large number of girl students belonging to the Scheduled Tribe and Scheduled Caste of the CSI Community were housed in the residence of an elderly woman, whom we called Peramma, mother of Rev. T.S. Ninan, the diocesan clergy secretary and one of the central figures in the caucus. He was also in all the top diocesan committees including the College Governing Board. Hostel accommodation provided in private residence was against the norms of the Scheduled Caste and Scheduled Tribe departments disbursing hefty amounts towards the hostel and educational concessions of the students. In the joint meeting of the Diocesan Executive and the college governing board of 19 April 1985, I suggested that the hostel be shifted to the Principal's quarters after it was extended and furnished. The suggestion was immediately approved and in due course implemented. Very soon the hostel students were shifted to the college hostel with an educated responsible lady appointed as warden. The hostel, when accommodated with and managed by Peramma, was a considerable source of income to Rev. T.S.

Ninan's family by way of rent and on other accounts. With the shift to the new college hostel one of the family's veritable sources of income came to be closed. Perhaps I might be on the wrong to think that this piqued Rev. Ninan and created in him bitter blood against me, the distaste of which was felt in all his activities as member in all the top level diocesan committees. Later when he failed to get selected as successor to Bishop Michael John, he left priestly service and the service of the diocese, I heard it rumoured.

## Principal on Compulsory Leave Dismissed

Through my report dated 12 August 1985 I explained to the Bishop-Manager the dismal and chaotic condition of the college office. 'As a part of my attempt to get a clear and definite point to start with,' I reported, 'I have written to the Collegiate Education Department, Trivandrum, to the District Welfare Officer, Kottayam, and to the Tribal Development Officer, Kanjirappally, requesting them to audit their respective accounts and fix liabilities if any.' On receipt of my report he decided to initiate disciplinary proceedings against Principal Arbey, then on compulsory leave, and served on him 'Memo' dated 16 August 1985 containing seven charges of mismanagement and dereliction of duties. In fact the Bishop-Manager was acting far in advance of the direction from the Commissioner& Secretary to Government No. 30871/D1/85/H. Edn. dated 16-12-1985 asking the Manager to initiate disciplinary Proceedings as 'the audit on accounts of the H.B. College, Melukavu, conducted by the Dy. Director of Collegiate Education, Kottayam, has revealed that there is clear case of misappropriation of government money in the college for the period during which Sri Arbey was the Principal. The gross irregularities and defalcation of government money amounts to grave misconduct for which the delinquent has to be suitably proceeded against'. Eventually the delinquent was dismissed.

## Selection of Grade IV Librarian Kicks off the Struggle

The IV grade librarian post was vacant and needed to be filled.

Applications were called for through due advertisement. The interview was fixed to 27 December 1986. The Interview Board, as per Statutes, consisted of the Government nominee (here, Mr P.C. John, Dy. Collector, Palghat), the Management nominee (here, Rev. T.S. Ninan) and the Principal as ex officio convener of the interview board. About a couple of minutes before the interview to begin, while I was exchanging pleasantries with Mr P.C. John and waiting for the arrival of the other nominee, the group of the three most-powerful members of all the diocesan council and other committees—Rev. P.V. Joseph, his brother-in-law Mr C.C. Jacob, the diocesan lay secretary and one of the local congress party leaders, both of them on the college teaching staff, and Rev. T.S. Ninan came in with the name of one G.P. Vijaya Kumar as candidate settled and therefore to be selected for the post of librarian.

These three formed the 'Three Pillars of the Diocesan Power Centre' and would have the last word on any matter. They had arrogated a kind of super-power over the entire diocese, particularly in matters concerning the college. I still have in my file the original of a complaint dated 25 December 1986 addressed to Prof in–charge by Mosa Joseph, one of the fourth grade employees, against another last grade staff. The complaint was marked with copies marked for the Bishop-manager, Rev P.V. Joseph and Mr C.C. Jacob! 'Here is the name of the person we are to choose from the candidates for the librarian's post' they told me giving me a slip. 'He is a little short of the required qualification. But that can be made up by a special order from the government,' they said. Mr P.C. John, who is another in-law of them, seemed to take for granted that their role in the affairs was decisive. 'Have you made the commitment to him?' I enquired. 'Yes, of course.'

'Before the interview?' I put in. 'Yes, before the interview. Interview! It's we who conduct it!' After a few seconds of silence I continued: 'In that case, the two secretaries and the government nominee may conduct the interview, complete the formalities and make the rank list. I shall keep off the interview affair', I said. 'Oh, no,' they insisted: 'You have to be on the interview board as the Principal is the ex officio member of the board'. 'If I have to be on the interview board, the selection of candidates will be made strictly on merit determined by their performance in the interview and other required qualifications. I cannot fool and cheat the candidates and their guardians with the show of a meaningless interview farce. It's me who advertised for and invited them to the interview'. The pillars of the diocesan authority were not without a shakeup at this unexpected resistance from what they thought a small creature like me against their self-assumed supremacy. A short but sharp altercation followed. Finally, finding that I was firm and unwilling to relax, they agreed to form the rank list on the basis of marks awarded. The interview was accordingly conducted and the mark lists signed by the three interviewers are still in my file.

The college governing board was soon convened and it discussed the problem. After hearing both sides the Bishop-Manager gave a ruling and proposed a compromise formula: 'It was wrong on the part of those who decided the candidate to be selected before the interview and committed to the person concerned to appoint him. It should not be repeated in future. However, the prestige of the diocesan secretaries has to be salvaged some how or other. So, Achen,' the Bishop told me, 'Prepare a rank list placing the candidate to whom commitment has been made in the first place, and the candidate who scored the highest marks in the second place. We are not going to apply for any special government order in favour of the first candidate who is declaredly a little short of the required qualification. So he will automatically be eliminated and the second on the list will automatically be approved and validly appointed. Thus the prestige of the secretaries could be salvaged and the deserving candidate will get appointed'. I decided to accept the Bishop's compromise formula, prepared the rank list accordingly and sent to Palghat for Mr P.C. John's signature.

On 2 March 1987 Rev. P.V. Joseph rushed to my office bringing Mr Vijaya Kumar with him. 'Why didn't you send this man's approval proposal?' he questioned me. 'Because I haven't got the minutes signed by Mr P.C. John'. 'Why did you send it to Mr John before getting T.S.'s signature?' 'To save time'.

'No, you're telling a lie. I am not convinced'. 'I refuse to talk with you any more. I don't feel bound to convince you of my decisions'.

On 30 December 1986 the three 'pillars of the power centre' rushed into the Principal's office with a rank list signed by Rev. T.S. Ninan and said: 'You are to sign this rank list'. 'Who prepared the rank list?' I enquired. 'We did it'. 'But the mark lists are with me. Upon what basis then did you make the rank list?' 'You only need to know that we have prepared the rank list'. 'I'm sorry, then,' I said, 'I refuse to sign rank lists arbitrarily prepared'. Pat came their reply: 'If you refuse to sign this, we will be constrained to proceed with disciplinary actions against you'. 'Please get out of my office,' I was provoked to say. 'I shall face them as they come'.

On 9 March 1987 another college Governing Board meeting was held. It was a preplanned attack on me by a pack of wolves. The members headed by the trio insisted that I should sign the rank list, arbitrarily prepared. Rev. P.D. John got up to express his views. But his son-in-law Rev. P.V. Joseph cut him across: 'Appachan, sit down. There is nothing more to talk about the decision. It is final'. Rev. P.D. John sat down. And the Board decided that I should sign this rank list, but refused to have it recorded in the minutes. 'Has the decision any purpose to serve other than to break me to the satisfaction of Rev. T.S. Ninan and group?' I helplessly asked the Bishop. 'Achen', the Bishop tried to sympathize with me, 'I have been broken several times'. 'Yes, Thirumeni', I said, 'I too am ready to be broken'.

## Ultra Vires Interference

Rev. P.V. Joseph had often interfered with college affairs including even with the class schedule. On 4 March 1987, he got the warden to send the second-year hostel students home citing a water shortage—ignoring the fact that staff were struggling to get more classes to complete the syllabus before the students left on the usual study leave. I came to know of it only when some students came to me for special permission to stay back. My complaint to the Bishop-Manager dated 11 March 1987 against this interference was seemingly ignored.

Another instance was his highly irregular interference with the process of admission, going against all the norms and stringent rules issued by the Directorate of Collegiate Education and the University. I noticed serious irregularity in the interview cards kept ready to be dispatched to the candidates. When questioned, the office staff reported to me that Rev. P.V. Joseph sat with them and dictated to them to issue cards to candidates of his choice for the most coveted and already nearly filled second group. On scrutiny I found that some of these candidates had not even applied for the second group. I instructed the office staff to adhere strictly to the norms and checked the irregularity. Upon this Rev. P.V. Joseph rushed to my office room in a storm of fury shouting abuses and snatched papers from my hands threatening that he would pull out my tongue. However, I refused to be intimidated or provoked. In my complaint to the Bishop-Manager dated 21 June 1987 I wrote: 'Rev. P.V. Joseph has also interfered several times with the office accounts by having secret dealings and transactions of business with officials dealing with money and accounts without my knowledge. This has caused a good deal of confusion already. Now that we have been able to bring the accounts of the college office up to date, I request that P.V. Joseph be told not to interfere with the working of the office staff'.

## The College Governing Board Decision Recorded

Referring to the events of the Board meeting of 9 March 1987, the Bishop said: 'They were making a planned attack on you....By defending you, I too get isolated. They are plotting against me'. In reply I said: 'After two years you will retire. I will have to face them wielding ultra vires authority and in-law politics'.

On 12 March 1987 I wrote to Bishop Michael John, resigning my membership in the Diocesan Executive Committee with immediate effect on ground that the caucus in the College Governing Board 'prevailed and decided that I sign the rank list of the Librarian candidates arbitrarily prepared...and wanted me to yield to their decision, though they would not have it recorded….Please recall my request made in the Board meeting of 31 October 1986 to relieve me of my duties as Prof.-in-charge and to make alternative arrangements for me to hand over charge to without further delay.'

The diocesan secretaries avidly published my resignation in the diocesan reports for the forthcoming diocesan council, but, understandably enough, they thought it clever to obliterate the ground on which I resigned. On Friday 20 March, Bishop Michael John called me to discuss the librarian rank list problem. On my repetition that I would be disentangled from this sordid college office affairs before signing the rank list, Thirumeni said: 'I am made to bear the brunt'. These words made me sad and on Sunday 22 March I told him: 'You will not have to suffer any more on account of me. I am ready to sign the rank list.'

## Preparation to Hand over Charge

On 25 March1987 The Bishop-Manager issued instructions to me to hand over charge of the college to Prof N.C. Joseph of Mar Athanasius College, Kothamangalam, who had been appointed Prof in-charge on deputation for one year with effect from 1 April 1987 'or any other day he comes to take charge'. 'I take this opportunity', the order continued, 'to thank you most sincerely for your kind and efficient services as Prof.-in-charge for the last two years. The affairs of the college were in a big mess when you took charge. But by your sincere efforts you have made things almost in order. May God bless you.'

In the context of the total mess the college office affairs were in when I took charge, all I could do immediately was to assign the various sections of the office work to different officials instructing them to maintain adhoc records until a permanent accounting system was installed. The system was completed and started to function thanks to the help of the expert team from the Manarcad College. And I instructed the office staff to transfer their respective section entries from the adhoc documents to the permanent ones. On scrutiny I found irregularities in the accounts of the various educational concessions including stipends, hostel grants and scholarships given to the S.T., S.C. and O.B.C. students by the government departments concerned. The section had been assigned to Mr K.G. Samuel, who was also a member of the College Governing Board. He was expected to hand over the hostel concessions to the warden and keep vouchers duly signed by the warden. Having volunteered to help the warden in the purchase of goods he neglected to maintain accurate accounts. In fact, later, he was dismissed from service for attempting to filch the monthly salary of the staff under the false story of a wayside robbery by unidentified persons on his way back from the Treasury. He failed to give any satisfactory reply to the several notices sent by me. The Manarcad expert team who came for the final inspection of the accounts and the records and registers prior to my handing over of charge also detected serious irregularities and mala fide negligence on his part in the maintenance of the hostel accounts. Hence I reported the matter to the Bishop-Manager on 5 June 1987. I concluded the report thus: 'In the context I suspect K.G. Samuel of want of bona fides in the delay in completing the educational concessions accounts and in submitting the hostel accounts. I fear that large amount of money including grants from the government departments as AB and LC [Actual Boarding and Lodging Charges] and the cash balance of the educational concessions accounts has to be accounted for by K.G. Samuel, the dealing official. I report the matter for information and recommend immediate necessary actions to get the amounts accounted for'. Again my complaint to the Manager dated 3 October 1987 pointed out irregularities of considerable amounts. But I was not informed of any follow up action on these reports. And I have reason to suspect secret connivance on the part of the embittered caucus who had a secret agenda to make use of these irregularities as possible means to realize the vow of some of them as it was rumoured to me later on: 'As long as there is life throbbing in my throat I will see that Rev. Abraham Vellamthadathil never gets his pension and retirement benefits'.

Prof *N.C. Joseph,* who was appointed as Principal on deputation for one year, came and I handed over charge to him on 1 July 1987 with all the formalities completed and papers and records signed and counter signed by the New Principal and Rev. P.V. Joseph in his capacity as Bursar of the college, who was looking forward to take over charge as Lecturer-in charge [L.i.C.] after the one year deputation period of Prof N.C. Joseph.

## My Night Visit to Ladies' Hostel

This episode may serve as a comic relief to this saga of tragic-comedy. As already mentioned the hostel students were shifted from the residence of Rev. *T.S. Ninan's mother* to the then vacant Principal's quarters. After the dedication of the quarters and inauguration of the new hostel, Bishop Michael John told me: 'Achen, now that the hostel has been shifted to a new residence within the campus, you are to take paternal care of it as if all the inmates are your children'. I was at that time residing in the Caily Land parsonage close-by. A young doctor from Andhra Pradesh, (I forget his name), fresh from his studies, was appointed medical officer in a diocesan health clinic. Being a bachelor he was staying with me in the parsonage and we had our meals from the hostel. The warden Saramma was a young graduate from the same East Kerala Tribal Community. One of her kitchen staff, Leelamma too was from the same community. Once, at about 11 p.m. information reached the parsonage that Leelamma was suffering from asthmatic breathing trouble. Both the doctor and myself rushed to the hostel and the doctor gave her medicine and the necessary first aid and allayed her discomfort. Fearing a possible relapse we advised the warden and Leelamma to spend the rest of the night in the parsonage for the easy and immediate attention of the doctor, if found necessary.

Later at the suggestion of my wife Ammal, I went to Kottayam with Leelamma on Friday 13 March 1987 for more expert treatment. The next day Ammal took Leelamma to Kottayam Medical College for consultation with Dr Mathew Paracken and after necessary tests and check up returned to my home. The following afternoon Leelamma left for Melukavu and reached the hostel. Again on Saturday 21 March Leelamma came with me to Kottayam and Ammal accompanied her for further check up with Dr Paracken. The next day after noon Leelamma returned to the hostel.

The adventure took place on 31 December 1986, the eve of the Papal Visit of Pope John Paul II to India. I locked the parsonage and was walking to catch the 4 p.m. bus on my way home to Kottayam. I did not want to miss the thrill of watching the touchdown of the plane carrying, the first-in-the-history, guest at the Kottayam Police Ground. On the way to bus stop I found a few hostel students returning from home followed by their young warden Saramma. She stopped seeing me approach. I saw it reflected on her face that something was deeply disturbing her mind. Her eyes were red with prolonged shedding of tears, I thought. 'Coming from home?' I enquired 'Yes, Achen,' she answered. 'Are you going home today?' 'Yes,' I explained. 'I would like to watch the touchdown of the plane carrying the Pope tomorrow'. Upon this Saramma seemed to burst into sobs and passed me by hurrying on her way to the hostel. I reached the bus stop. While waiting for the bus, I mused: 'Something very ponderous must be weighing her heart down. Joy shared is joy doubled, and sorrow shared is sorrow allayed', I remembered. But who is there to share and understand the weighing agony of this young, Scheduled Tribe graduate girl? Whimpering all alone during the whole sleepless night might lead her to some mental distraction and serious nervous breakdown and cause permanent damage to her mind. Suddenly I recalled my own terrible experiences of mind-breaking tension and the consequent long period of insomnia which I suffered during my seminary life in Poona. I recalled how my intimate friend and senior colleague, Brother George Mangatt (later Professor in the St. Thomas Seminary Vadavathoor) spent several nights with me in the chapel, cheering me up from my depressing, concentrated mental tension and how I felt consoled and saved from serious mental disorders. But who is there in the hostel to understand Saramma and share her woes and allay her tension? No. I cannot leave her in her terrible loneliness that night. But I'm not any expert psychologist. That doesn't matter, I thought. Even an illiterate mother can give the consolation and sense of security needed by her ailing child. God has equipped her with the maternal love and care, though not with any profound psychological expertise. Suddenly I also recollected the words of Bishop Michael John, uttered on the occasion of the shift of the hostel to the newly accommodated quarters: 'The hostel should be under your paternal care'. I did not care for any other sinister thoughts of rumour spreading – thoughts about the possible gossips and the row and noise that could be set in motion by the embittered caucus with their blind sweeping influence over the very gullible people of the community. I dropped my Kottayam programme and returned to the parsonage. I informed Saramma to expect my visit after about 10 p.m. I spent a couple of hours sharing her love for and confidence in me, sharing my own experience and the little wisdom I had derived from it as to how to face moments of intense mental tension in life. After I saw her calm down and ready to leave her future to the All-loving God, and to sleep the rest of the night, I returned to the parsonage.

Early the next morning I left for Kottayam and saw Pope John Paul II's plane touch down, saw the Pope from a distance and returned to the college the following day. I came to know that the rumours about my night visit in all its sinister sense had been flashed wide – strong bit of news in the hands of my bitter friends the trio to poison the people against me. I felt pity for poor Saramma. Had my effort to calm her mind down given her the feeling of a leap from frying pan into the fire? Will the good Bishop Michael John not think I had betrayed the trust he reposed in me and feel embarrassed before the simple and plain-thinking people? I decided to face the imminent turbulence with the peace and assurance of my conscience.

As expected, the Bishop summoned me and I had a frank interaction with him. In the wake of the simple people's inability to understand anything more than the 'sinister' side of the 'night visit', as painted by my clever embittered friends, I wrote to him requesting him to take any action he thought suitable to justify and clarify his position before the wondering people. Bishop Michael John had far greater understanding and decided to simply wink at me with his usual smile and to ignore the whole affair rumoured around.

**Post Prof-in-Charge Period**

I handed over charge, as mentioned above, on 1 July 1987. The phase of my struggle with the caucus-ruled church regime which followed was largely one of legal fight, but not any the less turbulent for that matter. Rev. P.V. Joseph, the expectant incumbent for the next Principal's post, his bother-in-law Mr C.C. Jacob, the local political Congress party leader, and Rev. T.S. Ninan, the expectant incumbent for the next Bishop-appointment were members in almost all committees concerning the diocesan affairs. The reports from all these committees were published for the information and consideration of the coming diocesan council. As I found out later from these reports printed and distributed in the council held in November 1987, practically every report contained a charge against me, most of them related to my association with and involvement in the communist party sponsored social issues like AIPSO [All India Peace and Solidarity Organization] Yuvakala Sahithi, Human Wall Formation, Human Chain Formation etc. Each charge was concluded with 'direction' to the Bishop to proceed with 'suitable' disciplinary action against me. Only while attending the council did I come to know that the effect of these repeated one-sided charges against me was that they could poison the gullible members of the council against me.

As directed by the Bishop on 15 September 1987, I made a report of the college affairs during my tenure of office and gave it to the council secretaries Rev. T.S. Ninan and Mr C.C. Jacob to be published in the concerned diocesan council report for the information and consideration of the forthcoming diocesan council of November 1987. When I read through the report during the council, I was shocked to see that my report had been mischievously distorted through interpolations and mutilations so as to betray me as confessing myself unworthy for the post of Principal. That was one of the ways the secretaries pursued to inject their venomous bitterness on the council against me. Although the Bishop-Manager tried to defend them under cover of their right to edit matters published for the council, I questioned their competence and bona fides to distort my report so as to make it defamatory and derogatory to me and then publish it in my name. On request, my advocate and friend, Mr K. Sankunni Menon, served a legal notice dated 1 December 1987 on the diocesan secretaries pointing out the mischievous distortions deliberately made by them and published in the diocesan reports for the year 1986-87. 'By [thus] publishing the report,' the notice read, 'the diocesan council secretaries have lowered the dignity, status and credibility of my client among the public and the entire congregation of the believers in particular'. It continued: 'They are, hence, responsible for the defamatory report published in the diocesan reports for the year 1986-87 claiming to be the report prepared by my client....Hence, I hereby call upon you to publish the report prepared by my client in full text with a statement of apology in the next issue of the official organ of the Diocese 'Jnanadeepam'. Otherwise my client will be constrained to set law in motion against the responsible secretaries'.

Rev. T.S. Ninan, in his reply to the legal notice dated 17 December 1987, denied the charge and agreed to 'request the Diocesan Executive to make it clear while publishing the reports for the ensuing year that the reports pertaining to the diocese and the Institutions are being published after they are edited by the officers of the council....'

However, Bishop Michael John, fully aware of the implications in the notice, through his letter dated 18 March 1988, invited the two secretaries and me 'to come to the Bishop's House at 11 a.m. on Tuesday 22 March '88...to create a friendly relationship' between us. Of course I accepted the Bishop's invitation for conciliation. In his subsequent letter dated 30 March 1988 the Bishop expressed his satisfaction in my accepting his invitation. After a vague attempt to defend his secretaries under cover of the 'right of editing' he promised that 'Rev. T.S. Ninan's apology shall be recorded in the minutes of the diocesan council....I hope you will agree to these promises and will withdraw yourself from your intention of drawing the diocesan authorities to the court of law unnecessarily'.

On 9 March 1988 my colleague Mr M.K. Kurian told me 'The Principal [Prof N.C. Joseph] says that he is utterly disillusioned with the behaviour of the CC-PV-TS axis'. In fact on 16 May 1988 Prof N.C. Joseph consulted me to know my willingness to take over charge again. 'Not interested at all' was my reply. Mr Raju D too on 25 May told me of 'the rumour that the last Management Board meeting had suggested your name to the post of the Principal'.

On 6 June1988, I called on Rev. E.J. Isaac for a short term loan of Rs. 300 as our May salary had not been disbursed yet. Mrs Rev. Isaac then told me of their neighbour Rev. T.S. Ninan: 'He and his wife threw stones at me for walking my cow near his compound, uttering obscene words, unmentionable to you. I told him: 'Are you a priest, you?' His son bound his grandmother's [Peramma's] hands together and slapped her on the face'. I said: 'When Rev. T.S. Ninan becomes the next Bishop, that will be the 'consummation''.

## Furore in the 1987 Council

I had a premonition as to the climate of the coming diocesan council of 1987 and a possible attack on me. So on 6 November 1987 I had a long talk with Bishop Michael John the details of which I got recorded through my letter dated 7 November 1987 and duly acknowledged with copies marked to the CSI Moderator and to the caucus partners. To quote a few lines: *'I always expected a group in the diocesan executive to jump upon my association with the communists and with the recent communist party sponsored civic solidarity programmes such as 'the formation of human chain', the anti-corruption pledge, the National integration pledge etc. as a convenient pretext to pressurize you to proceed against me....*

'I hope I am not mistaken in identifying the pressurizing group with the caucus centred round the diocesan secretaries

Rev. T.S. Ninan, Mr C.C. Jacob and the bursar Rev. P.V. Joseph. I have made reference to this caucus in my letter dated 12 March 1987, submitted to you resigning my membership in the Diocesan Executive. I question the bona fides of these officials and have great doubt about their competence to question my convictions and dealings. I repeat that they, from their vantage position, have been unscrupulously manoeuvering and manipulating to keep me outside the walls of the 'sons of the soil' they have been at pains to raise and to relegate me to anonymity and prevent me from growing into light. They seem to labour under an unhealthy fear that I might grow fat in their soil.

'You know that I opted to serve in this diocese with the all and only ambition to place at your disposal my priestly service for you to command it when and where you feel the need...expecting no earthly remuneration whatsoever. You have loved me and cared for me for which you have had to suffer undue pressure. You entrusted me with responsibilities which I have discharged to your satisfaction. To make matters worse for them the diocesan council of 1985 elected me to the executive and to the synod with the highest margin of votes. At this the officials mentioned seemed to have caught an unhealthy fear that I might take roots in this soil under the favourable climatic conditions of your love and trust in me and grow fat. And they have successfully schemed to keep me outside the wall and dig at me constantly to prevent me from taking any root. They, being at the helm of affairs, make the decisions and policies which the general council only unwittingly endorse. Often they have assumed powers that seemed to supersede those of the Bishop, so much so that I have felt myself ordained to serve under several parallel or super-bishops....Several actions and decisions I had to take, have, understandably enough, made me a 'persona ingrata' to them: for instance, my firm refusal to be a signature – stamp...and my resistance to their illegal interferences....The shift of the hostel from the rented house of Rev. T.S. Ninan to the management's own new building personally affected Rev. Ninan's family income adversely....These together with the consideration of my being considered an alien, mistakenly thought to be trying to grow fat in their soil, led them to manipulate so as to keep me outside the wall....Besides, using the vantage position they have been indulging in black-mailing and back-biting me with a view to tarnish and damage my person. Agonizingly enough, I have been denied chances to defend myself in the name of peace and smoothness. I chose to stand silent out of the picture in their animosity, only because my ambition of priestly ministry requires no indulging in church politiquing....By dint of hard-faced experiences, I have become wise enough to hate indulging in ugly church politiquing to push one's ambitions through. *I may be left alone by these officials to live my personal conviction where I am appreciated and to enjoy the peace of my conscience and the quiet of my home away from the turmoil of the church politics....I am well prepared to substantiate with facts every observation made herein, if I am called upon to do so. On the other hand if these officials have any complaints or grievances against my dealings in the diocese as a priest, teacher and professor-in-charge, I want them to speak out in the open forum unattenuated. I am equally well prepared to face them. In stead, attempts on their part in their vantage positions to cast aspersions on me or spread behind my back calumnies and rumours calculated to tarnish my image are only mean, very mean'. Highlighting my politico-social involvements I continued: 'The great majority of men fall victims to the ruthless power and exploitation of a handful of millionaires and the wealthy. If the church is incapable of moral indignation and reaction to the ruthless suppression of the human rights of the majority, something is radically wrong with such a church....The church of Jesus Christ has to reach out all the spheres of human life in order to bring all the spheres of human activities to the Rule of the Spirit of Truth and Justice.* (Emphasis added).

'I should like the secretaries and their group to know that one's faith is not dictated or ordered by another human, be he a diocesan secretary or even greater....My offer of priestly ministry is born not out of a need for grub, but out of my religious conviction and sense of vocation....The secretaries and their group may not understand or relish this. I thank the secretaries for their observation that I have not been loyal to the church I was born and bred in and that I will not be different in the church at the helm of which they sit. I thank them for their tacit admission that those of the church I left and those of the church I came in were not any different either'. And I concluded my letter: 'I assure you that my priestly services stand offered for you to order it for use whenever you feel the need, though, I understand, I should in no way be a cause of disagreement between you and the officials'.

What I feared would happen in the forthcoming diocesan council was far short of what actually happened in the council hall on 19, 20 and 21 November 1987. Uproarious scenes and furore were let loose on me for what charge or reason I was not told of. Neither was I given any opportunity to counter the uproarious scenes. I thought the Bishop felt to have been given the hard choice between the council and me and, understandably enough, I was given no opportunity to speak any thing in self defense. I got really annoyed. On 21 November while the council was still in session, I wrote to the Bishop with copies marked for the secretaries requesting him to direct the secretaries to give in writing their allegations if any for this uproarious furore and to give me opportunity to answer if I had anything to answer. I got no favourable response. I began to suspect that the Bishop was making his inevitable but definitive choice in favour of the council and I decided to choose the path of Natural Justice and law.

In the shade of the Bishop's choice against me, the caucus group grew bolder and continued their malicious back-biting propaganda against me even more vigorously than before through various reports for the next council and through the diocesan organ without, again, giving me any opportunity to respond to this one-sided mud slinging. The net result of all these was that the uproarious furore of 1987 council was fanned ablaze into a veritable attack of many misguided and gullibly embittered members upon me during the council session of 1988. Towards the very fag end of the council session in mounting restlessness on the part of the members, Bishop Michael John called upon Rev. Ninan to make his apology for the illegal and highly derogatory interpolations and mutilations as he had promised after the conciliation. He then patiently listened to Rev. Ninan who made a travesty of his 'apology' Under the pretext of apology he indulged in whitewashing himself clean and further digging at me through crafty remarks before the council members. The rest of the time was a free-for-all except me. Adding fuel to fire, and appeasing the embittered caucus and justifying, perhaps involuntarily, the sordid scenes that were being re-enacted, the Bishop came to conclude with a declaration much to my crude shock that he had administered an admonition-cum-rebuke on me!

I could see it only as a sudden change of mind on his part withdrawing his love and trust, I thought he had placed in me hitherto, in face of the stiff animosity and conspiracy of the caucus against me, whom, I understand, he could not afford to offend or alienate without grave ill-consequences upon the management of the diocesan affairs.

On 25 June 1988 itself I wrote to the Bishop: 'It pained me deeply to have heard you declare at the fag end of yesterday's council session, to my utter consternation, that you had administered an admonition-cum-rebuke on me. I am baffled as to why you had to make such a false statement in the council, since you and I know that there never was such an occurrence'. I continued reminding him of the several instances of the stiff animosity of the secretaries pressurizing him to take a stand against me. I reminded him of my previous request to call for the Secretaries' allegations if any against me and provide me an opportunity to explain my position and then concluded the letter: 'Under the circumstance I submit that your declaration of having rebuked me when, where or for what offenses I am not yet told, was false, unfair and illegal, the most poignant part of it being that it came from you. I also request that the declaration shall not in any form be recorded any where in the minutes of yesterday's proceedings'.

The Bishop, of course, responded on 16 September 1988, well after three months interval, through a letter sent by registered post with A/D justifying his declaration:

He denied having told me of the stiff animosity of the

secretaries (thank God he did not deny the fact of their animosity nor their pressurizing him to take a stand against me)

My reference to the diocesan council as 'misinformed one' [beguiled] was unbecoming of a priest of the diocese.

I sought his permission to solemnize the marriage of a non-Christian in a pandal at Vaikom (!)

I accommodated the hostel cook (the asthmatic patient Leelamma) 'an unmarried young woman in the parsonage on pretext that she was sick' and allowed a few young girls to live in the parsonage' [as by-standers for Leelamma] quite unbecoming of a priest!

My 'night visit to ladies' hostel' of the college 'after mid-night'.

I served legal notice on the diocesan council secretaries through an advocate (!)

He concluded his letter administering an 'admonition-cum-rebuke' saying: 'that making false allegations against the church hierarchy is quite unbecoming of a priest and would serve only to tarnish the image of the church....'

Going through the letter, for the first time sent under registered post with A/D, I got a suspicion that this belated reply was sent to me with the secret agenda of creating documents to counter my appeal before the University Appellate Tribunal filed against the appointment of the L.i.C. overlooking my right. [Fortunately, by that time the University Appellate Tribunal had been re-instated] The appeal matter is related later below. Hence I maintained a legal attitude in my reply to it dated 26 September 1988, and sent under registered post with A/D. I prefaced it with my observation: *'Dear Thirumeni, I was shocked and deeply pained at heart to understand that your higher sacred offices have been used [in this belated reply] to allege false and malicious charges against me for the purpose of building up an untenable and false counter case against me. My suspicion seems to be confirmed by the fact that you have directed to have your letter sent to me under registered post with A/D'*. For fear of undue prolongation and out of my respect for the enlightened readers I abstain from repeating the reply I gave to allegations relating to events that took place in the fag end of 1985 and at the beginning of 1986, but now raked up and framed into the shape of an 'admonition-cum-rebuke' to present before the University Appellate Tribunal for my character assassination. However, I should quote my reply to the third charge, not mentioned any where else so far: *'You know that I never sought permission to solemnize the marriage of a non-christian at Vaikom. You also know that I was only informing you that a respectable Hindu friend of mine from Vaikom wanted me to bless (solemnize) the marriage of his daughter with my presence. For such an action I never wanted permission from any authority. As a Christian priest I am duty bound to bless a couple when the parties concerned request me to do so. I wonder why you stated that you had an occasion to rebuke me in connection with the above marriage story. You never rebuked me, nor was there any reason either to rebuke me on that account. It was only because of some unavoidable inconvenience that I could not attend that marriage'.*

The first draft of this my reply had the following preface remarks: '...Your present letter is even more poignant as you are seen at labour to transpose into the form of an admonition-cum-rebuke even the most pleasant and cordial communication we had as a disguised design, I suppose, of building up a counter case in the context of my appeal before the University Appellate Tribunal. I feel with an anguish that it must have been a strain indeed on your conscience to sign this letter, you who loved me as a father and whom I loved, as I do even now, with filial love and devoted loyalty. It is indeed a tragic victory on the part of the caucus to set us as complainant and respondent as you are taking upon yourself as an inevitable task the case of the secretaries. I have no case against you, but I have one against the secretaries, whom, understandably enough, you cannot afford to offend. On my part I will continue to be what I have been to you, a Kent to Lear'.

# 22

# My First Legal Move

It is true I had concluded my report on the condition of the college during my tenure of its charge in the words of Simeon: 'Lord, now lettest Thou Thy servant depart in peace' [Luke 2,29]. But my credibility and competence was presented self-destroyed through the highly derogatory distortion of my report through interpolations and mutilations maliciously made by the secretaries. The promise and assurance given by the Bishop for the secretaries' apology and to have it recorded in the next council, was flouted by the clergy secretary who made a travesty of the assurance and added insult to injury. On Tuesday 14 June 1988, when Prof N.C. Joseph's period of deputation was soon to be ended, Bishop Michael John called me to his office and said: 'The diocesan executive considered the appointment of the next Principal. In my opinion you are the only qualified candidate. And you know that at heart I wanted you to retire as Principal. But the Executive is not agreeable to it....I sounded in the executive further that it would be better to appoint you Principal now than be compelled to do so as a result of any possible litigation'. To solve the Bishop's understandable predicament, I said: 'I have no desire to be Principal again. But I expect to be invited though I would refuse'. 'But Achen', he said, 'the executive does not want to invite you and have decided to appoint Rev. P.V. Joseph as Lecturer in-charge,' [L.i.C.] 'Your enquiry,' I said, 'as to my intention for any complaint is irrelevant in the wake of the executive's decision. Now that the decision has been taken, I suppose, they will have the ways and means to execute their decision'. 'Yes, you are right there', the Bishop said, and I came off.

They proceeded with the appointment of Rev. P.V. Joseph as Lecturer in-charge and I filed my appeal before the University Appellate Tribunal. In the final disposal of the appeal dated 18 February 1989, the Tribunal noted: 'It has been admitted by the respondent that the appellant is the senior most Professor in charge of the Principal of the college on the basis of seniority-cum-fitness in the vacancy of the Principal; the service rendered by the appellant during that period has been appreciated by the respondent. Then no rational ground is brought out to deny the chance of the appellant to be appointed as the Principal of the college or put him in charge of the duties of the Principal'. The letter dated 26 September 1988, intended to be a record for 'having administered an admonition-cum-rebuke' and presented as counter carried absolutely no weight. 'In the result', the Tribunal concluded, 'the appeal is allowed. The appointment of Rev. P.V. Joseph...is hereby set aside, and the management is directed to appoint the appellant as Professor in-charge of the duties of the Principal of H.B. College, Melukavu'.

The management went in appeal before the High Court against the Tribunal's verdict on the technical fault of not having impleaded Rev. P.V. Joseph as 'the affected party'. The High Court admitted the appeal and directed my appeal to be re-adjudicated after impleading 'the affected party'. The re-adjudication was finally completed on 21 December 1991, the eve of my superannuation and the revised judgment was issued on 2 January 1992, barely 90 days before my retirement on 1 April 1992. The final disposal observed: 'But it is seen that the date of retirement of the appellant is 22-12-1991 and as such he will be on superannuation till the closing of the college'. The clear conclusion is not that I had no claim to the post of the Principal, but that it ceased to be with my superannuation on 22 December 1991. My claim ceased to be thanks to the delay in disposing the appeal.

### Furore Exploded in the November 1988 Council

Following the shade of the Bishop's leaning, the executive

under the inspiration of the secretaries-centred caucus formulated a few resolutions to be passed in the November 1988 council. Their legal worth may best be adjudicated by the readers. The following were some of the resolutions:

> If any member attempts at any litigation against anybody in the service of the diocese, he should resign his membership in the diocese. Otherwise he would be excommunicated and his re-admission would be at the discretion of the Bishop.

If any one dares to file judicial proceedings against the Bishop, he will be subjected to the punishment awarded by the diocesan court. [Council Notice, pages 4 and 5]

The minutes of the 17-6-1988 'Education Board' published the additional information: 'The appeal filed by Rev. Abraham Vellamthadam against the L.i.C. is still in process'.

The executive of course were fully confident that the council would unquestionably vote for the resolutions. They were aimed at me and were intended to be detonators to explode the next council into an uproarious furore and it did explode. But before that:

### The First Disciplinary Proceedings against me

On 6 July 1989, the Bishop issued a memo of charges containing five allegations calling for my explanation. They were:

Active participation in the programmes of a political party: 'I have paper reports with your photograph as evidence'.

Appeal before the University Appellate Tribunal against the management.

Lawyer's notice sent against the diocesan secretaries against the distortion of my college report, adding: 'If you had told me your objection, I would have taken action to redress your complaint'

Dereliction of pastoral duty on a Sunday in Chovoor Church as per the report of the Church Catechist [Upadesi] Mr K.S. Samuel. 'I was shocked to hear that you did not go to

Chovoor Church on the appointed Sunday only because you had to attend the meeting of a political party on that day at Kottayam'.

I had gone to Chovoor Church on Sunday 29 January. When I was told that my arrival had not been announced by the Catechist on the previous Sunday, I came away without attending Sunday service. 'It seems that a worship service on a Sunday is not an important matter for you'!

In my reply dated 12 July 1989, referring to the first charge I wrote: 'Please note that this is the third time you make the same general [nebulous] allegation of my involvement in political activities obliging me to answer. Refer to my letter to you dated 7-11-1987 being my first detailed explanation to this same old allegation. In that I have already stated that involvement in the political activities of my country is a moral imperative laid on my conscience by my faith in Jesus Christ. If the Christian Faith has any relevance to and concern for human life, then it becomes the bounden duty of a Christian to get actively involved in politics that deals directly with human life....The Supreme CSI Synod that met in Trivandrum in January 1986 in which you and I were delegates, through one of its resolutions, moved by me and passed unanimously by the synod, pledged its support and cooperation to the government's move to introduce a common civil code. The same CSI Church earlier condemned the state of national Emergency imposed on the country by the then Prime Minister, late Mrs. Indira Gandhi. And was the CSI then not Christian and were these not meaningful and timely involvements of the Church in the civic and political activities of the country?'

I then pointed out how the diocesan lay secretary, Mr C.C. Jacob spent more time in the Congress party politics than in his duties as a college lecturer. I added: 'Your observation...that it is against the discipline of a Christian priest to take active part in politics identifying with a political party baffles me as ...Rev. K.J. Samuel (subsequently elected as clergy secretary, successor to Bishop Michael John and eventually as Moderator of the whole Church of South India but still later caught up in the ugly imbroglio of the highly scandalous and corruption-tainted issue of the Episcopal ordination of Evangelist K.P. Yohannan allegedly on hefty bribe) having identified himself with the Kerala Congress had gone canvassing votes for P.C. George against Prof N.M. Joseph. He went to the extent of provoking mob violence in Mechal. No charge of any violation of any church discipline has been brought so far against these officials. Since when, then, Thirumeni, has active involvement in the political life of the country become a taboo to a Christian priest?'

To the second charge I replied: 'I had submitted my written petition dated 15 June 1988 requesting you not to go ahead with the illegal appointment, overlooking my claim. But you chose to go ahead with it despite my request. Thereby you constrained me to go in appeal....Now that the Tribunal allowed my appeal, I hereby reserve my right to sue you further for compensation....'

I need not expatiate here on my answer to charge No. 3 in the light of what has been said about it earlier As to the fourth and fifth charges, too nebulous and short of necessary specifications, let alone the necessary details even to identify the charges and to make an explanation possible, I denied having cancelled any Sunday service, usually conducted in Chovoor Church. After explaining the gamut of the events leading to the catechist's own cancellation of the communion service on Sunday 29 January 1989 - although I had come prepared for it – on the plea that communion service had been conducted as usual on 22 January consequent upon the unexpected availability of another priest, I added: 'I assume that it is the events of January that you have been at pains to construe into the shape of a charge sheet and sling it at me. Did Mr K.S. Samuel think that one more Holy Communion service to the large congregation of Chovoor church especially when a priest [myself] arrived ready for it, would be an unnecessary luxury?

'How sad that you are so easily shocked by silly rumours as the one you say, you heard that I did not go to Chovoor church only because of my political programme....The shock was totally unnecessary as the rumour is baseless.

'The saddest aspect of your memo of charges is that you chose to construe – with how much strain on your conscience I cannot imagine – into the shape of a charge those very efforts I made to be utmost faithful to the surplice duty you assigned to me'. I reminded him of the powerful lobby in the executive committee including the secretaries, referred in my letter dated 7 November 1987, who had turned hostile towards me and added: 'I can see the memo of charges only as a desperate search of this hostile lobby using you as instrument for a cause to harass me. But should you have stooped to that level, Thirumeni, as to take up the cudgel of their animosity into your hands to strike me down – you who had loved me and cared for me for which you had had to suffer undue pressure… you whom I loved as I do even now as a loyal and dutiful son?. Please drop, and tell them to drop vindictiveness, I pray, and let me alone….I shall feel obliged to you and to these officials if you care to point out any detail in my priestly ministry that is contrary to the Christian Faith and conscience. At any rate, if any further vindictive move is made with a view to harass me because my priestly ministry is not found subservient to anybody's vested interests, I beg to submit that I shall have to have recourse to legal remedies against it'.

## An Investigation into the Dark Conspiracy

I wrote a letter to the members of the Chovoor church committee about the fourth and fifth allegations, as these pertained to the committee's purveyance. Baffled at the news of my 'dereliction of pastoral duty' they convened an emergency session and made an elaborate statement, dated 27 July, signed by all the members and sent to me by special messenger. The statement blankly denied even any trace of neglect of pastoral duty on my part and clinched every point of my reply to the Bishop. I got the further relevant and serious information about the homework done to obtain the catechist K.S. Samuel's report on the basis of which the fourth and the fifth charges were fabricated. In my letter dated 31 July 1989, forwarding to the Bishop a photocopy of the statement, I added:

'The statement, signed by all the nine members of the committee, witnesses that I am in no way guilty as the committee have found the charges baseless.

'The statement thus also proves that K.S. Samuel made a false report against me. The fact that he had been asked to retire...but now has been given extension of service and posted to Kothamangalm church, gives me ample reason to suspect that the false report, calculated to obstruct my priestly ministry, was brought through dubious means implying corruption.

'I therefore request you to take immediate steps to inquire into the circumstances which led to the procurement of the false report and measures to see that such false reports are not repeated'. Of course I have heard nothing more about it since then.

### September 1989 Council: Furore Bordering Physical Violence

The executive committee activated by the caucus was in hectic effort to prepare the forthcoming council to eliminate me. I knew that the one-sided flow of vindictive lava would swallow me up. Through the reports of 1987-88 year I was targeted nearly fifteen times through various kinds of allegations, highly defamatory and damaging to my image, each ending with the repeated chorus: 'The Bishop has been instructed/directed to take appropriate actions'. It is clear there were super-bishops or some superpower giving Bishop Michael John directions and orders! I also recollected how I was denied opportunity to counter any of the venomous darts directed against me in the previous council. So I decided to have a statement printed explaining facts with a view to distribute among the council members, though I doubted how far my statement would prevail over their blind, but beguiled loyalty to those super-bishops. The facts enumerated with unimpeachable evidence were pointed enough to pique these super-bishops. To add fuel to the fire of their unquenchable vindictive urge came the latest abortive disciplinary action on 'the Chovoor church issue' that further threatened to boomerang. But the 'most serious criminal misconduct' that was discussed in the council was my distribution of the printed statement of facts among the council members. It brought fire and flame upon me from all corners of the council hall including the Bishop on the dais. After the evening prayer service conducted and opening message delivered by Rev. K.C. Mathew at 6.30 p.m. on Thursday 14 September 1989, the council session began its official business. The blind loyalists and henchmen of the caucus in a strong passion of 'my country right or wrong' began the outburst of ire and poison directed against me. Just to feel the stink that was let out, let me quote: 'How it is that Rev. Vellamthadathil comes to sit in the council, even after two years of the diocesan officials' proceedings against him?' was the first query. Some one made reference to the report published in *Desabhimani* about the latest charge sheet served on me and my reply to it. 'How is it that the diocesan officials failed to get Rev. Vellamthadathil out of our scenes? Should we step in to handle him out physically?' was the loyal offer from one M.S. Devasia. 'Defrock him,' said the Moonilavu member and Congress activist, Mr T.M. (?) Joshua. Upon this the Kattappana man, Mr K.M. Thomas, burst the shell of 'the distribution of leaflets in the council venue', ensued and fuelled by the Bishop's 'strong' condemnation of this 'black, unprecedented crime of distributing leaflets in the C.S.I council venue'. That was a green signal indeed and the eruption of ire and fire began uninhibited, each one indulging in remarks and words of abuse according to each one's cultural milieu and educational level. I admired my own self-control to have sat through the mud-slinging, much to the full satisfaction, gratification and appeasement of the engineers of this explosive operation. A number of them demanded that I should explain myself. I sat undisturbed with my lips closed tight 'Why doesn't the Bishop order him to speak?' some shouted. 'So many members asked him to speak out. But he doesn't. Then will he speak if I ask him?' the Bishop queried. 'I'm to be ruled not by the crowd but by the President,' I said. 'No, the Bishop need not ask him to speak. So many of us asked him, but he refuses, insulting all of us,' Rev. T.S. Ninan interjected rather cleverly to rule out in advance the possibility of the Bishop's asking me and my responding! 'We shall move a resolution and unanimously pass it, expelling Rev. Vellamthadam from the council' suggested one. 'Last year you were reluctant to approve the constitutional amendment censuring court proceedings against the Bishop or the diocesan officials with the punishment of expulsion. But if you propose now a new resolution to expel him from the council, what will be his reaction? We have to be careful. He consults lawyers and so we have to move cautiously,' the Bishop counseled the member. And then he continued: 'Has Rev. Vellamthadathil nothing to state in the council?' 'I came with my statement, last time', I responded, 'But you refused me permission on the pretext of shortage of time to complete the council's scheduled agenda. Hence I got it printed at my own expenses and distributed so that the members may read and understand the facts at their leisure. I fail to see the reason for this furore over a printed statement.' 'I could not permit you to speak falsehood', the Bishop intervened. 'You want me to speak', I said, 'and then when I begin to speak you disallow me. What else have I to do then, except make printed statements where falsehood, if any, may be pointed out.' 'If the diocesan officials fail to get him out, then for God's sake, let him go out himself and save this poor diocese,' came the plea from some one. Only Rev. C.I. Joseph and K.G. Daniel (now Bishop, second successor to Bishop Michael John) seemed to speak somewhat soberly and logically. The Rev. P.D. John got up: 'Look, now he is getting support from the public,' he said. 'See, the Papers [Desabhimani of the date] take up his case. He is thus growing at our expenses and on our own proceedings and reports. Let us therefore stop all further mention and reference against him altogether, and leave the affair there, lest he grow further on our reports and proceedings.' Belatedly arrived wisdom! I thought. 'If our proceedings did not succeed,' some one enquired, 'then when will the diocesan court handle him? What is its power?' To this the Bishop replied: 'The diocesan court is not very strong. And I do not know what to do next, if he refuses to honour the summons of the diocesan court'.

Practically the whole evening session was concluded with this furore. It was followed by a rush for my printed statement, though some pusillanimous pious loyalist priests wouldn't even look upon the statement. Outside the hall Mrs. Rev. K.G. Daniel, a non-Malayalee lady, confronted me with questions, with the poor helpless Rev. K.G. Daniel looking on. Generally, I felt pity over the plight of this crowd, blind with outbursts of irrational smoke and rumbling of blind emotions. Next morning, Friday 15 September, I had breakfast at a hotel and at about 11.45 a.m., I came off with a copy of that day's Desabhimani bought from Pala.

On 18 September 1989, I wrote to Bishop Michael John heartily congratulating him for his candid presidential address delivered during the tenth council, declaing his decision not to give up his convictions on account of pharisaic criticisms, 'but to honour again invitations from other groups such as S.N.D.P. Viswakarma Maha Sabha etc., criticize who may, because you consider these invitations as God-given opportunity for you as Bishop to witness Christ - great heroic and noble decision. I am particularly grateful to you for it because it articulates why I too honour invitations to take part in social, cultural and political events and movements'.

Referring to the furore raised over the distribution of my printed statement among the council members I continued: 'I have my right to let other members know what I have to say. The council secretaries had printed innumerable one-sided, insinuating references and allegations against me casting aspersions in the reports for the November 1988 council. My attempt to explain myself before the council last year was disallowed by you on pretext of want of time to complete the business before the council agenda. It was therefore proper and well within my legitimate right and the only choice for me to commune with the other council members through a printed authentic statement of facts to defend myself against the slanders of the council secretaries. It was regrettable that you chose to publicly condemn this perfectly legitimate step, thereby giving the green signal to the joint attack on me that followed. They stuck together the lot of them in insulting and abusing me. The call made by the treasurer (Rev. P.D. John) to burn my printed statement was a cowardly act, calculated, I suppose, to prevent my side being known. The offer of one M.S. Devasia, which went unobjected by you, to physically handle me out...was indeed telling enough.

'The next proposal to keep me out forthwith through a resolution to be moved for the purpose, was reluctantly given up by you declaredly for fear of further legal after-effects of such a hasty step. Was the diocesan council the proper forum and machinery to handle disciplinary proceedings against me, Thirumeni, and to sit in judgment over me?

'There was then the suggestive remark thrown up in the council that I leave the service of the diocese on my own. The remark, I think, is irrelevant. I had written to you as far back as 7 November 1987 that 'I opted to serve in this diocese with the all and only ambition to place at your disposal my priestly ministry for you to order it when and where you feel the need of it. The ball is therefore in your court. As you have made abundantly clear (*in your presidential address*), now that you have ordained enough priests from among your own people for ministry congenial to your people, if you think that my priestly ministry is no more required in the diocese, you have only to say so, and there will be nothing to stand in the way of my withdrawing my offer. That would be honest too. Instead, attempts on anybody's part to adopt dubious ways and proceedings devoid of bona fides [memo of charges dated 6 July 1989 regarding Chovoor Church] to tarnish me and smother me out and at the same time gratify somebody's vindictiveness, will necessarily have to be resisted'.

Taking this as convenient escape from the Scylla and Charybdis he found himself in between, the Bishop wrote to me on 30 October 1989 requesting me 'to withdraw your offer to serve in the East Kerala Diocese. I shall be obliged if you would do so before 3 November 1989 as the pastoral board is meeting on the 4th'.

To this I replied on 1 November itself thus: '...When you decided that my priestly ministry in the Diocese was inconvenient to some officials and therefore to be terminated...your first move was to initiate disciplinary proceedings [on the basis of the report bought from catechist

K.S. Samuel] as a means to solve the problem... keeping further assignment of priestly duties suspended, pending consideration of my reply to the charges which I submitted as far back as 12 July 1989....

'Under the circumstance I regret my inability to oblige you by withdrawing my offer...as long as the proceedings initiated by you is still pending disposal'. And till date I have not heard anything more about it.

### Rev. K.J. Samuel Installed as the New Bishop

Rev. P.V. Joseph continued as L.i.C. during the re-adjudication of my appeal against his appointment. Bishop Michael John's time of retirement was fast approaching. The election of the panel of bishop candidates was held on 11 November 1989. I refused to participate in the election process. The period from the panel election to the installing of Rev. K.J. Samuel as the next Bishop was a very eventful one, following the heated atmosphere of the life-and-death competition among the candidates, particularly between Rev. T.S. Ninan and Rev. K.J. Samuel. It was reported to me by Rev. P.D. Joseph on 2 February 1990 that Rev. P.D. John and group were fooled by some of the K.J. Samuel group by a telegram conveying the false information that Rev. A.J. Varghese had been declared as bishop-elect. The group reached Rev. A.J. Varghese with congratulations, garlands and elaborate fire works and they rang the church bell before the congratulation ceremonies were conducted. The 7th February dailies announced Rev. K.J. Samuel as Bishop-designate. On 15 February on the way back from the college I attended Adv. Mathews P. Mathew arguing in the Pala Munsiff Court defending the Bishop-designate in the case questioning the validity of his election to the Bishop-panel and the case was posted to 5 March 1990 for judgment. On 19 February Mrs. Rev. E.J. Isaac informed me that the CSI Moderator and Bishop Mani came to Melukavu CSI Cathedral reportedly to settle the Cathedral Church congregation's grievances against Rev. T.S. Ninan. The latter was removed from being pastor of the Cathedral and was prohibited from participating in any active priestly service. 'God is good, Achen,' Mrs. Isaac seemed to console me, 'and makes retribution then and there'.

At a grand and solemn ceremony held at Melukavu Cathedral at 3 p.m. on Saturday 10 March 1990, Rev. K.J. Samuel was consecrated bishop-successor to the Rt. Rev. K. Michael John. The installation was anticipated before the communion service lest it be disturbed and disrupted by an impending stormy rain, symbolic or ominous I do not know, as threatened by the looming dark and cloudy atmosphere. What made the ceremony most solemn and stately was the presence of a large number of policemen deployed to maintain law and order that was threatened by the two rival parties of the successful bishop candidate and the thwarted candidates! On Monday 12 March, on my arrival at the college, the Cailyland sexton's son Mr Kochu told me that Rev. T.S. Ninan was on suspension for two months by Bishop M.C. Mani for dereliction of Sunday duty. Bishop M.C. Mani had been given charge of the diocese during the interim period between Bishop Michael John's retirement and Bishop K.J. Samuel's installation. At any rate, the very presence and the former enthusiastic activism of Rev. T.S. Ninan faded slowly until eventually he relinquished the very priestly service and the diocese itself, banished himself from the privilege of the 'sons of the soil' and betook himself and sought refuge and better prospects, I hope, in America. I had no more problems from him.

Bishop K.J. Samuel was eventually catapulted to the highest echelon of the C.S.I. Hierarchical escalator, the Moderator, the first ever one from the Scheduled Tribe community. I am not sure whether Indian Constitutional Provisions on 'Reservation' was applicable to the C.S.I. Constitution. At any rate, as the C.S.I. Moderator, he had to face a bitter period of scathing criticism and condemnation and bitter protests from all quarters for renting his Episcopal ritual privilege of 'imposition of hands' to the Evangelist K.P. Yohannan whom he made the Most Rev. Archbishop K.P. Yohannan at an easy stroke by 'imposing hands on him', allegedly on a hefty rent.

It was the unprecedented and the most notorious open-marketing of the Episcopal ritual privilege of 'imposition of hands' to manufacture 'ritual priesthood' or episcopacy in the open market. Bishop K.J. Samuel's action led to widespread vehement protests, sending a quaver across the whole C.S.I. It morally forced at least one C.S.I. bishop, to resign his episcopacy – the Rt. Rev. Dr George Isaac of North Kerala Diocese. In his letter of resignation dated 11-02-2003 and submitted to the C.S.I. general secretary Prof Mrs. Pauline Sathyamoorthy, he remarked: 'The event of the C.S.I. Moderator [Bishop K.J. Samuel] consecrating a person – Dr K.P. Yohannan – as 'Archbishop' at Thiruvalla on 7 February…in a most stealthy as well as dubious and hasty manner, has totally shattered my trust in the leadership of C.S.I. The press release which came in *Indian Express* and *Malayala Manorama* by the C.S.I. Moderator is an absolute lie for which I am sure he is answerable before God….

'Now the Moderator's act of officiating the consecration ceremony of Dr K.P. Yohannan as Bishop cannot be viewed other than as a deliberate and preplanned act of cheating the entire CSI and thus literally shattering the dignity and credibility of the Bishop's office in C.S.I.

'In this context the painful course of action left before me is to relinquish my office as the Bishop of North Kerala Diocese'. If Bishop K.J. Samuel gained a hefty profit out of renting his Episcopal ritual privilege, I have no grudge against him. Similarly if he as Manager of H.B. College, joined the L.i.C. Rev. P.V. Joseph and the influencial caucus to form an axis to work out the already resolved project or the secret agenda of seeing to it 'that Rev. Abraham Vellamthadathil does not ever get his pension or retirement benefits as long as life throbs in our throat,' I have no surprise either.

### The L.i.C.-K.J.S. Axis

My appeal against the appointment of Rev. P.V. Joseph as L.i.C., no doubt, piqued all those concerned sharply. And they decided to put every opportunity to the best possible use for the purpose of preventing me from reaching superannuation and retirement from service. Only too late did I come to suspect of an axis formed between the L.i.C. and the Rt. Rev. K.J.S. to work out their secret agenda.

**On the Lookout for Chances**

On Thursday 5 June 1990 I happened to reach college only at 10.15 a.m., fifteen minutes late, owing to unexpected delay of the bus. Though I had duty only in the afternoon as per time-table, on coming to mark my attendance I found 'casual leave' marked. The very next day quite a few teachers came at 10.20 a.m. But they were not awarded this largesse of 'casual leave'. Besides, there were instances of certain teachers, particularly those in the in-law caucus, permitted to mark their attendance on several days of continuous total absence. I complained to the new Bishop-Manager on 8 June 1990 against this illegal and discriminatory award of 'casual leave', not applied but sanctioned. But my complaint fetched no response and the award of 'unapplied casual leaves' to me went on unabated. On 31 July I complained again pointing out: 'Today when I came to mark my attendance I noticed that several sessions of my attendance in the Register have been crossed out with red ink by the L.i.C. or by which miscreant I am not sure and for what reason I am yet to be told. Please note that I have availed myself only of three casual leaves this month. On all other working days of the month, I have come and attended to my duty in time without any failure...More than three casual leaves, if marked against me for this month, will be objected to....'

My request to get the L.i.C. rectify all the illegal tampering with my attendance in the register was ignored. I had also brought to the attention of the Manager the serious irregularity of combining various divisions of several batches of students into large unwieldy gatherings, reducing the number of periods in order to suit those (in-law) politicians to find more free time for party political works. It was in violation of the University Statutes governing the sanction of pattern and number of teaching staff in accordance with the number of classes. Combining divisions of batches into classes of large crowds caused grave damage to the academic life of the students and intolerably heavy burden of physical strain to teachers having to address classes of mammoth size. As the senior most Professor and former P.i.C, I informed the Manager that 'rectification of (these serious) irregularities cannot be deferred without grave consequences. The receipt of my written complaint with copies marked for the Vice Chancellor, the Dy. Director of Collegiate Education and the L.i.C. was duly acknowledged by the Bishop Manager. In my letter dated 17 August 1990 forwarding the copy of my complaint to the Manager I referred in detail to the tampering with my attendance and brought to the attention of the Dy. Director, Kottayam: 'Under the circumstances more than three casual leaves from 1-7-'90 to 17-8-'90 would be unauthorized and therefore illegal on the part of the L.i.C.'

## Complaints to Higher Authorities Prohibited

Having found no response to my complaint dated 31 July 1990, I sent complaint dated 17 September 1990 to the Registrar, M.G. University, with copy of the former, requesting to take cognizance of the irregularities and enquire into:

> The irregularities in the arrangement of classes,
> The illegal tampering with my attendance and
> The false statement of the casual leave account submitted along with the salary bills for August, and to protect the interests of the staff and students.

Having received no response to my complaint to the University, dated 17 September 1990, I sent another dated 30 January 1991 as usual through the Management. This time I handed the letter over to the Bishop-Manager in person on 4 February with a request to forward it to the University and to sign copy thereof in acknowledgement. The Bishop then told me that he would first present the complaint to the consideration of the Management Board, scheduled to meet that day evening to examine and remove the causes for complaint. On 11 February I called on the Bishop-Manager and was told: 'I reject your complaint to the Registrar because the Board has refused me permission to endorse or acknowledge any complaint against the management'! In my subsequent response dated 11 February 1991 and sent by registered post with A/D with copy to the Registrar, sent directly, I humbly warned him: 'It is my legal right to complain against the Management before higher authorities and that you are duty bound as per the same right, to forward it to the authority addressed to'. The letter might have induced the management to forward it, as the University Syndicate later acted on it with the seriousness it deserved.

## The University Enquiry

The University Syndicate Commission consisting of Prof K.G. Paulose and Dr C.V. Cherian visited the College on 6 September 1991 for enquiry and observed the following: 'Combining classes with large number of students is against all principles. In the discussion with the representatives of the management it was made clear that the management should find out accommodation for all the twelve batches; otherwise affiliation granted to the existing pre-degree batches and to the new B.Com course will be reviewed. The management should be strictly instructed that admission to First Year Pre-degree and First Year B.Com can be made in 1992 only after satisfying the condition regarding accommodation. The L.i.C. has misguided the University by sending work load for twelve batches and getting the teaching posts sanctioned accordingly, whereas actually the batches were only eight. It is a crime against the University and the Government and is viewed seriously'.

With regard to the complaint of tampering with my attendance, the commission report made it clear that 'The Lecturer-in-Charge assured that he will look into the details and reply lapses if any'.

## Series of Vindictive Steps in Retaliation

My complaint to the University dated 17 September 1990 added fuel to the fire. The deep-rooted vindictiveness exploded into a series of steps targeted to achieve the secret agenda of eliminating me from the service at least one day prior to my retirement and thereby of preventing me from getting any retirement benefits and pension.

### Slander and Malign Campaign

On 26 January 1990 the Hostel staff Leelamma visited me at home when she came to visit Dr Mathew Paracken for her routine check up. She indicated how she was being pressurized by the L.i.C. and the warden Mrs. Chachi to join them in the project of slandering and maligning me. Again on 28th she explained to me her bitter experiences at the hands of the two officials, scheming and conspiring to smother her out of the hostel. On 5 February, Leelamma's father and sister visited me at the college to report that the L.i.C. told him to have seen me and Leelamma together at Pala. When confronted on the issue, he flatly denied the reported fact and said that Leelamma and family were capable of fabrications.

### Promotion Pushed to Abortion

The manager issued order No. HBC/G.3/90 dated 18 September 1990, promoting me as First Grade (non-cadre) Professor, but with a decision to get it aborted. To this day I have not got any benefits 'for want of the University's approval'. The fact is that the promotion order was never followed up with the subsequent necessary formalities for approval.

### First Memo

I had protested against the management's ignoring the complaint about combining classes of mammoth proportion by refusing to engage such classes arranged one next to another in a long corridor enclosed by three-foot high brick walls and separated with movable bamboo screens. And they recorded it in the reports of the diocesan executive committee of 31

October 1990 for consideration of the next council: 'The L.i.C. served memo of charge on Rev. Abraham Vellamthadathil for not engaging classes for months. However he has started engaging classes following the management's handling the problem in the presence of the University Syndicate member'. (Minutes presented for the 11th diocesan council meeting, page 24-25).

## Audit Report Kept Hidden in the Arsenal

As soon as the L.i.C. took charge there was an audit of the college accounts for the period from my taking charge till that of the L.i.C. A disorderliness in the accounting of nearly Rs. 92, 000 received towards S.T., S.C. and OBC hostel fee was detected and recorded in the audit report. The problem was not about due utilization for the benefits of the students concerned, but for want of proper vouchers from the staff official K.G. Samuel and the warden Mrs. Chachi. The reader may remember that I had taken up the matter and reported to the manager for due proceedings. However, the L.i.C. kept the report hidden from me to use it against me when it came to my retirement and consequent benefits. During the long period of three years of my service as Professor and Head of the Department from the date of the audit report till my retirement I was not informed of this 'audit objection' nor was I called for any explanation. The L.i.C. had decided to fire this dreaded missile at me to achieve the final victory in ousting me.

## Ballistics of Memo Fired One after Another

In the ballistic warfare declared against me, the first missile was fired in the form of 'The Memo dated 19 September 1990' served on me containing nine charges including 'false complaints sent to the manager and higher authorities without intimating me. These are very serious misconducts and dereliction of duty'.

In due time, I answered all the charges as they deserved. By way of prefacing the detailed explanations, I stated: 'In the wake of your combining divions into classes of mammoth size I felt constrained to point out the illegality of your decisions...and request you to re-arrange classes batchwise... and to reset the time table accordingly. This my well-intentioned action unfortunately incited you to greater animosity and you have been indulging in a series of vindictive measures against me such as illegal and indiscriminate tampering with my attendance, marking against me leave that was neither availed nor applied for...crossing out my attendance marked on several sessions without caring to intimate me of the reason thereof if any, sending false statement of my casual leave account along with the salary bills etc....' Denying the mischievous charge of instigating and misguiding the students I added: 'I protest against such wild, mischievous and baseless allegations....'

Only four months had passed when the next memo, dated 5 February 1991, was served on me. Of the seven charges listed, the sixth one read: 'You may refer to the memo issued to you on 19-9-'90 for committing these same irregularities. In spite of your undertaking to behave well, given in the presence of Prof K.P. Sarachandran, member of Syndicate, you have deliberately refused to keep your word or do your duties.' At a stroke he tries to establish through implied inferences that I confessed myself guilty of the previous allegations and that too under the witness of a syndicate member, but obstinately continued the offences!

The above memo was served on me on 13 February 1991, though backdated 5 February 1991. In my reply I pointed out: 'You have, happily, referred to the presence of the honourable syndicate member. Kindly recall that on his surprise visit on 1 October 1990 he pointed to you the grave irregularities found in the arrangement of classes and gave strict instructions to take emergency steps to correct irregularities. Kindly recall also that in the context mentioned in the present memo he advised you to shun animosities and counseled a spirit of understanding....But you have chosen the path of fabricating allegations'. In due time again I gave my reply to the memo in the manner it deserved.

**Ban to Address Students**

As requested by the College Union officials, I was called upon by the Union Chairman during the college day functions to give a message. As soon as my message was over the L.i.C. rushed on to the dais, took up the microphone, and started pouring out the hot lava of his distaste in a language of first rate abusive idioms: 'There are people having no shame to come on public stage uninvited'. I was stunned as to the reason for this eruption. The next day, I was cleared of my wonder and wounded sentiments when the chairman, Johney Cherian, in his letter dated 25 February 1991, expressed his deep apology on behalf of the student Union for the highly abusive words of the L.i.C. He explained in the letter how after getting my consent to give a message during the function he included my name on the programme and presented the programme to the L.i.C. for information. The latter scolded him thoroughly for inviting me to speak. He cut off my name from the programme list. 'But,' Johney continued, 'I pretended to obey him and decided to use my discretion as chairman of the meeting and called out your name for the message although he had deleted your name.' I gently scolded Johney for defying the L.i.C. and cautioned him against possible future 'rewards'. I felt amply rewarded when I read the following in the chairman's letter of apology: 'After listening to your message, we really felt that it would have been a loss indeed for us if I had not invited you and if we had been denied the opportunity to listen to your very valuable message'.

# 23

# The Final Battle to Work out 'The Agenda'

There was barely one more year for my retirement on 1 April 1992. Before that 'the agenda' had to be worked out: to eliminate me from service and thereby prevent me from getting the retirement benefits including pension. A lot of formalities had to be gone through by the pensioner signing options and other related papers, and by the Principal forwarding them to the departments concerned. On my part I had completed all the formalities, and I requested the L.i.C. to forward the papers in due form. But he continued tampering with my attendance and cutting down the number of my unused casual leave. So in my complaint dated 19 September, addressed to the Dy. Director, Kottayam, I pointed out details of the casual leave I had taken. 'Again,' my complaint continued, 'the option forms and other papers relating to my pay-fixation in accordance with the latest State Revised Pay Scale were presented to the L.i.C. on 8 September 1991. But he told me he had chosen to delay it....I request you to use your good office and call for my option forms and related papers for necessary processing, and thus save me from the necessity of going for the arduous and time-consuming court proceedings to protect my retirement claims and benefits'.

### Common Memo Served on Five of Us

On 13 August 1991 the Bishop-manager served a joint memo on me, Mr Raju D. of the Malayalam Department, Mrs. Annie George of Physics, Mrs. Mariamma Varghese of Commerce and

Chellamma P.M. of Hindi – all Heads of the respective departments. The background of the memo is as follows: Mr K.U. Elias of the department of Malayalam was as loyal to the management as Prof. M.C. Mathew was to the Uzhavoor College management, perhaps a little more. He was one of the prosecution witnesses in the domestic enquiry soon to follow. Mr Elias was absent on three consecutive days – Wednesday, Thursday and Friday, being the 24th, 25th and 26th of July 1991. But on Thursday, 1 August, he marked his attendance on these days of total absence. Contrary to the usual practice of marking casual leave on the days of absence, the L.i.C. kept the attendance columns of Mr Elias vacant for these three days of absence. The five of us mentioned above filed a complaint dated 2-8-91 to the L.i.C. with copy to the manager against this blatant violation of the standing rule often invoked by and adhered to in the case of other members of staff. Copies of the complaint had also been sent to the Dy. Director and to the Registrar. The complaint observed: 'We wish we were mistaken in thinking that Mr Elias waited, or was counseled to wait, till the 1st of August to mark the attendance on those days of total absence only to avoid the chance of being detected by others, because the page of attendance for July would be turned back for the page for August. Are we to believe that your keeping Mr Elias' attendance columns for 23, 24 and 25 July blank up to 1 August and Mr Elias' marking the attendance of these days of total absence on 1 August was a mere coincidence? On the contrary several factors constrain us to think that this is favouritism, dangerously bordering corruption, doled out to foster unhealthy groupism among the members of staff, at the expense of the solidarity and unity of the teaching fraternity.

'In the circumstance we request you to cancel the attendance marked by Mr Elias on days of his total absence and take deterrent disciplinary action against him for this patent and grave act of irregularity'.

Pat came the Bishop-Managers joint memo dated 13 August 1991 jointly served on all the five of us calling for our explanations on or before 20 August 1991 and ordering us to explain:

> 'On what ground did you make the false complaint? Why you did not discuss it with the lecturer-in-charge, or give him in writing

Why did you send the false complaint to the Dy. Director of Collegiate Education and Registrar of the M.G. University?

These acts of fabricating false and fictitious allegations against the head of the Institution as well as against colleagues and reporting them to higher authorities mentioned and to the head of the Institution are serious offences'.

And our joint explanation dated 16 August 1991 we did give to the bishop-manager with copies marked to the same higher authorities mentioned. Prefacing our joint explanation we observed: 'Your show-cause notice is based entirely on your assumption that our memorandum...was false and fictitious....With deep regret we are to submit that before assuming so, you did not care to hear us or require us to produce evidence in support of our memorandum of complaint, which, we feel, ought to have been your first step in the course of Natural Justice. We repeat our complaint that Mr K.U. Elias...marked his attendance of those days of absence on 1-8-'91 with the clandestine concurrence of the lecturer in charge. Further we maintain that our memorandum of complaint, bona fide made, is quite in order and expect suitable legal action by those concerned to get the irregularities rectified and future ones prevented....

'Under the circumstance we submit that any proceedings initiated on the basis of the one-sided report of the lecturer in charge, cited in the show-cause notice, the contents and details of which we are still kept ignorant of, will be totally unmerited by us'.

### Request to Forward Pension Papers Rejected

On 16 September 1991, I submitted the papers related to my pension/gratuity in quadruplicate and duly filled in along with a copy of the government order No. G.O.(P) No. 477/9D/(60)/ Fin sanctioning two annual increments and one biennial increment with request to forward them along with the necessary non-liability certificate 'so as to avoid delay in sanctioning my pension on my retirement on 1-4-92'. Knowing the unfriendly attitude of the L.i.C., I submitted the papers through Mr M.E. Mani, one of the office clerks, as a record of evidence. Again on 24 September 1991 I wrote to L.i.C. reminding him that the increments mentioned above are overdue for sanction, and its sanction is to be reckoned with in preparing the pension papers and in entering it in the pension book. 'Kindly take steps,' I requested him, 'to get my increments sanctioned so as to include it in this month's salary bill and to forward to the higher authorities my pension papers without further delay.' But, with 'the secret agenda' of torpedoing my very retirement, the L.i.C. probably thought it unnecessary to accept the pension papers. So he sent them back to me through the same clerk who told me: 'He refused to accept them and asked me to return them to you'. This last letter of 24 September was returned to me through my colleague Mrs. Lissamma Isaac without assigning any reason. In my letter dated 26 September I protested against this as 'nothing but pursuing your programme of harassing me through deliberately delaying the papers for which you alone are responsible'. I then sent all the papers and the letters dated 16-9-91 and 24-9-91 by registered post with A/D. Back came his response brandishing at me the last fatal missile sent from the headquarters, the Bishop-Manager's memo dated 18 September 1991 which was on the postal transit.

## The Final Memo

The final and calculated to be 'fatal' memo of charges dated 18 September 1991 was fired by none other than the Rt. Rev. Bishop-Manager himself well in advance of my retirement that would take place six months from thence. The L.i.C. probably had this battle in mind which would bring the war to its intended finale and therefore render the moving of pension papers unnecessary. All that was necessary was the completion of the statutory formalities of a domestic enquiry. The memo included all the charges twice leveled earlier and answered. In addition to these was the ninth allegation: 'On 2-8-1991, under your initiative some unfounded allegations were raised against the Lecturer in Charge and forwarded the same to the government and University authorities otherwise than through the proper channel'. This was in fact a clubbing of two allegations, namely that of taking initiative to fabricate false allegations against the L.i.C. and of sending it otherwise than through the proper channel. The reference obviously was to the joint complaint dated 2 August 1991 and signed by five of us, all heads of various departments. It was a war tactic to dissociate and isolate me from a group for the easy final attack. The memo required 'to submit your explanation in writing ...on or before 1 October 1991, failing which disciplinary action will be taken against you in accordance with law'.

On 20 September I received the memo. I submitted my 8-page explanations highlighting some of the important episodes of this saga of hostility and concluded it thus: 'In the light of the above I submit that the charges in the memos cited above are based on reports and allegations fabricated by the L.i.C. and his in-laws in the diocesan executive committee and the College Governing Board to wreak vengeance and therefore without bona fides....I may also add that these acts of harassment and vindictiveness have caused me very great hardships and damages, mental and otherwise, for which I reserve my right to demand adequate compensation through legal means'.

## Intense Mental Agony

Intense mental agony I indeed had to a level far above ordinary endurance. I was sure the management's inveterate hostility would end up in my dismissal at least one day before my retirement and both the management and myself were equally sure of appeal. But the level of mental agony was raised by the thought of the possible agony and embarrassment my wife and two little kids would have to face. My wife then was, as she is even now, a teacher on the Girideepam High School staff and my children Jeslie and Maymol were studying in the same school. Jeslie and Maymol were on the list of the School's Roll of Honour, both having won innumerable district level top awards in school youth festivals. Maymol at the age of bare twelve won the State level top award for the classical dance form 'Bharat Natyam' during the State School Youth Festival held in Kasergod. Dismiss me they would and publish the news in all the prominent dailies, in order to enjoy the infernal satisfaction of seeing the agony of my family and immediate relatives, be it even temporary. I anticipated the agony of my wife and children facing the staff of nearly a hundred, and more than three thousand students, who would be looking at them with one question in their eyes: 'Your husband, your dad has been dismissed?' While our innocent children, unaware of the impact of the dawn of publication of my dismissal, were gently snoring under our enfolding hands, my wife and I spent several nights – literally sleepless nights-wetting our pillows with tears and sobs suppressed lest they should wake up our sleeping kids.

In my letter to the Bishop-Manager dated 20-11-1991 I pointed out: 'Enquiry ordered by an agency into allegations made by the same agency is tantamount to the prosecutor deciding his case against the prosecuted. This is violence to the very foundation of Natural Justice and a travesty of the very judicial process and therefore unjust, even though perhaps legal....I wish to make it very clear that I am absolutely willing to cooperate to have the allegations enquired into by a competent authority, preferably by the authority of the University Syndicate, but not an authority appointed and paid for by the vindictive management seeking to eliminate me.

'A private college teacher must have, by virtue of Natural Justice an authority to whom he can take his grievances against a vindictive management for redress'.

In my petition of even date addressed to Kerala's Governor, who was Chancellor of the University, I expressed my entire willingness to face an impartial enquiry. But I got no response to either of my pleas. I understand that they stick together, the lot of them – political and religious leaders in clandestine alliance. In our democracy, they are governed not by Justice, but by law they make for their own wellbeing.

### Steps of Formalities Ahead

Submission of explanation to the memo was only a preliminary formality. On 18 November 1991, just three months before my retirement, I received the notice of enquiry dated 15 November from advocate P.J. Kurian, requiring me to appear in his office at Thodupuzha, nearly sixty kilometers from my place of residence. I was to appear at 2.30 p.m. on 23 November, leaving hardly five days of notice. The schedule was strategically and minutely calculated. On the part of the management, it had made an advocate's legal service available through the M.A; L.L.B. inquiry officer, and the L.i.C. and of course Mr K.U. Elias were presented as management witnesses. I was denied permission to avail myself of legal advice through a lawyer. In the course of the enquiry, I applied three times for prorogation of the date of hearing: once because of my hospitalization for cardiac problems; two other times to complete the valuation of the University Exam answer books according to the University Exam schedule. The loyal and efficient enquiry officer concluded the enquiry according to the schedule preplanned, with an observation that I was not cooperating at all with the enquiry. He presented his report dated 27 January 1992 with the remark that he had to conclude because of my 'non-cooperation with the process of enquiry'.

The report concluded thus: 'Since out of the nine charges leveled against the DE [Delinquent Employee: my special thanks to him for awarding me with this new title] Rev. Abraham Vellamthadathil by the management, seven charges [including that of instigating the four other Heads of Departments to fabricate false case against the L.i.C.] are proved beyond doubt, I hold that Rev. Abraham Vellamthadathil is GUILTY'.

Equipped with this [indubitable] enquiry report, His Excellency Rt. Rev. Dr K.J. Samuel issued notice dated 19-2-92, the final formality left before the issuance of order of dismissal.

(I don't know who conferred on him this 'doctorate' and when. Perhaps it was a necessary accompaniment to the purple cassock, red sash and golden chain with golden pectoral cross he was vested with on the day of his installation.) The notice sounded like the Son of Man's Judgment on Doomsday: 'The enquiry report found the charges and they were very serious offences invoking the imposition of dismissal from service'. To quote fully, 'The disciplinary authority is of the opinion that the charges proved against you are of very grave nature calling for severe punishment. It is therefore proposed that the punishment of dismissal from service be imposed on you with immediate effect.

'If you have any representation to make against the proposed action, you my submit the representation in this regard within one week of the receipt hereof by you, failing which final orders will be passed as if you have no representation to make in this matter'.

My wife and I looked forward to 28 February 1992 to see the dawn of the day to receive the order of dismissal and to watch the celebration thereof through the media flashing in large head lines the news of my dismissal. The silent but inevitable prayer that came to our minds was the words of Jesus: 'Father, if possible, let this chalice pass from me. Yet not my will but Thine be done'.

## Heaven Intervened

Who has seen the inscrutable mind of God? Nobody, not even the Rt. Rev. K.J. Samuel. One of my friends, I forget who that angel from heaven was, advised me to show the notice to the then practising advocate in the High Court, Ernakulam, Mr Abdul Gafoor, who would later be an Honourable Judge in the same High Court. Mr Gafoor brought his legal and judicial mind to bear closely upon the notice. He detected a legal flaw which neither the acute vindictive minds of those in the College disciplinary authority, nor the Bishop's brother advocate saw. Accordingly Mr Gafoor dictated to me the following notice dated 26 February 1992 in reply to the notice of dismissal: '*The show-cause notice cited above proposing to inflict on me the punishment of dismissal from service with immediate effect and asking for my representation against such proposal was served on me on 19-2-92. The time limit specified therein is only one week. The said notice makes it clear that the management had made a detailed consideration of the report of enquiry. Therefore this notice is as contemplated in clause 73(12) of the Mahatma Gandhi University First Statutes 1991 issued in G.O.M.S. 23/91/H.Edn dated 8-2-91 and published in Kerala Gazette dated 11-2-91.*

The penalty of dismissal proposed is the one provided in clause 71(VII) of the said Statue.

Clause 73(12) (a) of the said Statues providing the procedure for imposing major penalty makes it obligatory on the part of the manager, in case it is proposed to impose such a penalty, to furnish the delinquent a copy of the report of the enquiry authority and to give him reasonable time which may not exceed one month.

As the proposal in the notice cited is based on the details, conclusions and finding of guilt contained in the enquiry report, necessarily I can put forward my valid explanation only on studying the said report. Furnishing a copy thereof to me is a statutory requirement as submitted above which cannot be avoided. Therefore I humbly submit as a first point that as the copy of the enquiry report is not furnished to me, I am practically disabled to make my representation against the proposal to impose the maximum penalty on me.

As a second point, I urge that the period of one week specified in the notice is unreasonably too short a period, as several documents, facts and evidences are involved in the case. Therefore I deserve reasonable time of at least three weeks to submit my reply to the show-cause notice, after the receipt of the copy of enquiry report.

A show-cause notice as the one cited above without furnishing the copy of the report is not a show-cause notice in the eye of the law and it has no legal efficacy. I further submit that the show-cause notice gets its validity only if the enquiry report is attached thereto. Therefore it is made further clear that the notice will be effective only from the date of furnishing me with the copy of the enquiry report referred to and relied on in the said notice.

In the above circumstance I humbly request the management:

'To furnish me with a copy of the enquiry report referred to in the show cause notice cited above so as to enable me to submit my representation against the proposed penalty, and, to grant me three weeks time from the date of receipt of the copy of the said enquiry report to submit my representation against your proposal'.

The notice must have hit them like a devastating anti-missile, bringing to a sudden halt the hellish momentum taken on by the management machinery heading for my earliest possible dismissal before my retirement. The reading of this notice worded in easy but very sharp and poking legal thrusts must have been an unending torture of a painful ordeal. Every minute ahead is decisive and they could not afford to miss any more minute. Back came the Bishop-Manager's second notice dated 18 March 1992. Only thirteen days more for dismissal because on the fourteenth day, that is, 1 April 1992, I would be a retired professor. The second notice along with the required enquiry report was dispatched on the 18th itself by registered post with A/D. But they made a very clever mistake which, God forgive, I put to my best possible advantage. After all, tactics and quick devices are permitted in an emergency period of declared war.

On the 18th itself the management served me with a copy of the notice sent by registered post. It was served on me through a peon for my information and acknowledgement. I took the information thanking God for it, but gave a false acknowledgement by scribbling something instead of usual signature, no doubt, with the intention of denying acknowledgement. Killing a man is a crime, I thought, but killing some one in self defense is not. Further more, I regarded this emergency war strategy as a new practical application of the Catholic theologico-moral principle of the 'occult compensation'. The copy served on me informed me that the concluding stipulation of the notice was: 'Your representation, if any, should reach me within one week of on [sic] the receipt of this notice. No further request for extension of time shall be entertained'. I calculated: the notice, sent by registered post could reach me on the 21st or, sure, on the 22nd March. The ultimatum would require my reply by 29 March. And I could expect the dismissal order by 29th itself. I planned a short but final strategy in this ballistics.

On 19 March I met my friend the local postmaster and said: 'Sir, I understand that a registered postal article addressed to me is in the postal transit. I shall call at your office and take delivery of it on the 25th'. 'All right, Fr Abraham. We shall retain the letter here till you come to take delivery'. 'Thank you, Sir' and I proceeded to college. I again calculated: one week from 25 March will end on 1 April when I would be out of service by retirement. My dismissal then would perhaps be legal but irrelevant. I reached college happier and more cheerful than usual and I found the L.i.C. and his in-laws rather gloomier than usual.

31 March 1992. The last day of my service in H.B. College. The Bishop-Manager's letter dated 30 March 1992 with copies marked for the Director of Collegiate Education, the Registrar M.G. University, the Secretary, Higher Education Department and the Dy. Director, Kottayam was handed over to me. It was typed in a hurry as can be seen at first reading. The letter was to inform me:

1. You are guilty of the charges
2. You deserve severe punishment of dismissal as proposed
3. You have refused to submit any representation till 29 March 1992...[but I was legally bound to give it only on 1 April 1992 and I did give it on the due date. See below]
4. In spite of the above facts, the college governing body...decided to take a very lenient view in the light of the fact that you are retire (sic) on 31- 3-1992.

'However, in view of the serious dereliction of duty and misconduct the governing body decides that:

> the two stagnation increments due on 1-9-90 and 1.9.91 be withheld
> It is ordered that you are not entitled for the increments in view of the punishment imposed on you'

The fifth reference given in the order of 30 March was to 'OUR letter dated 18-3-92' [emphasis added]. Till 31 March I had thought the letter dated 18 March 1992 was from the bishop-manager. But the new information of 'our' letter confirmed my allegation that there were *other* miscreants also behind the mischief – the politician caucus of the in-laws, if I am not mistaken. The letter dated 30-3-92 was a silent proclamation that this belated leniency was the least and last way to conclude the proceedings they initiated and to check the ghost of vindictiveness they let loose without further disfigurement of their faces and damage to their wounded pride. With deeply-felt sentiments I took leave of my other colleagues and members of office staff who had shown me so much love, understanding but silent support and sympathy during the days of my second phase of struggle with the Christian Institution and came off with the decision of my own course of legal procedures to resolve the ugly dramatic climax.

## My Explanation to the Dismissal Order

I submitted my explanation to the dismissal notice in due time, with copies marked to all the four higher authorities who had been served with copies of the dismissal order. In my forwarding letter dated 1 April 1992 I made it very clear that I was required to submit my representation 'within one week from receipt thereof'. The notice reached me at 3 p.m. on 25 March 1992. 'As such the submission of my representation is due only on 2-4-1992. You had therefore no legal and valid reason to assume on 29-3-1992 that I refused to submit my representation and accept the charges and findings in the enquiry report.

'Enclosed herewith is my representation...showing that the whole enquiry proceedings, concluded ex parte deliberately denying me to have my case and supporting evidences heard and recorded in the enquiry report, is violative of Natural Justice and illegal and that any action proposed to be taken against me on the basis of mala fide proceedings will be illegal.

'I have persistently denied all charges as I do even now, and submit that your present order, issued on the basis of your unwarranted assumption, is invalid and illegal'. I concluded my 8-page representation against the show cause notice of dismissal saying: 'Further more, the mala fide proceedings and the prolonged acts of harassment and vindictiveness have caused me untold damage, financial and otherwise, and mental anguish for which I am entitled to claim adequate compensation. I hereby call upon you to show-cause if any within 10 days from receipt of this why I should not initiate legal proceedings against you for adequate compensation. Copy to the Enquiry Officer'.

## Appeal before the Tribunal

Now it was my turn to take the course of legal proceedings. In April 1992 itself I filed my appeal No. 2/92 before the Appellate Tribunal through my advocate Mr. M. Gopinathan Nair. The counter affidavit filed by the Bishop-Manager contained the following blatant lie as his last resort. In the sixth paragraph he remarked: 'Before the Appellant entered the service of the Respondent College, the appellant was employed in another private college. Disciplinary proceedings were initiated against him by that Management for very grave acts of misconduct and the same was dropped by that management on the appellant agreeing to resign from the service of that college. Little did the respondent realize that the appellant would not learn from past experiences and would continue to indulge in acts of misconducts'! [Yes, the character of the appellant and the nature of the two managements continue the same, as I have already pointed out.]

## Disciplinary Proceedings Swept Clean Out

My appeal No. 2/92 before Tribunal was finally heard and

adjudicated by the Tribunal, Mr P. Ramachandran Nair, on 3 March 1993. The judgment awarded was a clean vindication of my long-tortured righteousness and honest service and a clean sweep out of the travesty of disciplinary proceedings. Let me quote: '...as per the terms of the covering letter which accompanied the copy of the (enquiry) report, the appellant was entitled to a week's time from 25-3-92 for replying the show-cause notice. But it is seen that before the expiry of the above period on 30-3-92 the respondent passed the impugned order. This is not only illegal, but also against basic concept of the rule of Natural Justice....

'8. Although the proposed punishment was dismissal from service, the punishment actually imposed as per the impugned order was 'withholding' of two increments due to him on 1-9-'90 and 1-9-'91. This punishment was that imposed on 30-3-'92, one day prior to the date of his retirement from service.

'9. 'Withholding of increment' is one of the several penalties prescribed in Statute 71 of Part D of chapter 45 of the M.G. University, First Statute 1991....If it is to be withheld, it has to be done before it is accrued....Therefore the order of the respondent dated 30-3-'92...was illegal and ultra vires.

'10...The records further show that the appellant answered both the memos dated 19-9-'90 and 5-2-'91. After his explanation the matter was not proceeded with. It was only on the eve of his retirement that all these charges were raked up again, another memo of charges was framed and an enquiry was held in undue haste and a punishment imposed just a day before the retirement of the appellant from service. In the circumstances there are strong reasons to think that the disciplinary proceedings which culminated in the order under appeal was lacking in good faith. That apart, it is vitiated by basic error of law and violation of rules of Natural Justice.

'11. I therefore allow the appeal setting aside the impugned order of the respondent'.

The news was flashed across in big heads in almost all the prominent dailies. *Indian Express* dated Tuesday 23 March 1993, for instance, reported the news in two columns with the remark: 'The Tribunal in its verdict...concluded that the Manager's order was vindictive, illegal and violative of the principles of Natural Justice'. I am not certain whether the L.i.C., the Bishop-Manager, his brother advocate and their in-laws politician caucus were shocked at the news. But I thanked God, the Spirit of Truth and Justice, Who led to the total vindication of my prolongedly tortured righteousness.

**Legal Steps for Retirement Benefits**

The long cherished and strong nourished 'secret agenda' having failed, the inextinguishable vindictiveness still continued bubbling and fermenting. The next step was to obstruct or at least delay my last month (March) salary, release of Provident Fund and retirement benefits. On 4 May 1992 I sent a notice to the L.i.C. pointing out the deliberate and therefore culpable delay in moving the papers 'in spite of the fact that I had submitted my pension books (and required papers) duly signed as far back as 16 September 1991. To the best of my knowledge I have no liability whatsoever towards the college nor have you informed of any so far.

'Under the circumstances your neglect can be seen as pursuance of your vindictiveness to harass me even after my retirement.

'As such I request that within two weeks from receipt of this notice I may be informed of your reasons, if any, for your refusal to draw and disburse my salary for March and to forward my papers relating to my retirement benefit, failing which I shall be constrained to take necessary legal steps and you will be held responsible for the costs and other losses consequent thereto'. Copies of the same were marked to the higher concerned authorities including the Bishop- Manager.

On 15 May the bills and the related papers were submitted to the Deputy Director, but not in proper form. So the office of the Deputy Director returned them on 25-5-92 requiring to re-submit them in proper form.

On 31 May 1992 I forwarded to the Director of Collegiate Education a copy of the petition to the Manager to have the formalities expedited and requested the Dy. Director's urgent intervention.

Intervene indeed the Deputy Director's office did through its letter No. D1-6.600/92 dated 4-6-'92, enquiring about 'pensionary claims of Rev. Abraham Vellamthadathil'. The L.i.C., already appointed Principal, in his reply dated 10-6-92 put the blame on me saying: 'In spite of repeated requests he has not cared to return the declaration forms duly signed which is essential for passing the bill'! Besides, 'He has filed a petition before the University Appellate Tribunal against the punishment of withdrawing two increments which is pending disposal'. I received the Deputy Director's letter No. D1-6600/92 dated 23-6-'92 informing that as per the management's 'report to this office, action is being taken regarding the claiming of last salary bill, the closure of Provident Fund, the pensionary claims etc from the college. The copy of the letter is also enclosed herewith'. Yet there was no positive result. Time was wasted in useless exchange of several letters between the Principal and me. In my letter dated 31-7-92, for example, I wrote: 'I fail to understand by any stretch of imagination why you should be so obstinately bent on scraping from my declaration form my designation as First Grade Professor sanctioned by the Manager through order No. H.B.C./G3/90 dated 18-9-90 particularly because the validity of the declaration in no way depends upon the designation, as I have been given to understand by the Dy. Director's office.

'I also understand that orders have been issued to you from the Dy. Director's office fixing my U.G.C. basic pay to Rs. 1075 as on 1-4-90'. I concluded the letter requesting to forward my pension papers and to draw and disburse the salary arrears including the U.G.C. Scale arrears without any further delay. Still to no positive effect. So on 15 September 1992, more than six months after my retirement, I appealed to the Directorate, Trivandrum, to definitively intervene and get my salary and pension arrears and benefits disbursed. I pointed out the emptiness and irrelevance of the Principal's contention that disbursing the salary of March and computing pension and preparing pension papers would be illegal while my appeal No. 2/92 before the University Appellate Tribunal was pending disposal.' The appeal is against the Manager's order dated 30-

3-'92', I pointed out, 'purporting to impose the punishment of withholding two stagnation increments due on 1-9-90 and 1-9-91. The punishment can have no effect as no stagnation increments are due to me under the U.G.C. Scale sanctioned with effect from 1.4.'90'.

I knew that the management would be brought to act only under threat of legal procedures. So my advocate before the Tribunal Mr M. Gopinathan Nair issued a legal notice to the Principal dated 3 October 1992, pointing out the facts I have mentioned above and concluding: 'Your action (of deliberate refusal to forward his pension papers…) is patently mala fide and your motive is to harass my client because of personal ill – will.

'This is to inform you that if you fail to forward the pension papers of my client and disburse his salary for March 1992 and arrears of salary from 1-4-'90 within fifteen days, he will be forced to resort to legal steps for realizing the same with interest at the rate of 18 per cent per annum for the period of delay and the compensation for the suffering he had to undergo due to the denial of his pension and other benefits. You will be responsible for the cost and consequences of any such legal steps….'

The Government department of Collegiate Education too intervened in answer to my appeal dated 15-5-92. Mr K. Hamza, under secretary, Government of Kerala, Finance department, in his letter to the Dy. Director, Kottayam, D.O. No. 73488/PWC-D3/92/Fin dated 15-10-92 with copies marked for the Principal and for me asked the Dy. Director ' to please look into the case personally and arrange to forward a reply urgently in the matter. Please return the representation along with your reply'.

The Principal in his reply dated 21 November 1992 to the legal notice dated 3 October 1992, after his usual pleas wrote: 'If it is agreeable to your client, the above papers can be processed, sans the two increments and if only it will in no way affect the case before the Appellate Tribunal or warrant any contempt of court on our part'.

# 24

# The Denouement through the Courts

## Pension Papers forwarded under High Court Direction

Finding no effects of appeals and legal notices, I filed OP No. 15164/92-E before the Honourable High Court. The case was heard by the Honourable Mr Justice K.B. Balakrishnan and direction was given on 24 February 1993: 'Under the above circumstances, the third respondent [Principal] is directed to submit the pension papers to the second respondent [Dy. Director, Kottayam] on 10-3-93....Along with the pension papers the third respondent shall also forward the arrear bill relating to the arrears of Salary due to the petitioner consequent on the revision of pay scale by the implementation of the U.G.C. scheme. (The petitioner) is entitled to get arrears of salary from 1-4-'90 to 31-3-92. Arrear bill for this amount also shall be sent along with the pension papers'. I thanked God for this clean sweep out of the management's rubbish entirely in my favour.

## Vindictiveness Wriggles under Court Lashes

The poison of vindictiveness had not been spilled out in full. The Principal of course submitted all the papers related to the salary, arrears and pension benefits in accordance with the court order, but incomplete in formalities so that they were sent back from the Higher Education Department Offices concerned for correction and re-submission. His neglect to send up papers in proper form for processing invited another legal notice from Advocate K. Sankunni Menon dated 5 June 1993. With reference to the verdict of the Tribunal and to the High

Court order of 24 February 1993, the notice pointed out: 'The Principal, however, complying with the High Court Order in its letter, but intending to defeat its spirit submitted the pension papers, but in defective form and presented the arrears bill after withholding two increments in direct violation of the court direction. The pension papers were returned by the Dy. Director...for rectification of defects and re-submission. But it is understood that to this day the Principal has not rectified the defects and re-submitted the pension papers to date....

'You have thus violated the court order in its spirit...and persisted in the path of vindictiveness; you are therefore liable to be prosecuted against for contempt of court....

'In the circumstance you are hereby given notice that unless you comply with the orders of the honourable High Court also in the light of the Tribunal's verdict, within two weeks from receipt of this notice, my client will be constrained to set law in motion....'

### Provident Fund Released

On 17 May 1993 I received a copy of the intimation No. P.F I 11(1) 38051/92 of the Director of Collegiate Education to the Principal informing him: 'that KPCSPF Account No. 2076 in respect of Rev. Abraham Vellamthadathil, retired Professor of your college has been closed and authorization for Rs. 54509 is enclosed herewith. The amount may be drawn and disbursed to the subscriber and date of encashment intimated to this office.'

### Release of Gratuity: Another Long Episode in the Saga

As far back as 23 December 1993 I had requested the Principal to take steps necessary for the issuance of the Last Pay Certificate (L.P.C.) and the Non-Liability Certificate (N.L.C.) by the Higher Education Authorities concerned for the release of my gratuity. On 27 December I reminded him of the same and of the report of the Departmental audit for the period from 1-6-85 to 31-3-1990, i.e., including my tenure of office as Professor-in-charge. In my letter dated 23 December 1993 I had pointed out: 'The management has not so far sent any reply clearing audit objection, if any, nor have I been so far informed of any audit objection relating to the period of my tenure of office. In the light of the management's own appraisal of my tenure of office during which the chaotic condition of the college office was restored to order and charge was handed over to the Principal on deputation with all the records and accounts written out in order, and signed by me and countersigned by the in-coming Principal and by the present Principal then in his capacity as Bursar 'there is no reason why any of my pension benefits should be delayed or withheld against any departmental audit objections related to my tenure of office'. So I requested the Principal to take steps necessary to clear the departmental audit objections, if any, to clear the way for the Deputy Director to release the N.L.C. for drawing my pension and gratuity. 'Please take notice,' I concluded the letter, 'that if the management refuses to comply with my request, as above, it will be treated as disregard of the order of the honourable High Court dated 24 February 1993...and the matter will be proceeded against legally....' A copy of this notice was forwarded to the manager and another to the Deputy Director with request to take cognizance of the facts and take necessary action in the matter.

Acting on this my notice the office of the Deputy Director sent to the Principal notice No. F2-6708/92 dated 10-1-94 reminding him that 'the non-liability certificate can be issued...only on settling the audit objections contained in the departmental audit reports....This office has already called for your further reply to the various objections in the audit report for the period during which Fr Vellamthadathil was the Principal of the College. Any laxity in furnishing the reply and clearing the objections may cause delay in getting his gratuity and such delay will lead to payment of interest on the pension claims. This office will not be responsible in case such a contingency happens, as it is the Principal who is to settle the objection in the audit report....You are therefore instructed that priority should be given to settle the objections in the audit report as expeditiously as possible'.

Though I was in the service for two more years after the said audit report was received by the Principal, I was kept ignorant of the fact or of the details of the audit objections. Probably the then L.i.C. kept it as a last minute secret bomb to explode on me as the 'big bang'. It is only from the Deputy Director's letter No. F2/6708/92 dated 13-12-96, addressed to the Principal with copy marked for me that I came to know of the details of the 'audit objection' against me. The details were:

| | |
|---|---|
| Want of payee report for Boarding and Lodging: | Rs. 63813.85 |
| Tuition Fee and Fine (Short Collection) | Rs. 955.50 |
| P.D. Account (special fees) | Rs. 28275.59 |
| Total | Rs. 93044.94. |

The objection regarding the boarding and lodging charges was not about its utilization for the purpose intended, but the want of payee receipt or vouchers from the warden, Mrs. Chachi, and the college office staff, Mr K.G. Samuel, assigned to handle student grants. I had warned both of them several times demanding to furnish vouchers, served memos on both of them and not satisfied with their replies, I had reported the matter to the manager for further action against them even before I handed over charge. As for the short collection of tuition fee and fine and P.D. Account maintenance it was the failure on the part of the Office staff concerned and in due time I had reported the matter to the manager for further action. But the manager and the caucus put the matter on the cold storage to be taken out for the last 'big bang' against the pension benefits.

On receipt of the copy of the Deputy Director's said letter dated 13-12-96, I wrote to the Principal on 20 March 1997 with copies marked for the Director of Collegiate Education and the Deputy Director and explained: 'I handed over charge of the college on 2-7-87 with all the documents, registers, records and accounts including a detailed statement of accounts for Rs. 54501.25, being office–cum-management expenditure which I met during the two years of my tenure of office. The papers were duly signed by the in-coming Principal and counter-signed by you in your capacity as Bursar....All details and documents are with you since 1-7-1987.

'Further I continued my service as Professor and Head of the Department of English for five more years till I retired from service on 1 April 1992. During all these five years of my continued service in the college, I was neither intimated of any audit objection nor called for any explanations thereof. Even four and a half years after my retirement I was not intimated of any audit objections or liabilities nor called for explanation.

'Under the circumstance the Management alone is able and bound to reply to the audit objections.. And therefore I may be favoured with a copy of the reply that you might have sent to the authorities concerned'.

## To High Court Again

As was to be expected, I got no information as to how and why such a liability was fixed against me. So I filed OP No. 10094/94B before the honourable High Court with the State of Kerala represented by the Chief Secretary, Deputy Director of College Education, Kottayam, Principal H.B. College and Accountant General (A&E) Kerala as Respondents. The Hon'ble Mr Justice C.S. Rajan having heard my case, presented by advocate Mr V. Divakaran Potti, gave his verdict on Wednesday 18 February 1998: 'The petitioner has pleaded that he has not yet been served with any communication either fixing up liability or quantifying the amount of liability, though he retired from service on 31-3-1992. A reading of Ext P8 [Liability certificate dated 8-8-1994 issued by Accounts officer-in-charge for the Director of Collegiate Edn.] will go to show that no prior notice was issued before the fixation of liability. No explanation was also called for from the petitioner.'

'The statement filed on behalf of the second respondent did not show that prior notice has been issued to the petitioner before fixation of liability. Therefore it is obvious that Ext P8 [Liability Certificate] has been passed in total negation of the Principles of Natural Justice. Therefore I quash Ext P8 [Liability

Certificate]. The second Respondent is directed to fix the liability against the petitioner in accordance with the law. The petitioner is also free to take up the plea of bar of limitation under the KSR against the fixation of liability at this distance of time'. The intended 'big bang' bomb ended up as a bubble in a cup of soda. The court also showed me the way out if any liability happened to be fixed, i.e., the plea of bar of limitation of 'this distance of time'.

Acting upon this verdict, the office of the Deputy Director issued notice No. F1-6708/92 dated 13-5-98 providing details of a proposed liability of Rs. 91721 [Rs. 1325.94 less than the liability of Rs. 93044.94, fixed earlier!] with the conclusion: 'Therefore you are directed to report within thirty days of receipt of this notice, your explanation if any for not fixing the amount as liability against you... (failing which) the undersigned will proceed further presuming that you have no explanation to offer'.

As the High Court order above showed me, I could have pleaded 'bar of limitation of this distance of 11 years'. Besides, I was under medical instruction of bed rest after an operation for cataract done on 15 May 1998. But no. Instead I submitted my explanation dated 8 June 1998 and pointed out. 'De facto there is no liability against me and I handed over charge with my hands clean. That the management was satisfied with my discharge of duties as Principal stands out from [innumerable] testimonials'. Then coming to the three items of liability, namely, want of vouchers from the hostel warden for the hostel charges of Rs. 63813.85, short fee collection of Rs. 906 and P.D. Accounts for Rs. 27001, I arrayed my explanations with documents to show that I was in no way responsible for these defects. With regard to the first item: 'There is no case that the amount was not utilized for the purpose for which it was given. The objection is that the payee's receipts [vouchers] are wanting'. Here I explained the actions I took and the report I submitted to the management about the warden Mrs. Chachi and the college office staff K.G. Samuel – a member of the college management board and later dismissed for attempt to filch the one-month salary of the Staff on the way back from

Erattupettah Treasury. With regard to item no. 2, I submitted: 'A Principal with the full load of teaching work in addition to his other duties as Principal cannot be expected to collect fees from the students. It was the duty of the concerned clerk to collect fees in time and to report to the Principal cases of default if any for further action. No case of default has ever been reported to me during my tenure of office or later. It is for the management to ask explanation from the clerk responsible for the short fee collection'. Item no. 3 too was adequately explained. I concluded requesting the department: 'to kindly take cognizance of the above facts and get the management comply with the requirements of the audit and issue orders releasing my gratuity with interest at the bank rate till disbursement'.

In reply, the Deputy Director's letter no. F1/6708/92 dated 1-8-'98 informed me: 'Your reply has been forwarded to the Principal and manager for obtaining their remarks. The matter of issuing N.L.C. is expected to be finalized shortly on receipt of the reply from the Principal for which he has been instructed'. Three months passed before I received a copy of the Deputy Director's 'Revised and Final Liability Certificate' dated 3-11-'98 fixing a liability of Rs. 270 as 'short collection of tuition fees and fine'! Earlier as per the detailed notice dated 13-5-'98 it was Rs. 906. Again in my reply to this 'Revised Liability Certificate' dated 12 November 1998 I responded: 'Kindly explain how the short fee collection of Rs. 906 came to be reduced to Rs. 270 and how and why this reduced amount came to be fixed as liability against me'. I was fed up with filing suits and I did not want to tread unendingly long legal steps for this trifle of Rs. 270. It is only a little late that I realized this was another bureaucratic trick to some how or other keep me under some 'liability', even if it is for as paltry a sum as Rs. 5, in order to escape the possibility of any suit for interest for the delay. Through my reply to A.G. Trivandrum, dated 12-11-98 I accepted 'to remit Rs. 270 to the Treasury 'Under protest', reserving my right to question the validity of the revised and final L.C. in the court of law'. Then followed the usual pest of redtapism that rules the government offices. After having been shunted back and forth between the Dy. Director's office, the A.G.'s office etc, finally on 30 March 1999 I got the Gratuity Payment Order absolutely, unhurt and entrusted it to the manager, Central Bank of India, Kottayam for encashment. All my pension benefits were made available for me, which I continue to draw even now. I don't know whether life is still throbbing or getting choked in the throats of some in Melukavu.

## Suit for Compensation Dismissed

Having got all my retirement benefits including pension, I turned to the indemnification for all the damages, mental, physical and economic, caused by the persistent harassment and vindictiveness. I filed OS no. 67/99 in the Pala Sub Court against the Bishop Manager as the respondent. The OS was finally heard by the sub-judge Sri K.V. Thampikutty and he decided it dismissing my petition mainly on the ground of article 72 of the Limitation Act, stipulating that the various episodes in this saga of struggle were episodes of years of distance of time. The second ground was somewhat weird. The defendant argued that he was acting as Trust Representative of the C.S.I. Church Association. And the C.S.I. Church Association was not marked as respondent in the OS. So the OS was dismissed on the ground of 'non-joinder of necessary parties'. I wondered whether I should have included as Respondents the CSI Moderator, all the CSI Bishops and pastors of all the Churches of South India as members of the 'CSI Church Association'! But the third and most important ground on which the OS was dismissed was that 'even at the last moment his liability is there of an amount while he was working as a Principal of the college. So it is settled position of law when liability is there and if the liability is not clear [sic] off, then the non liability will not be issued by the concerned authorities'. Only when I read this did I realize the mischief behind the Deputy Director's 'revised and final liability certificate' dated 3-11-98 fixing a liability of Rs. 270 as 'short collection of tuition fees and fines', even though I had protested against this anonymous liability, questioning the order as to 'how the short fee collection came to be reduced to Rs. 270 and how and why this reduced amount came to be fixed as liability against me'. Even if they had reduced the amount to such a negligible amount as Rs. 5, it would have served their purpose of keeping me under liability and escaping from the possible burden of the penalty of interest upon the gratuity amount of Rs. 65000 and more at the rate of 11 per cent for nearly 11 years! In the practice of dishonesty and crookedness they stick together the lot of them, be they politicians, bureaucrats or religious higher ups of the 'heavenward escalator'! I felt too tired to run to court with another OP against this 'liability of Rs. 270'.

## Final Suit for Recovery of Money

However I had one more OS No. 11/95 before the Sub Court of Pala against the Bishop Manager for realization of the loan of Rs. 48600 including the office expenses of Rs. 15056I had spent for the day-to-day college office and management. It is to be remembered that I assumed charge on a nil-balance in the wake of the totally disorderly state of the office affairs and of Principal Arbey's refusal to hand over charge. Since the management dishonoured the guarantee they had undertaken to refund the amount with interest on or before my retirement, I filed OS no. 11/95 dated 10 April 1992 before the Sub Court of Pala. The case was presented by the veteran and venerable advocate Mr V.T. Thomas (Sr.) The OS having been finally heard on 17-10-1997 and 22-10-1997 by the Sub Court Judge Sri N. Mohandas, the judgment dated 22 October 1997 was given allowing my OS and directing the defendant Bishop-Manager to pay me 'Rs. 76302 with interest at the rate of 6 per cent per annum on the principal amount of Rs. 48000 from the date of suit till realization of the amount with proportionate costs from the defendant and its assets'.

The defendant went in appeal and filed AS no. 612/1998 before the Honourable High Court. I presented my own case as party-in-person along the flawless line of arguments followed by the able advocate Mr V.T. Thomas in the Sub Court. The AS having been finally heard on 9-11-2006, the Honourable

Mr Justice V. Ramkumar dismissed the AS and decreed: 'The decree of the lower court be and is hereby confirmed and the Appeal Suit be dismissed with costs'. Quoted below are a few observations made by the Honourable Mr Justice Ramkumar. They are quoted not in the least to cast aspersions on any one but to acknowledge the great compensation and comfort they brought to alleviate the intense mental agony and the thick darkness of uncertainty which my family and my immediate relatives had to face in this my unequal struggle with a powerful group equipped with power and blind though beguiled followers, and enraged with deadly venom of hostility and unquenchable and unscrupulous vindictiveness.

'The Board of Management had taken an unreasonable attitude [interview and selection to fill the non-teaching staff vacancies] and when the plaintiff was requested to affix his signature in the minutes he wanted his objection to be noted. When that was not acceded to, he tendered his resignation [of membership in the diocesan executive]....There was an interview conducted for the selection of non-teaching staff. Contrary to the result of the interview, the management wanted to give first rank to a particular candidate. Since the plaintiff was against that, the diocese became antagonistic towards him. They started a tirade against him'. [Paragraph 8, page 9]

'DW1 the successor Bishop (father K.J. Samuel)...confessed that he is a defendant in a suit filed before the Munsif court, Pala as OS 84/1990. The allegations in that suit were that he was guilty of misappropriation of fund, abuse for foreign aid, falsification of documents etc. and he was sought to be injuncted from becoming the Bishop. DW1 also confessed that there is another case against him in which the plaintiffs are father A.J. Varghese and K.J. George'. [Paragraph 9 page 10.]

'DW1 confessed that after 1986 the officials of the diocese were not on good terms with the Plaintiff' [Page 10]

'A perusal of Ext. A13 judgment of the University Appellate Tribunal will show that DW2 [Principal Rev. P.V. Joseph] had an axe to grind against the plaintiff who successfully challenged the appointment of DW2 as officiating Principal of the College'. [Paragraph 10, page 13]

Referring to the Former Manager, Bishop K. Michael John's appreciation of my service as published on page 3 of the Diocesan Official Organ 'Jnanadeepam' vol. 4 for the month of June 1987, produced as Ext. A 35, the judgment remarked: 'The above extract bears ample testimony to the fact that matters concerning the college were in a bad shape and it was the plaintiff who after taking over the charge of Principal brought orderliness and financial propriety to the affairs of the college and the Bishop has expressed his appreciation and gratitude paying rich encomiums to the Plaintiff. It is such a person who is sought to be characterized a person guilty of fabricating documents to substantiate the claim made by him....

'A person who had virtually sacrificed his career for the betterment of the college and who had transformed the college from a total mess and disarray into a coverable [sic]. Institution was rewarded in the most unjust and unbecoming manner. Exts A13 and A33 [judgment in AS 2/92 M.G. University Appellate Tribunal] judgments will clearly show that the plaintiff who had rendered admirable service to the Institution as a loyal servant was subjected to vindictive and hostile treatment by the defendant. The allegation that the letters particularly Ext A5 were fabricated by the plaintiff was a blasphemous one leveled without any basis whatsoever'. [Page 15-16]

These candid observations and remarks of the Honourable High Court brought me heavenly joy and compensations adequate enough. They were divine curative balm to my deeply wounded soul and shattered sentiments and unimpeachable justification of my righteousness. I thanked God, Who is the Spirit of Truth and Justice in whom I trusted and continue to trust. The judgment concluded: 'The trial judge who had the unique advantage of seeing the witness (es) and assessing their credibility was inclined to accept the plaintiff's case as true.... The result of the foregoing discussion is that this appeal is devoid of any merit and is accordingly dismissed with costs.

## The Final Resolution: Mark the Difference

Let me be mercilessly brief and bring this long saga to a finale with a difference. The OS No. 11/95 dated 10-4-92 was now back in the Sub Court of Pala for execution. By now, the Bishop-Manager K.J. Samuel had been succeeded by the new Bishop the Rt. Rev. Dr K.G. Daniel as the Bishop-Manager. As expected, my advocate, Mr V.T. Thomas, on my behalf together with the Management's advocate worked out the calculation according to the directives of the court and came to the conclusion that an amount of Rs. 128500 was due to me from the Management. Out of this Rs. 15000 in cash was accepted by advocate Mr V.T. Thomas on my behalf as the first installment.

The new Bishop, Dr K.G. Daniel then sought the mediation of my good friend and guide Rev. K.C. Mathew, retired Principal of Bishop Moore College, Mavelikkara, to negotiate with me for a settlement of the issue through a few easy installments as the East Kerala diocese was under financial strain to settle the execution of the court order at a stroke. As invited by Rev. K.C. Mathew I met him at his residence and after a short but cordial exchange I gave him the following assurance: 'Achen, please tell Bishop K.G. Daniel not to plead financial stringency of the diocese in the court. Ask him to write a cheque for the balance of Rs. 113500/- on my behalf and present it in the court in full settlement of the case. I will see to it that he is freed from all strains related to the settlement of this issue'. Rev. K.C. Mathew conveyed the message to Bishop K.G. Daniel. The latter signed a bank cheque for Rs. 113500 and presented it in Pala Sub Court. Advocate V.T. Thomas took delivery of it on my behalf in full settlement of the execution of the court verdict and handed the cash and the cheque to me. Out of this I paid a nominal amount of Rs. 10000 as advocate fees and took the balance of Rs. 5000 in cash and the cheque for Rs. 113500—a total of Rs. 118500—and went straight to Rev. K.C. Mathew, cancelled the cheque and handed it over to him along with Rs. 5000 in cash with request to return the whole amount to Bishop K.G. Daniel. I then returned home to share my joy and peace with my family and immediate relatives to their entire satisfaction and cordial approval of the settlement. Within a few days I received a letter from the new Principal of the College Rev. K.J. Samuel (Jr.) dated 14-5-2007, sent on behalf of the Manager and the College Management Board expressing: 'Our sincere thanks to you in settling the financial obligation, consequent on the court order in the OS 11/95 (EP89/98) at Sub Court Pala. I also acknowledge the receipt of the cheque returned and Rs. 5000 handed over through Rev. K.C. Mathew'. It was followed by the letter from Bishop K.G. Daniel dated 23 May 2007 addressed to Rev. K.C. Mathew with copy marked for me. It read: 'On behalf of the diocese I extend our sincere thanks for settling the financial case with Rev. Abraham Vellamthadam in a most peaceful and Christian way of reconciliation. I am very happy that Rev. Abraham Vellamthadam showed the Christian maturity of peace and harmony at this stage. Once again we appreciate your mediatorship and prayer for settling the matter'. To this I responded on 8 June 2007 thus: 'I thank you for acknowledging that I have shown 'the Christian maturity of peace and harmony' at least at this stage, although your remark is overshadowed by an oblique rebuke that it was belated. If you are prepared to agree that 'Christian maturity of peace and harmony' is a bilateral and not just one-sided obligation, you will please consider the following facts among many others, and let me know what Christian peace and harmony the college management on its part has shown me and where it is that I should have shown it earlier'. I need not repeat those facts any more.

## Farewell to the CSI East Kerala Diocese

In continuation of the letter of Bishop K. Michael John dated 30 October 1989 requesting me to withdraw my offer of priestly service in the East Kerala Diocese, I thought I should relieve the diocese of the 'burden' of my offer. So on 6 May 1997 I wrote to the then Bishop K.J. Samuel (whether he was the CSI Moderator then, I am not sure) thus:

> '...Bishop Michael John through his order dated 2-6-'84 authorized me to serve as a priest in the diocese. However, when some of the officials of the diocese,

> including the then secretaries, found my service inconvenient to them, the Bishop thought it convenient to eliminate me through the formalities of a disciplinary action and served on me memo dated 6-7-'89 of allegations including dereliction of pastoral duty [the Chovoor Church Episode concocted on the basis of the deviously bought report from Catechist K.S. Samuel]. In my reply dated 12-7-'89, I denied all the charges....

'Ever since then nothing has been heard of the fate of the proceedings even to this day, whether for fear that the whole affair would boomerang and prove counter productive or for what other reason, I am yet to be told. However the Bishop through his letter dated 30 October 1989 requested me to withdraw my offer of priestly services.... Again in my reply dated 1-11-89, I submitted that it would have been honest on his part to make this request and easy on my part to immediately oblige him, had he done so before resorting to the devious means of a mala fide disciplinary proceedings to get me out. As the matter then stood, I regretted my inability to oblige 'as long as the proceedings...is still pending disposal....' It is fairly eight years now, and the diocesan authorities have not, even to this day, shown the courtesy to either withdraw the proceedings or to take it to its logical conclusion... [according to] the accepted principles governing disciplinary proceedings....However, in case the diocese does not care either to pursue it or withdraw it, I shall feel justified to presume that the diocesan authorities [decide to] keep mum over the affair because of fear to face the consequence of mala fide proceedings. In this case please take this communication as my letter of formal withdrawal of my priestly service in your diocese'. And with that I bade farewell to the CSI East Kerala Diocese.

# 26

# From Dark Dungeons to Dazzling Dawn

After four years of study in Philosophy, the Poona Jnana-Deepa Vidyapeeth awarded me its M.A. in the first class with distinction. There I was taught the divine halo of the Light of Reason with which God endowed and equipped man to distinguish and choose the path of righteousness based on Truth, Justice and Love. Thereafter I joined the same Jnana-Deepa Vidyapeeth for Theology. And the dean of the faculty of Theology, the venerable Rev. Fr Joseph Neuner, S. J., introduced me to theology with the theological adage: 'Philosophy ends where Theology begins'. In philosophy I was taught to follow the God-given light of reason to pursue the path of God-set human destination. But the theological adage is a defiant clarion call to black out this God-given light of reason in the life's path to God-set destination and to tread a darkened path of destination set by the dogmatic teaching authority of more or less ambitious human hierarchy of ritual priesthood. They hold out, as substitute for the God-given light of reason, the blind man's rod of the self-arrogated divino-jure dogmatic infallibility. Obedience to this hierarchy was instilled in the gullible faithful as a religious duty from their very infancy and the rod of blind faith in the dogmatic authority was extended to them to rely on against tumbling over hard rocks of existential problems in the path of life – path blackened out with the thick darkness of dogmatic faith formulae because 'Philosophy ends where theology begins'.

Speaking of 'Gandhi and the Western world', Louis Fisher wrote: 'Had Gandhi been born in India three thousand years ago, his birth would have been wrapped in myths and his youth in miracles and he would have been worshiped as a God'. What Louis Fisher wrote of Gandhi became true in the case of Jesus. Jesus was born two thousand years and more ago. He preached to the humanity a gospel of the pure Godly truth of Natural Human Morality, a gospel of two-fold dimensions: a vertical dimension of the relationship of 'the love of God, the Moral Imperative' and a horizontal dimension of the relationship of 'the love of one's neighbour as oneself'. God is Truth, Justice, Love, Grace, in short, the fullness of Goodness. The unselfish love of man is the horizontal relationship of man's solidarity and sense of identity with each other, hinged on the vertical relationship of the love of God – Love of Truth, Justice etc. And the New Testament summarizes all the laws and prophets in this two-dimensional relationship of man. [Mathew 22, 37-40]. The New Testament adds: 'It is more important to obey these two commandments than to offer animals and other sacrifices' [Mark 12, 33]. This two-dimensional natural human morality is the religion with a capital 'R'. But we have nth number of religions with all sorts of weird sacrifices, rituals, poojas, mantras, archanas, pilgrimages and what not except the two-dimensional love which Jesus preached. Jesus condemned the ritual priesthood of his time in the most bitterest and vituperative words calling the high priests and their hierarchy in terms such as 'brood of vipers', 'hypocrites', 'whitened sepulchers' etc. He cleansed the temple of Jerusalem of all the ritualistic rubbish of religious business for which they decided to eliminate him. These very high priests, conducting the religious business, successfully planned for the death of Jesus on the Cross under cover of the clandestine alliance with the political power of Pilate, the Governor. Even the power-blinded Pilate found Jesus not guilty of any crime to humanity and tried twice to set him free. 'He knew very well that the chief priests had handed Jesus over to him because they were jealous' [Mark 15, 10; Luke 23, 13-16] But each time the religious high-priestly class foiled Pilate's attempts by blocking the path of judicial process for Natural Justice. At first they blocked the path through political threat: 'If you set him free that means that you are not the Emperor's friend' [John 19, 12]. The second time by whipping up blind fanatic religious sentiment of the beguiled, gullible followers of the high-priestly class to violence: 'The chief priests and the elders persuaded the crowd to ask Pilate to set Barabbas free and Jesus put to death'. [Mathew 27, 20] Then comes the irony: The next generation of these very high priests presented Jesus as God the Son, sent by God the Father to be sacrificed in atonement for 'the sins of the world' and threw the blame of the crucifixion of Jesus upon the anonymous criminal 'the sins of the world'. This story was again distorted and given shape to in the ritualistic form of the sacrifice of Eucharist and they arrogated it as their monopoly to perform this ritual as the Redemptive Sacrifice and used it as a regular source of income. They also restored back to position the very religious edifice of the weird ritualistic system which Jesus overthrew and replaced by his two-dimensional relationship of Love of God and Love of Man. Even more ironically they positioned Jesus as its basement! The religion of the two dimensional natural human morality was flooded with the divine light of reason. But the ritualistic priestly hierarchy blacked it out and shaped it into mysterious faith formulae to be administered to and swallowed by the gullible believers from their very infancy. These faith formulae drugs are insulated within the 'infallible magisterium' against any light of reason penetrating them. These drugs regularly administered, keep the believers faith-addicts and consequently religious fanatics. Each ritualistic religion boisterously proclaims its set of faith formulae as above reason and those of others as against reason, but in either case they are *alien to reason.* If alien to reason, which rational creature can benefit by them? What criterion is there to choose which ritualistic religion as true?

Jesus declaredly came to establish the Kingdom of God here on Earth, a just, peaceful, prosperous kingdom of divine love and ruled by the principles of natural human morality. Jesus came that the humans 'may have life and have it more abundantly'. But the ritualistic religions with their faith-formulae drugs have created a world around us, completely drained of all moral values and divine grace, made turbulent with blind fanaticism generated by faith-addiction, terrorism and communal riots. The theology of churchianity distorted the two-dimensional cross of Jesus' discipleship into 'cross a symbol of sacrifice and privation' during life here on earth. It then turned this distortion of the two-dimensional relationship brought by Jesus into a 'symbol of sacrifice and privation' as the foundation for a skyward looking or other-worldly spirituality and asks the blind followers to look up to heaven for reward after death and offers the ritual practices of the high-priestly hierarchy as escalatory service to heaven, while they themselves look sharp downward on luxurious life here on Earth. A German theologian and researcher, Holger Kersten, says: 'The message of Jesus has been distorted beyond recognition'. Dr James Kottoor, a theologian and great journalist, in an e-mail message circulated on 14-9-2007 says: 'Churchianity must die if Christianity is to live, so that the brotherhood of all humans under the fatherhood of God, which Jesus dreamt of, may come true. Only then can we honestly, boldly and prayerfully say the 'Our Father…' because at one stroke it proclaims our brotherhood with the rest of humanity, transcending all religious, irreligious, political, social, cultural, racial, national, linguistic, class and caste affiliations which keep humans divided into ever so many conflicting camps'. What is this distortion of Jesus' message beyond recognition? Rev. Dr Roger Gaikwad, general secretary, N.C.C.I., in his paper on 'the Need of Rethinking' [keynote address delivered in the first session of the two-day conference 'the First Kerala Presbyters' Koinonia' held in the CSI Holy Trinity Cathedral, Kottayam, on Thursday 6 September 2011], explains: '[Christianity] has *transformed the gospel into a religion.* (emphasis added) just as it has happened else where'.

It is indeed high time we started to rethink, to give up groping in the narrow dark dungeons of the areas alien to reason, holding the rod of blind faith, extended by the self-arrogated 'divino jure' infallible teaching authority of the ritualistic priestly hierarchy and come out into the dazzling dawn of Jesus' message of the 'Kingdom of God here on Earth' following the God-given light of reason. Following the God-given light of reason is the religious duty par excellence precisely because it is God-given. It is high time we freed ourselves from the mere rotating and not anywhere reaching 'giant wheel' of the 'escalatory service' of the ritual priestly hierarchy with the board of destination 'Heaven after Death'. To quote Holger Kersten once again: 'It is simply a matter of the greatest importance today to find a way back again [from the dark dungeons of the blind faith formulae drugs] to the [dazzling dawn of the] universal and central Truth of Christ's message, which has been distorted almost beyond recognition by the profane ambitions of more or less secular institutions that have arrogated to themselves a religious authority ever since the early centuries of the so-called Christian era...Jesus sought to create an immediate link between God and human kind, not to set up bureaucratic channels [escalatory services] to go through....The divinity is not remote from us at some mystically infinite distance, but inside each one of us. It should inspire us to lead our lives in harmony with the Infinite to recognize our short existence on earth as a part of the eternal whole'.

The years of my struggle with the catholic management of St. Stephen's College Uzhavoor and the Christian CSI management of H.B. College, Melukavu was a period of groping in the dark dungeon created by the gigantic structure that had taken shape in the name of Jesus Christ and at the expense of His lucid message of natural human morality. But it has also helped me to distinguish between Christianity and churchianity. The net result of this long ordeal is the realization of the difference between the dark dungeon of the blind faith formulae giving shape to the high-income-generating and addiction-inducing ritual system, built up under these faith formulae, and the lucid Religion of the two-dimensional relationship as preached by Jesus. These dead ritualistic practices have created a hell of the beautiful God-created world, and blacked out the dazzling dawn of the two-dimensional relationship brought by Jesus to create a heaven, the Kingdom of God out of this hellish world. In this Kingdom of God Jesus wanted the vertical relationship of faith in God –Truth, Justice, Love, Grace, Goodness – to rule the horizontal relationship of the human solidarity and sense of identity of each one with the whole human fraternity. This saga of my traumatic experiences ended in a healthy catharsis. Here I came across many characters who played their characteristic role. Let me mention some of them.

The dogmatic Catholic infallible teaching authority and Uzhavoor college management asked me: 'Who are you to think when we are here?' A Catholic leading lawyer, decorated with the insignia of chevalier title advised the same management that the brief time of the non-existence of the Appellate Tribunal was 'the right and safe time to do away with Fr Vellamthadathil through the mere formality of a domestic enquiry'. Authority, invested with the ritual priesthood exhorted their faith-addicted 'faithful sheep' [or rams?] to get united to strengthen the hands of the Bishop against me. To this the sober Mr Cyriac replied; 'Try to meet ideas with ideas and not with rods and clubs'. Outwardly simple, but inwardly honest and just, Kuriakochettan visited me as my opponent and left me as my life-long friend. The Bishop-Manager with high ritual priesthood, refused me an N.O.C. to leave the service of the college and join another, and gave me the choice to resign my service, while the then Vice-Chancellor advised me not to resign and helped me by issuing a notice to him which induced him 'to show mercy' and issue the N.O.C. While the first Bishop-Manager of the H.B. College, with the ritual high priesthood found me unworthy and his candidate worthy for appointment on general merit, the Government nominee Dr Babu Paul I.A.S. and the University nominee, Dr Andrews Valentine, insisted on my appointment on general merit. Again, while the same Bishop-Manager delayed my monthly salary for about 20 months because of his refusal to appoint me as a lecturer, but only as a junior lecturer, his lay-secretary Mr Sunny Kallupalam who had no ritual priesthood, but shared abundantly in the 'Royal Priesthood', got my appointment as lecturer and payment of my salary with arrears. Under the inevitable influence of a caucus that ruled the next Bishop-Manager I was required to sign a rank list of candidates for appointment, arbitrarily made, contravening the merit assessment through the interview. On my resisting it this caucus of ritual priests and associates let loose a long tirade against me, including a domestic enquiry on a memo of charges, framed by them and enquired into by their paid enquiry officer. They found me guilty of the charges and issued notice of dismissal on the very eve of my retirement. They had the secret agenda of depriving me of all my retirement benefits including pension. And most of them were participants in the ritual priesthood imparted through the unbroken traditional Episcopal imposition of hands! It was the then advocate and later honourable Justice Mr Abdul Gafoor who extricated me from their clutches and placed me back in the path of justice and saved me and family from the embarrassment, at least temporary, of a dismissal. The University Appellate Tribunal, Mr P. Ramachandran Nair who heard my appeal, adjudicated the whole disciplinary proceedings and declared me innocent of all charges and pronounced the whole procedure illegal, violative of Natural Justice and vindictive. The Honourable High Court Judges, Justice K.G. Balakrishnan, Justice C.S. Rajan, and Justice V. Ramkumar intervened on each one's turn and made all my retirement benefits and other arrears and dues available to me without any damage whatsoever. These venerable persons certainly do not share the Christian ritual priesthood imparted through the unbroken traditional imposition of Episcopal hands. But can any one deny that they share the royal priesthood imparted through the internal anointing of the grace of Truth, Justice, Love and Goodness? I leave it to the readers to think and draw their own mature conclusions.